Studies in Urban and Social Change

Published by Blackwell in association with the *International Journal of Urban and Regional Research*. Series editors: Chris Pickvance, Margit Mayer and John Walton.

Published

The City Builders
Susan S. Fainstein

Divided Cities
Susan S. Fainstein, Ian Gordon, and Michael Harloe (eds)

Fragmented Societies
Enzo Mingione

Free Markets and Food Riots
John Walton and David Seddon

The Resources of Poverty
Mercedes González de la Rocha

Post-Fordism
Ash Amin (ed.)

The People's Home?
Social Rented Housing in Europe and America
Michael Harloe

Cities after Socialism
Urban and Regional Change and Conflict in Post-Socialist Societies
Gregory Andrusz, Michael Harloe and Ivan Szelenyi (eds)

Urban Poverty and the Underclass: A Reader
Enzo Mingione

Capital Culture
Gender at Work in the City
Linda McDowell

Forthcoming

Urban Social Movements and the State
Margit Mayer

Contemporary Urban Japan
A Sociology of Consumption
John Clammer

The Social Control of Cities
Sophie Body-Gendot

CAPITAL
CULTURE

GENDER AT WORK IN THE CITY

Linda McDowell

First published 1997

Blackwell Publishers Ltd
108 Cowley Road
Oxford OX4 1JF
UK

Blackwell Publishers Inc.
350 Main Street
Malden, Massachusetts 02148
USA

British Library Cataloguing in Publication Data

A CIP catalogue record for this book is available from the British Library.

Library of Congress Cataloging in Publication Data

McDowell, Linda.
    Capital culture : gender at work in the city / Linda McDowell.
       p.   cm. — (Studies in urban and social change)
    Includes bibliographical references and index.
    ISBN 0-631-20530-6. — ISBN 0-631-20531-4
    1. Sexual division of labor—England—London.   2. Sex role in the
work environment—England—London.   3. Financial services industry–
–England—London.   4. Women employees—England—London—Interviews.
5. Male employees—England—London—Interviews.   I. Title.
II. Series.
    HD6060.65.G72L66   1997
    306.3′615′09421—DC21
                                                                              97–7780
                                                                              CIP

Typeset in 10½ on 12 pt Baskerville
by Ace Filmsetting Ltd, Frome, Somerset
Printed in Great Britain by Hartnolls Ltd, Bodmin, Cornwall

This book is printed on acid-free paper.

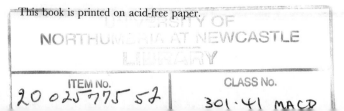

In memory of my father, F. H. Leigh 1917–1995

Contents

List of Illustrations

FIGURES

PLATES

MAPS

Series Preface

In the past three decades there have been dramatic changes in the fortunes of cities and regions, in beliefs about the role of markets and states in society, and in the theories used by social scientists to account for these changes. Many of the cities experiencing crisis in the 1970s have undergone revitalisation while others have continued to decline. In Europe and North America new policies have introduced privatisation on a broad scale at the expense of collective consumption, and the viability of the welfare state has been challenged. Eastern Europe has witnessed the collapse of state socialism and the uneven implementation of a globally driven market economy. Meanwhile the less developed nations have suffered punishing austerity programmes that divide a few newly industrialising countries from a great many cases of arrested and negative growth.

Social science theories have struggled to encompass these changes. The earlier social organisational and ecological paradigms were criticised by Marxian and Weberian theories, and these in turn have been disputed as all-embracing narratives. The certainties of the past, such as class theory, are gone and the future of urban and regional studies appears relatively open.

The aim of the series *Studies in Urban and Social Change* is to take forward this agenda of issues and theoretical debates. The series is committed to a number of aims but will not prejudge the development of the field. It encourages theoretical works and research monographs on cities and regions. It explores the spatial dimension of society including the role of agency and of institutional contexts in shaping urban form. It addresses economic and political change from the household to the state. Cities and regions are understood within an international system, the features of which are revealed in comparative and historical analyses.

The series also serves the interests of university classroom and professional readers. It publishes topical accounts of important policy issues (e.g. global adjustment), reviews of debates (e.g. post-Fordism) and collections that explore various facets of major changes (e.g. cities after socialism or the new urban underclass). The series urges a synthesis of research and theory, teaching and practice. Engaging research monographs (e.g. on women and poverty in Mexico or urban culture in Japan) provide vivid teaching materials just as policy-oriented studies (e.g. of social housing or urban planning) test and redirect theory. The city is analysed from the top down (e.g. through the gendered culture of investment banks) and the bottom up (e.g. in challenging social movements). Taken together, the volumes in the series reflect the latest developments in urban and regional studies.

Subjects which fall within the scope of the series include: explanations for the rise and fall of cities and regions; economic restructuring and its spatial, class and gender impact; race and identity; convergence and divergence of the 'east' and 'west' in social and institutional paterns; new divisions of labour and forms of social exclusion; urban and environmental movements; international migration and capital flows; politics of the urban poor in developing countries; cross-national comparisons or housing, planning and development; debates on post-Fordism, the consumption sector and the 'new' urban poverty.

Studies in Urban and Social Change addresses an international and interdisciplinary audience of researchers, practitioners, students and urban enthusiasts. Above all, it endeavours to reach the public with compelling accounts of contemporary society.

Editorial Committee
John Walton, Chair
Margit Mayer
Chris Pickvance

May 1997

Acknowledgements

This book is the result of field work in the City of London. While the banks who opened their doors to me and the people who talked to me must remain anonymous, I want to thank them for their interest and frankness. It was a pleasure for me to learn about their ideas and their everyday lives and I hope they think the results have been worth it. I have also been fortunate to be able to share this work with colleagues and friends in a range of institutions in many parts of the world. The study was started in the company of social scientists, mainly geographers at the Open University, funded by an ESRC grant. I acknowledge the support of this institution and the companionship, intellectual stimulus and advice of John Allen, Allan Cochrane, Chris Hamnett, Doreen Massey and Phil Sarre, but especially Gill Court who is now working in the USA. I am indebted to her not only for carrying out many of the interviews on which this book is based but also for the analysis of personnel data from one of the case study banks. Some of the argument in chapters 2 and 3 is drawn from working papers that Gill and I wrote together, and chapters 6 and 7 are rewritten versions of jointly authored papers.

Rosemary Pringle was a key influence. Her work on secretaries (Pringle, 1989), which I read before I came to know her, helped me to think about sexuality, power and desire in the workplace. I was then fortunate to be able to work with Rosemary at the Open University in 1991, and her friendship, along with that of Sophie Watson, was vital in influencing my ideas about power at work. I am also grateful to many of the feminist colleagues inside and outside geography departments who have talked, discussed and argued with me as I worked on this book. In particular, I thank Susan Christopherson, Susan Hanson and Margaret Fitzsimmons in the USA and Liz Bondi, Suzy Reimer, Hazel Christie, Jennifer Rubin, Sylvia Walby, Jane Wills and Michelle Lowe in the UK. I also thank all those people who heard me give papers drawing on parts of this work. Although I cannot acknowledge you all individually, your comments made a difference. The debt I owe to Nigel Thrift should be evident in the text. It was he who first provoked me to an empirical investigation of the social structure of the 'new' City. A longer debt to Ray Pahl must also be gratefully acknowledged. I first met Ray as the 'boss' of the Centre for Research in the Social Sciences at the University of Kent years ago and since then he has become a friend as well as a colleague. His stimulating work 'on work' throughout the 1980s has been a key influence.

While I started the research on which this book is based at the Open University, the main part and its completion occurred after I moved to the Department of Geography at Cambridge. In its congenial atmosphere, I found stimulus and space to write and the interest of Stuart Corbridge, Ron Martin and Alan Hudson in global money was a boon. So thanks go to my newer colleagues too. Margit Mayer, Chris Pickvance and John Walton, the editors of this series, read the whole of the book when it was longer than this and their insightful comments were a great help in the production of a leaner version. I am extremely grateful for their succinct, incisive but encouraging editorial advice. Finally, the insights I gained from texts and interviews into forms of masculinity and femininity were immeasurably strengthened by living with my adolescent children: to Hugh and Sarah I owe a debt greater than they know. I thank them and their father for their love and support – and all the meals they made when I was busy.

Parts of this book have previously appeared in earlier versions as: 'Gender divisions of labour in the post-Fordist economy', *Environment and Planning A* (Pion Ltd, London, 1994), 26, pp. 1397–418; 'Missing subjects: gender, power, and sexuality in merchant banking', *Economic Geography* (July 1994), 70:2, pp. 229–51; 'Performing work: bodily representations in merchant banks', *Environment and Planning D: Society and Space* (Pion Ltd, London, 1994), 12, pp. 727–50; and 'Body work' in D. Bell and G. Valentine (eds), *Mapping Desire* (Routledge, London, 1995).

The author and publisher are also grateful to the following for permission to reproduce the photographs: Emma Hallett (plate 2.1), the *Guardian* and the *Observer* (plates 2.3, 7.1, 8.5), Kippa Matthews (plate 8.2), Rapho (plate 8.4). Every effort has been made to trace copyright-holders, and we apologise for any errors or omissions in these acknowledgements.

Introduction: Money and Work

In the 1980s there was a huge expansion of employment in the financial services sector of advanced industrial economies. In Britain, the US and Japan, the deregulation of money markets, the development of new financial instruments and the introduction of new technologies that enabled the almost instantaneous transfer of vast sums of money between the monetary exchanges in each of these nations seemed to point to a new and exciting economic future based on the transfer of invisible sums of money – a sort of clean and virtual future in which older notions about the basis of economic growth and the nature of work would disappear. The urban theorist Manuel Castells argued that the technological innovations had created a deterritorialised 'space of flows' (Castells, 1989) in which what geographers refer to as the friction of distance had vanished. Money, advice and even people could be moved round the world at high speeds. Space and time had been compressed, according to David Harvey (1989a), and truly, as Marx had foretold, all that was solid – factories, goods, labour – seemed to have melted into air or, more prosaically, into the glass fibre cables of telecommunications. Other urban scholars suggested that the cities in which financial markets – the apotheosis of the new international economy – were based had become increasingly detached from other cities within their nation state, instead becoming 'global cities' with more in common with each other than cities lower down the urban hierarchy (Sassen, 1990; King, 1990b). In these cities, new forms of work were undertaken by an international elite who were as at home in London as Frankfurt, in New York as Tokyo – the new middle class of the late twentieth century. Changes in the world economy revolving around the expansion of an international financial services sector through deregulation and the globalisation of markets, trade and labour had led to the strong growth of a new category of professionals in the 1980s, with new ways of working and living and different cultural values and norms from their predecessors. Thus, as Featherstone has argued (1990):

> The globalisation of capital flows with 24-hour stock market trading, which gained pace after the 'Big Bang' of October 1986, not only deregulated local markets and made local capital vulnerable to the strategies of corporate raiders, it necessitated new norms for the market too. The globalisation of capital also entailed the globalisation of the market in services to finance, commerce and industry. A new category of professionals: international lawyers, corporate tax accountants, financial advisers, and management consultants were required as the various business and financial interests sought to chart and formalise the newly globalised economic space. (p. 7)

A small number of cities – London and New York among them – are at the apex of this globalised economic space. With their high-waged service-based economies they are important locations in patterns of international migration by the new service class and business elites (Beaverstock, 1994; Champion, 1994; Cohen, 1987; Daniels, 1993a, b; Salt, 1992; Sassen, 1990). Many of these new professionals are highly mobile, spending periods in a number of countries, moving within and between the internal labour markets of multinational corporations and banks based in the global cities. As Sassen (1990) has argued, international economic change, global patterns of migration of capital and labour, and the rise of a global service sector have led to the emergence of a new international division of labour in which the high-status and highly paid jobs in the upper echelons of control and professional functions are increasingly concentrated in the world cities from which the global economy is managed and controlled. Sassen and many others (Coakley, 1992; Coakley and Harris, 1983; Fainstein, 1994; King, 1990b; Noyelle, 1989; Thrift, 1994; Zukin, 1992) have argued that London, New York and Tokyo are the three most significant global cities, pre-eminent among other expanding financial centres with a full range of international financial services – commodity, currency and security markets, leading stock exchanges, banking and specialised business services, and the full range of advanced information infrastructure. In London between 1961 and 1991, 272,000 jobs were created in producer services and, as Marshall et al. (1992) noted, 'London alone possesses over 40 per cent of Great Britain's employment in business services (insurance, banking, finance and professional services)' (p. 454).

It has also been argued that this globalisation of the market for financial and legal services has altered the social relations of the financial sector, that the conventional ways of doing business based on personal contacts and networks between a bourgeois elite have been replaced by a more democratic or meritocratic system, often referred to as an 'Americanisation' of financial services. It has made space for a new generation of lawyers and bankers who are less tied to the quasi-aristocratic ideals and disdain for marketing that had characterised the 'gentlemanly' stock exchanges and legal practices of an earlier era (Beaverstock, 1994; Dezalay, 1990; Featherstone, 1990; Thrift, 1994). In the new global markets, the emphasis is increasingly on technical competence, aggressive tactics and a more meritocratic ethos.

But these theorists also recognised that the new global economy and global cities were themselves only too 'real' – places in which real people lived and went to work. Within these cities, social inequalities appeared to be increasing, as a growing number of the affluent, if not super rich, money makers working in the old and newer occupations in the global financial service sector and associated professions – lawyers, accountants and so on – lived and worked cheek by jowl with growing numbers of poor and immobile workers who serviced the newly affluent international middle class. While house prices spiralled to giddy heights in the late 1980s as old dockland warehouses were converted to bijou homes, and the affluent engaged in increasingly visible activities of conspicuous consumption, the poor in these cities became remorselessly poorer (Borrie, 1994; Philo, 1994; Rowntree Foundation, 1995; Sassen, 1990). The workplace and leisure needs of the 'masters of the universe' – the term is Tom Wolfe's from his satire on Wall Street, *Bonfire of the Vanities* (1988) – gave rise to growing numbers of restaurants, cafés, dry cleaners, hotels, cleaning firms, architectural salvage firms, small building contractors, nannies, cooks and domestic cleaners and so forth, all of whom were affected by the pronounced moves towards flexible, casualised and low-waged employment in these cities from the mid 1980s onwards (Allen and Henry, 1996).

The market rhetoric of the new right and, in Britain, Mrs Thatcher's various claims that 'there is no alternative' and 'no such thing as society' seemed to endorse Gordon Gekko's claim in the film *Wall Street* that 'greed is good'. Financiers and bankers typified the individualist attitudes and lifestyles that were celebrated in the 1980s. The poor were pushed to the margins both literally and in the political discourse of the time. Life was tough but exciting and Big Bang in London in 1986, when the deregulated markets were opened ever wider to foreign competition, seemed to validate the decade's rhetoric. But then, only a year later, on Black Monday, the pound and the dollar fell on the international exchanges and the markets panicked. House prices peaked in the same year and then stagnated in both London and New York, and an employment shakeout began. While Tokyo seemed impregnable at the time, its turn came too in a recession in the early 1990s, just as London and New York began to recover. These years of expansion and deregulation, followed by recession, clearly had an impact on social practices in the City of London and on Wall Street as the impregnable image of the 'masters of the universe' was tarnished by financial ruin, scandal and unemployment. I was curious to find out exactly what had changed for the men, and smaller numbers of women, who worked in the financial sector in the late 1980s and early 1990s. Had the remarkable changes of the heady 1980s shaken up older forms of workplace practices and social interactions in the City, only in turn to be affected by the more dour 1990s?

I was also curious about the effects of boom and then recession as I had lived in London myself between 1987 and 1992, benefiting and then losing in the crazy housing market of the capital. I was working at that time with a group of economic and urban geographers at the Open University, and there we began to investigate the dynamics that lay behind the remarkable spiral of growth and then decline in London and the South East of England in these years. While others looked at high tech work (Massey 1995; Massey and Henry, 1992), the catering and cleaning industries (Allen and Henry, 1996) and the effects of both on income inequalities (Massey and Allen, 1994), and at the housing market (Hamnett and Seavers, 1994), I wanted to understand how an institution like the City of London worked, viewing it through the lens of the lives and careers of individual men and women working in the City's merchant banks at the end of this period of radical change both in the global economy and in the City.

Despite working in a compressed global space made possible by new means of communication, and frequently moving between global cities, these new professionals spend their daily lives in more geographically restricted sets of spaces. King (1990b), for example, has pointed out that they often both work in and live in a specific type of urban space – the redeveloped inner-city areas – and it is it is by no means clear that working in a globalised sector necessarily generates a cosmopolitan outlook among the employees (Wouters, 1986, 1990). Indeed, as Hannerz (1990) has suggested, a range of responses are possible between the polarities of localism (territorially anchored or 'bounded' cultures involving face-to-face relations between people who do not move around a great deal) and cosmopolitanism (transnational cultural networks extended in space in which there is a good deal of overlapping and mingling which encourages engagement with the other). Some of the people who travel widely, such as businesspeople and financiers, may be locals at heart who do not really want to leave home or move between cities for work.

As Thrift (1994) has emphasised, for the workers caught up in the transformation of the City, everyday life is not carried out in the virtual space of deterritorialised flows of money, but instead involves social interactions among a particular group of men and women, working in the new electronically based dealing and trading rooms and in the back offices and corporate boardrooms of City banks. Thrift designated these arenas a 're-embedded set of meeting places', although in retrospect it is hard to see that the everyday working life of financial sector employees was ever carried out in disembedded spaces. It was just that the rhetoric of placelessness carried us with it at the time. But, as Robins (1991) noted:

> Globalisation is, in fact, also associated with new dynamics of re-localisation. It is about the achievement of a new global–local nexus, about new and intricate relations between global space and local space. Globalisation is like putting together a jigsaw puzzle: it is a matter of inserting a multiplicity of localities into the overall picture of a new global system. (pp. 34–5)

Fortunately academic geographers, myself among them, recognise that place always makes a difference, be it at the scale of the workplace, the city, the region or the nation state. Indeed, in this book I hope to demonstrate that organisational sociology might be strengthened if more attention was given to *where* things take place as well as *how* they do.

I was interested in seeing whether and where women might fit into this global/local jigsaw. I initially approached my investigation of change in the City from a particular perspective and at a particular spatial scale, however. As a geographer interested in the nature and reasons for gendered patterns of occupational segregation, I decided to work at the level of the workplace, although neither denying nor neglecting the structural and institutional factors that sort men and women into different occupations. I wanted to get inside a number of investment banks and look at the daily social practices and interactions between employees. While others had argued that the 'new' City of the 1980s had shed its old elitist image, recruiting workers in the period of expansion from a wider range of class backgrounds than had traditionally been the case (Budd and Whimster, 1992), I was interested in the extent to which the City had opened its doors to women. The 1980s had been marked by a rapid expansion in the number of women gaining higher educational credentials and a range of professional qualifications in law, accountancy and business, for example, that would seem on the surface to fit them for the range of expanding occupations in the City. But financial services, and particularly the more blue-blooded areas of investment banking, had long denied access to all but an exceptional minority of professional women and a legion of female clerical workers. My aim, therefore, was to assess the extent to which women had entered and progressed up the occupational hierarchy in investment banking in the City of London at the end of the 1980s and into the '90s.

Investment banking is the pinnacle of the British banking system, distinguished by its long history of family involvement, where generations of sons and nephews followed their fathers and uncles into 'the bank'. It was once a world of measured calm (Michie, 1992) which was apparently shattered by the events of the 1980s, when rapid expansion opened up the City to new ways of doing things, but detailed empirical substantiation of new forms of working, especially the impact on gender rather than class divisions, was lacking.

The 1980s and early 1990s have also seen an exciting explosion of feminist-influenced work on organisations, occupational gender segregation, power and sexuality, the social construction of femininity and, more lately, masculinity at work. Feminists realised that the unveiling of the unmarked, disembodied and universal individual in the western intellectual tradition as male was insufficient. It had become increasingly evident that, like femininity, masculinity took many more forms than the singular, oppositional character 'man' who appeared in many of our texts. Despite the dominance of hegemonic versions, both masculinity and femininity take multiple forms, which are defined, constructed and maintained not only by the institutional structures of capitalist economies but also through everyday talk and behaviour at particular sites. It was clear to me as I approached a number of banks for cooperation with my investigation that I wanted to look at the dominant forms of masculinity and the ways in which they excluded certain men, as well as positioning women in particular ways and places as the 'Other' in relation to dominant constructions of masculinity.

As well as the expanding feminist scholarship, the 1980s and early 1990s were a period marked by an extraordinary intellectual ferment in the social sciences and the humanities in general. Growing cross-disciplinary work, in which ideas about situated knowledge, positionality and reflexivity disrupted conventional ways of doing research within particular disciplines and approaches, became significant. A wide range of new ideas about the ways in which material social relations, meaning and symbolism were interconnected produced stimulating cross-fertilisation between literary and cultural studies, for example. Despite coming somewhat late to many of these ideas, geographers also experienced a 'cultural turn' in which the analysis of discourses, texts, symbols and meaning became part of the ways of understanding contemporary socio-spatial changes and behaviour. Influenced by this work and by the resurgence of a sociology of economic behaviour, I found the combination of an older materialist way of understanding the economy and new ways of thinking about economic behaviour as embedded and embodied, through symbolic meaning, representation and discourse, extremely liberating. I turned to a wide range of sources from several disciplines in order to explain what was revealed to me in the banks. I brought to bear a combination of approaches and methods, trying to show how different ways of seeing the City complement each other. In succeeding chapters, I move down through different levels or scales of analysis in turn. Drawing on a wide range of disciplinary perspectives and approaches is something that has perhaps distinguished good geographical scholarship for many years. Geographers reading my text should find the disciplinary eclecticism comfortable, or at least not at all unusual. I hope that others, more used to singular perspectives, will find my approach provoking rather than theoretically promiscuous. In chapter 1, I outline the changing nature of work in contemporary industrial economies and the different ways of thinking about it that have influenced my empirical work in the banks. The book then moves through analyses of the institutional structures of gender segregation, gendered patterns of employment, recruitment and careers, to an investigation of the culture of banking, media representations of bankers and daily social interactions between men and women on the shop floor, as it were, in this case in dealing rooms, corporate boardrooms and individual offices.

The book is divided into two parts. In chapters 2 to 5 of part I, I examine the major changes in the City of London since the mid 1980s and the ways in which they are related to its class and gender composition. Chapter 2 provides a short history of the development of London's pre-eminence as a financial centre, focusing in particular on the 1980s employment growth, social and technological changes and the impact on the built environment of the City. In the next two chapters, the patterns of gender segregation in investment banking in the City are established. In these chapters, I begin to draw on a large-scale survey and detailed field work in three merchant banks, undertaken between 1992 and 1994 in the City of London. In chapter 5, as well as looking at the current class and gender composition of the City, I also show how recruitment strategies reproduce its particular culture.

In chapters 6 to 8 of part II, the impact of the cultural as well as the economic and social aspects of those radical years of change in the City are the dominant focus, examined through the words of individual workers. In chapter 6, I look at the ways in which mechanisms of cultural imperialism, drawing on Iris Marion Young's (1990a, b, 1993) work on social justice and the politics of difference, position women in the workplace as inappropriate or vile bodies. I then turn, in chapters 7 and 8, to an assessment of how fictional images and representations of the world of money and its key players both reflect and affect 'reality'. What Thrift et al. (1987) termed the 'sexy/greedy' years of City expansion exercised a remarkable hold on the popular imagination, and the exchanges and dealing rooms of New York and London became the locus of a series of books, films and plays. In addition, both the tabloid and broadsheet press gave significant space to the antics of the key players of these years – the patriarchs and princes of the brave new world and the fallen heroes (and a longer and longer procession of the latter trooped through the 1990s). In chapters 7 and 8, I deconstruct the reality/representation dichotomy, showing how the discursive construction of masculinity and femininity in investment banks is partly based on these very images and representations. In these chapters, multiple gender performances, different ways of doing masculinity and femininity in different locations in the banks, are the focus, and here Judith Butler's (1990a, b, 1993) influence is apparent. Finally, in chapter 9, I attempt to bring the different levels and aspects of this analysis of gender at work together in an assessment of the prospects for women in City workplaces and in the labour market more generally.

This has been an enjoyable, but at times difficult, book to write. As I attempted to cross disciplinary boundaries, it threatened to become a baggy, almost boundless monster, escaping not only the discipline of my own discipline, geography, but also the publisher's word limit. I managed to tame it, but I am conscious that it is a work in progress, a set of reflections on complex issues that of necessity had to be terminated in mid 1996 when I thankfully returned the final manuscript to Blackwells. As I have intimated above, the literature about work, organisations, services, gender, sexuality and power is expanding exponentially in a fascinating way, and new lines of research and explanation are rapidly opening up to reinterpret older ways of understanding gender relations. If this book helps others to move beyond what I have tried to do here, then it will have achieved its purpose, although, of course, I hope it will also hold the attention of the reader through its intrinsic qualities. The world of merchant or investment banking – the terms seem to be used interchangeably – is a fascinating one, and it has been a delight to spend time in the company of people who work within it. The slight envy that I have always harboured of colleagues who are social anthropologists has now been laid to rest. I truly felt a stranger in a foreign land in these banks.

Part I
Gender at Work

1

Thinking through Work:
Gender, Power and Space

The fabric of the advanced economies has been enlarged to encompass new sectors, new jobs, and new ways of working, . . . taking shapes previously unimagined.
A. Sayer and R. Walker, 1992, p. 2

INTRODUCTION: ORGANISATION,
SPACE AND CULTURE

In this chapter, I want to counterpose a number of sets of literatures to draw out some questions about the changing organisation and distribution of waged work, especially its feminisation, that will be explored in detail in different ways in the chapters that make up this book. As many analyses have made clear, there is an evident, empirically demonstrable, trend towards the 'feminisation' of work in contemporary Britain. In using this term, I intend to indicate a great deal more than the numerical increase in the numbers of women entering waged employment in the labour markets of Britain's towns and cities. I also want to encompass the shift to service sector employment, where the attributes of growing numbers of jobs and occupations are based, in the main, on those purportedly feminine attributes of serving and caring, as well as what organisational theorists and management consultants see as a trend towards the feminisation of management structures and practices with a growing emphasis on less hierarchical, more empathetic and cooperative styles of management. The popular as well as the academic literature in these areas includes praise for non-hierarchical structures, for empathy and caring in the workplace and a range of other essentialised feminine attributes. Indeed, so lyrical has a stream of this literature become about feminised attributes that women have been dubbed 'the new Japanese' of organisational theory by one over-enthusiastic advocate (Helgasen, 1990). If these literatures are to be believed, if sheer numbers of women in the labour market are emphasised and the terms and conditions of many women's employment are ignored, it might seem that women are entering a new period of success and empowerment in the late twentieth century world of work. Some grounds for this optimism, as well as contradictory evidence, will be revealed in later chapters in the specific circumstances of merchant banking in the City of London.

The empirical evidence about the purported feminisation of organisations has been paralleled by a remarkable expansion in theoretically grounded studies of service-based economies. In a range of disciplines and from a range of perspectives, the changing nature of work and structure of organisations has been the focus of recent attention. A particularly noticeable trend in this work has been what we might term a 'cultural turn', in which the the perception of work and workplaces as active forces in the social construction of workers as embodied beings has become a prominent emphasis. Rather than seeing the workplace as a site which men and women as fixed and finished products enter to become labour power, the ways in which the workplace or the organisation play a key role in the constitution of subjects is becoming clear. It is this work that has been a major influence here, especially studies that have examined the gendering of organisations, the construction of work as emotional labour and the management of feeling and the significance of embodiment – of men and women as physical beings of different sizes, shapes, skin colours and sexual proclivities and preferences as well as gendered attributes – in workplace interactions. To this incisive and significant literature, I want to bring a specifically geographical imagination and suggest that the location and the physical construction of the workplace – its site and layout, the external appearance and the internal layout of its buildings and surrounding environment – also affects, as well as reflects, the social construction of work and workers and the relations of power, control and dominance that structure relations between them. Here a set of literatures from geography, architecture and urban sociology are useful. The link between these different literatures, between sociological and geographical imaginations, is the notion of performance, especially the new theoretical work on the body as a site of inscription and cultural analyses of the body. The social constructionist literature has, for several decades from Goffman (1961, 1963) onwards, fruitfully used the notion of the stage and performance as a way of understanding everyday behaviours and interactions, and this is mirrored in some of the earliest feminist writing about gender roles. More recently, feminist scholars have developed a psychoanalytically based notion of gender itself as a performance (Butler, 1990a, b). In the work on the built environment, the physical structures of the workplace and the street, Sennett's (1977) classic examination of the decline of the public arena uses the concept of performance as a key to unlock changing attitudes to public and private spaces. His argument that the significance of the street was reduced by the fear of others and otherness has parallels too with the long tradition in feminist scholarship on woman as 'Other'. This work has fruitful links with analyses of organisational culture and with detailed explorations of the ways in which the body is inscribed by these cultures and by specific workplace practices.

A focus on the body as culturally inscribed but also as occupying a range of different spaces in the city, both inside and outside, public and private, is one way of bringing together different theoretical, disciplinary and methodological approaches. All these themes are an important part of developing an understanding of social behaviour in merchant banks. My aim, therefore, is to bring together approaches that are too often kept separate with their emphases on different spatial scales, be it the individual or the economy as a whole, or at an in between scale, the organisation. I want to show how individual behaviour at work, the social construction of gender divisions, the redevelopment of the built environment in the City of London and the restructuring of employment in contemporary industrial economies like Britain may be linked together and so better illuminate the wide-ranging social and economic changes in the nature, organisation and distribution of work in Britain. As Sassen (1996) has recently suggested, in a schematic outline of new ways of thinking about the economy of global cities, it is work in 'the analytic borderlands' that seems provocative in explaining the complex and changing structure of the economies of global cities. New work is needed, she has suggested, in 'several systems of representation, [each] with its own definitions, rules, boundaries, narratives, constructing a dialogue across each' (p. 184), and she believes, as I do, that 'theoretical work on the body . . . opens up new possibilities for analyses of the sort I am exploring here' (p. 185).

MEN'S JOBS, WOMEN'S JOBS: EMPLOYMENT CHANGE IN THE 1980S AND 1990S

As well as a book about money, this is a book about gender, power and space and the ways in which they are connected to each other and to the changing nature of waged work in contemporary Britain. Like other advanced industrial nations, the last decades of the twentieth century in Britain have been marked by a series of remarkable changes in the nature and location of waged work. So great has been the impact of these changes that Pahl has suggested that waged work is the dominant but unresolved question at the end of the twentieth century: 'confusion and ambiguities about its meaning, nature and purpose in our lives are widespread' (Pahl, 1988, p. 1). The world as we thought we knew it has vanished. The post-war certainty about the nature of work, when it was assumed that full-time, waged employment for men was the norm, is now revealed as an exception, dominant only for three brief decades between 1945 and 1975 (Pahl, 1984). As in earlier centuries, it seems clear that waged work for growing numbers of people, perhaps even for a majority, was and will be discontinuous, interrupted and uncertain (Rifkin, 1996) – in short, a world of employment that has always been familiar to most women.

The remarkable series of changes that was set in motion in Great Britain, and indeed in other advanced industrial economies, from the mid 1960s onwards to their apotheosis in the late 1980s seems to have finally buried the belief in the permanency of work. In the 1980s, the nature and structure of waged work in these societies, its organisation and rewards, the types of tasks undertaken and the people who did them, as well as the places in which they laboured, changed irrevocably. The relative certainty of life-time employment, often for a single employer and frequently in the same place, that had faced men in the post-war decades was swept away in a rhetoric and reality of flexibility, restructuring, casualisation, polarisation and feminisation. The decline of manufacturing employment in western industrial economies that had been evident for two decades accelerated in the 1980s, and increasing numbers of people found themselves employed in the service economy in a range of occupations from selling haircuts to selling financial advice. These new jobs in the service sector – new only in the sense that they came to dominate these economies – were unevenly distributed across space and between the population. Old manufacturing heartlands suffered serious employment decline, whereas the sunbelt in the south and south west of the United States, and the golden arc or triangle joined by Bristol, London and Cambridge in Britain, increased their share of national employment and associated prosperity.

For a time Pahl's thesis about the changing nature of work seemed overly gloomy and, as the 1980s progressed, the huge expansion of employment in the service sector seemed to counter his pessimism. In the South East of England in particular, economic growth accelerated in the mid 1980s after a period of recession in the early years of that decade, and there was a widespread belief in the buoyant middle years of the decade that the expanding financial services sector heralded a new secure economic future for Britain. New forms of work based on the ownership, control, movement of and access to money led to the rise of new types of well-paid, middle-class occupations which in combination were dubbed a 'new service class' or a new cultural class (Savage et al., 1992; Thrift, 1989; Urry, 1986). This was the group designated 'yuppies' in popular culture. While the term 'yuppy' was used, without doubt, to include professional workers in the financial services sector, the label 'new service class' tended to be used more restrictively to distinguish a group of workers in what might be referred to as the cultural industries – in marketing, advertising and public relations as well as TV and radio producers and presenters, magazine journalists, fashion writers, and arts administrators and performers. The helping professions – social workers, therapists etc. – are also often included in this new class fraction. This group of middle-class workers were identified as being of key significance in the socio-economic changes that seemed to be sweeping 1980s Britain. Their attitudes to work, it was argued, were different from both the old bourgeoisie and the old manufacturing-based working class. For this new middle class or cultural class, work was fun: indeed, the boundaries between work and leisure were increasingly difficult to define as the social relations of production and consumption merged into each other (Du Gay, 1996). Questions of style and performance, of the ownership and possession of a range of 'positional' goods – the Filofax, a Peugeot car, Gucci shoes, a gentrified flat or house in an inner area that was, in estate agents' parlance, 'rapidly improving' – all marked out these work-ers as a distinct class fraction (Thrift, 1989). This group, it was argued, were also the leaders in a shift towards an increasing emphasis on cul-tural production, on consumption and lifestyle, on images and the aestheticisation of life, that had become a significant feature of late mod-ern capitalist societies (Featherstone, 1991a; Giddens, 1990, 1991). Working with the media, the new cultural class actively promoted the ideas of 'celebrity intellectuals' (Featherstone, 1991a, p. 45) who embraced the popular. Indeed, Bourdieu designated the class as a whole the 'new intellectuals' because of their adoption of a learning mode or attitude towards life (Bourdieu, 1984, p. 370). As well as ideas, this class was said to be 'fascinated by identity, presentation, appearance, lifestyle and the endless quest for new experiences' (Featherstone, 1991a, p. 44). It is also significant that a spatial referent was attached to the group. Paralleling geographers' arguments about deterritorialisation, Featherstone suggested that the new cultural class had a 'frequent lack of anchoring in terms of a specific locale or community' (1991a, p. 44), although other theorists identified a specifically local impact of the group who were among the key actors in the gentrification of inner area housing markets in the global cities in which they worked (King, 1990a, 1993; Sassen, 1990). Many of the new cultural industries were also located in inner areas (Zukin, 1995), resulting in new political alliances, bringing together 'professional politicians, government administrators, local politicians, businessmen, financiers, dealers, investors, artists, intellectuals, educators, cultural intermediaries, and publics [and] has resulted in new interdependencies and strategies that have changed power balances and produced alliance between groups that may previously have perceived their interests as opposed' (Featherstone, 1991a, p. 47). As I shall show in later chapters, high-status workers in the financial services sector increasingly identify with this configuration in their attitudes to work and leisure, and in their aetheticisation of everyday life.

The remarkably uncritical tone in which the new cultural class is analysed by some, however, was challenged by the reassertion of the cold world of economics in the celebration of consumption. As Harvey (1989a) never ceased to argue, the 'postmodern' turn to consumption was little more than 'the cultural froth of late capitalism'. The mechanisms of class division and exploitation ground on slowly and surely below the surface, and the emphasis on aestheticisation and lifestyle merely disguised the insecurity of many of those employed in the new service industries. The bubble of service sector expansion burst at the end of the decade. In Britain and the US, between 1990 and 1992, there was recession and a 'shakeout' of service sector employment, and Pahl's next examination of work had a pessimistic title: *After Success* (Pahl, 1995). Financiers, dealers, lawyers and cultural workers alike were reminded of the harsh world of economic reality as unemployment rose and the housing market suffered an almost unparalleled crisis as real prices fell. Many of those who had bought into the gentrified lifestyle in inner areas or dockland conversions were stranded in negative equity as the value of their property fell below the loan secured to purchase it. A new literature about downsizing and shakeouts and the advantages of a less pressurised lifestyle – an individual's choice to downshift matching enforced corporate downsizing – began to replace the more outrageous of the 1980s texts that had celebrated the 'greed is good' ethos. But even in the boom years, the expansion in service sector employment had not brought prosperity for all. While many of the new jobs were highly paid, demanding increasingly well-qualified employees who were rewarded commensurately, the greatest expansion of employment had been in poorly paid, often casual and temporary work at the bottom end of the service sector – perhaps more accurately called 'servicing' rather than service occupations. In the 1980s, the fastest growing jobs in the US economy, for example, included retail assistants, nursing auxiliaries, care attendants in old people's homes, janitors, truck drivers, waitresses and waiters (Castells, 1989; Christopherson, 1989; Sassen, 1990). The list in Great Britain was similar (Handy, 1994; Lawless et al., 1996). The net result was a widening pay differential between the well paid and the poorest paid. For those in the bottom decile of the income distribution, for example, the decade brought an absolute as well as a relative decline in their share of the total earnings from employment (Rowntree Foundation, 1995).

As well as growing income polarisation, the 1980s saw the continuation of a shift of employment from men to women which had begun with manufacturing decline in the 1960s. In the ten years after 1966, the net decline in manufacturing output led to significant job losses, of which 73 per cent were jobs previously held by men, but only 27 per cent by women. Over the same decade, the net increase in private sector services resulted in a 125 per cent increase in jobs for women, but a 44 per cent decrease in men's service employment (Dex, 1987). In the next 15 years, the loss from the manufacturing sector slowed down but the attrition of men's employment continued. Consequently, by the beginning of the 1990s, there were 3.5 million fewer men in waged employment than at the beginning of the 1960s and almost 3 million more women, although as women were more likely to work part-time, the total number of hours worked had fallen (McDowell, 1991; Walby, 1988).

These figures reflect a transformation in the labour market behaviour of women in Great Britain in the post-war era. In response to employment restructuring and to social changes from reliable contraception to new patterns of consumption (McDowell, 1989), more and more women entered the workforce. At the beginning of the 1990s, more than half of all women and almost 60 per cent of married women were economically active (Department of Employment, 1992b), compared to just over a third of all women and a fifth of married women in 1951. The time women spend out of the labour force is also becoming shorter, with 45 per cent of women returning to work and an additional 20 per cent looking for work within nine months of childbirth. While the overwhelming majority of women in paid work with young children still work part-time, an increasing proportion are returning to full-time employment after childbirth. The rate of return to full-time rather than part-time work rose from 5 to 15 per cent between 1971 and 1991 (McRae, 1991).

The feminisation of the labour market is not, however, an undifferentiated process. Just as work is becoming increasingly differentiated as a whole in its conditions and rewards, women as waged workers are also becoming increasingly differentiated (Crompton et al., 1996; McDowell, 1991; Phillips, 1989). Whereas a minority of well-educated women are able to enter and hold on to full-time work in professional occupations, the majority of women in waged work are in part-time jobs at the bottom end of the labour market. Thus, the proportion of women able to return to work after giving birth, for example, differs according to the type of work they do or are willing to accept. In comparison with other occupational groups, women professionals and associate professionals (the latter group includes teachers, health and social workers and librarians) are more likely to return and most likely to return full-time. Many of these women are in public sector employment where provision for working mothers in the form of flexible working and part-time work is more usual. Women managers and administrators in the private sector, on the other hand, have a lower rate of return, partly reflecting restricted opportunities for part-time employment at this level (McRae, 1991). Women professionals, as a group, are less likely than either managers and administrators or secretarial and clerical workers to experience downward occupational mobility (Brannen, 1989; Dex, 1987).

These trends reinforce arguments based on the analysis of pay differentials which suggest that women are becoming increasingly differentiated as a workforce. Throughout the 1980s, a growing proportion of women gained educational qualifications and they are beginning to constitute a substantial proportion of those entering professional occupations. Young women improved their performance in school-leaving examinations throughout the 1980s, and as the 1990s began, there was almost no difference between the proportions of men and women aged 20–24 gaining degrees (11 and 10 per cent respectively), although considerable differences still exist in the subjects they study (Department of Employment,1992a; Government Statistical Service, 1992). Such is the evident success of women in school, university and professional examinations, that a crisis of male under-achievement has been recognised as the popular and academic press begins to investigate 'boys who fail' and young men with little hope of steady employment (Campbell, 1993; Wilkinson and Mulgan, 1995).

These trends in the education sector and in the labour market have resulted in a rising number of women gaining access to professional occupations – once the bastions of masculine privilege. In some cases women's representation in the professions has increased dramatically. Examples include law, banking, accountancy, pharmacy and medicine. In 1991, for example, almost half the new entrants to the legal profession in Great Britain were women, up from 19 per cent in 1975 (Crompton et al., 1990; Rice, 1991). In banking, women accounted for just 2 per cent of successful finalists in the Institute of Banking examinations in 1970, but by the early 1990s almost a third of the finalists were women. In 1975 only 7 per cent of new chartered accountants and 6 per cent of the Chartered Institute of Public Finance Accountants members were women, but a decade later these proportions had risen to 25 per cent and 36 per cent respectively (Crompton, 1992).

A comparison of women's occupational distributions in 1971 and 1991 from national Census data reveals significant increases in women's participation in many types of jobs. In these two decades, women increased their representation in managerial occupations from less than 5 per cent to almost 11 per cent and also made inroads into professional occupations in general. In 1991, 15 per cent of all employed women were classified as professionals compared with 11 per cent in 1971 (Lindley and Wilson, 1993). However, there were also gains for men in professional categories; it seems that at least part of women's improved position was a result of the overall expansion of employment opportunities in these areas – many of them in the new middle-class occupations just outlined – rather than women taking jobs previously held by men.

Despite their growing presence in higher level jobs, few women make it to the top of the occupational hierarchies in the public or private sector. Although one in four junior managers in Britain was female at the start of the 1990s, at senior management levels the number of women remaining was down to one or two per 100 (Summers, 1991a). Less than 1 per cent of managing directors of large companies were women, and a similarly tiny proportion of directors of publicly quoted companies were women (Labour Research, 1992). Women are equally badly represented in the upper echelons of the public sector. They are, for example, almost completely absent at the highest level of the police force (the first woman chief constable was appointed in 1995) and the judiciary. As the '90s began, only one out of 14 regional health authorities was chaired by a woman; and just 7 per cent of top Civil Service posts, less than 2 per cent of local council chief executives, and only about 25 per cent of secondary school headships were filled by women (*Financial Times*, 1992; Goodhart, 1991; Summers, 1991b). Even in law and accountancy, which women have entered in considerable numbers in recent years, the number making it to the top is tiny. Women are approximately 12 per cent of partners in law firms, less than 2 per cent of the fellows of the Chartered Institute of Management Accountants and, as I began my work, less than 4 per cent of directors of the big four banks in Britain. As we see later, women's representation on the boards of merchant banks is remarkable only for their almost complete absence.

EXPLAINING ORGANISATIONAL AND WORKPLACE CHANGE

In the next part of this chapter, I want to shift from an empirical to a theoretical focus and examine the sets of theoretical literatures about work, organisational change and culture and gender divisions of labour that influenced this study of gendered patterns of recruitment, promotion and social interaction in the world of investment or merchant banking. I want to outline briefly the ways of thinking that have influenced me in the years in which I have been preoccupied with questions about gender and power. I hope to show that, rather than taking a singular or disciplinary-specific approach, a more complete understanding of why certain types of people are successful merchant bankers can be gained by bringing together a range of different theoretical approaches to occupational segregation and labour market segmentation, the culture of workplaces – literatures about the body, about clothes and personal presentation, about success, organisational structures and the meaning of work, and about the impact that the built environment has on how men and women situate themselves in spaces and places.

In this work, I have adopted a geographic approach in the sense of moving through progressively finer spatial scales in an attempt to build up, or rather uncover, the processes behind empirically evident patterns of gender segregation in the City, in the financial services sector and within merchant banks. Thus, I move from the general to the particular throughout the book, ending up with the individual and his or her body, a spatial scale not generally considered by geographers but much more familiar to sociologists and psychologists. In any study of service sector work, however, in which so much depends on 'the management of feeling to create a publicly observable facial and bodily display' (Hochschild, 1983, p. 7), the scale of the body cannot be ignored. Because my aim is to understand the gendered organisation of the financial services sector – at least to the extent that merchant banks are representative organisations in this sector – my focus remains on the City and the firms within it. This is not a study of the role of the financial services sector *per se* in restructuring Britain's space economy. But this is not to imply that I have completely ignored the overall significance of the financial services sector or the specificities of merchant banking.

In a study of gendered management and employment practices in the insurance industry, Kerfoot and Knights (1994) argued that, for them, 'financial services are merely a site for empirical research rather than the intrinsic object of investigation' (p. 124). I began this study of merchant banks in the City of London with a somewhat similar belief – my concern was not with the economic niceties of fluctuating interest rates, nor with instruments of deregulation and re-regulation, not even with the successive scandals that affected so many City banks in the 1980s and 1990s, but rather with the everyday practices of the men and women who worked in City banks. But, of course, the two cannot be separated. The specificities of financial services as an industry, the particularities of the City in the early 1990s and the environment, attitudes and culture of each merchant bank affected the ways in which gender differences in recruitment policies and career opportunities worked out. What economic sociologists term 'embeddedness' and geographers 'location' cannot and should not be ignored in the investigation of gender segregation at work. Looking back, I realise that even to think for a moment that place and specificity might not matter was foolish. Although the trend towards feminisation evident in the new service economy of the UK and other advanced industrial nations might be a general one, the ways in which it works out in different sectors and in different geographic locations are particular. Thus, this book is a detailed case study of the processes of gender segregation in three merchant banks which are distinguished as much by the differences in their workplace practices as by their similarities. Indeed, this recognition resulted in the dual notions of embeddedness and embodiment becoming important in my analysis.

The embeddedness of social and cultural institutions, firms and individual workplaces is now a key area of study in the new economic sociology or social economics (Granovetter, 1985; Gudeman, 1986; Zelizer, 1987; Zukin and DiMaggio, 1990), whereas Bourdieu (1984) used the term 'embodiment' to refer to similar processes at the scale of an organisation. In the main, however, in analyses of the ways in which national and local factors have influenced economic changes, geographers (Schoenberger, 1994; Storper, 1994; Thrift, 1994) have turned to the revitalised area of economic sociology, rather than to studies of organisational culture, not only to shed light on the location of industries and their position within national and local systems of political and financial regulation, but also to open up new questions about the cultural meaning of new products, new forms of workplace organisation and labour recruitment. Economic sociology focuses on issues of power, the social aspects of markets and business–government links, on social networks and the culture of organisations. It challenges conventional notions of rational economic actors, suggesting rather that economic action is embedded in the social context and the specific institutions within which it takes place. Like all social interactions, economic decisions are as much affected by tradition, historical precedent, class and gender interests and other social factors as by considerations of efficiency or profit. This is particularly evident in the world of merchant banking, in which networks of familial interests as well as the networks of social elites link directors of banks together and to directors of other British firms and the Conservative Party (Hutton, 1995b; Sampson, 1992; Scott, 1991; Stanworth and Giddens, 1974a, b).

Sets of common social assumptions and cultural understandings shape economic strategies and goals. As Zukin and DiMaggio (1990) have argued:

> culture sets limits to economic rationality: it proscribes or limits exchange
> in sacred objects and relations (e.g. human beings, body organisms or
> physical intimacy) or between ritually classified groups . . . culture, in the

form of beliefs and ideologies, taken for granted assumptions, or formal
rule systems also prescribes strategies of self-interested action . . . and
defines the actors who may legitimately engage in them (e.g. self-interested
individuals, families, classes, formal organisations, ethnic groups). Culture
provides scripts for applying different strategies to different classes of exchange. Finally, norms and constitutive understandings regulate market
exchange, causing persons to behave with institutionalised and culturally
specific definitions of integrity even when they could get away with cheat-
ing. On the one hand, it constitutes the structures in which economic self
interest is played out; on the other, it constrains the free play of market
forces. (p. 17)

In the 1980s, one of the Conservative government's achievements was to
reverse long-standing constraints, creating the circumstances for the spread
of a new set of cultural assumptions in the City and in wider society. An
ideology of individualism – that people are solely motivated by pecuniary
gain – and the associated claims for the efficacy of deregulation in freeing
the market from the stranglehold of the state and assuring economic
efficiency and success gained the high ground. How these notions progressively infiltrated discourse and practice in a range of economic institutions is a major research challenge for economic sociologists and
anthropologists. Merchant banking in particular, within the City as an
institution, was one of the prime locations for the successful promulga-
tion and diffusion of these new cultural assumptions; it therefore seemed
an exemplary site for research. Of all the middle-class occupations in
that new service or new cultural class that expanded in the 1980s, it was
bankers who were characterised as the personification of the era: the
apotheosis of individualistic, profit-oriented 'yuppies'.

Moving to a finer spatial scale of individual firms, rather than the
environment of the City as a whole in the late 1980s and early 1990s, it
is clear that changes in the nature of assumptions about ways of acting
and interacting affected different institutions in different ways, in part
dependent upon their earlier histories and cultures and the impact these
had on how and which people were recruited in the expansionist years of
the 1980s. Here, economic sociologists Zukin and DiMaggio suggested
that the notion of scripts that structure different types of exchanges is
useful for analysing behaviour within particular institutions. Their notion is close to earlier social interactionist and ethnomethodological approaches in sociology, and has a particular purchase on the ways in
which everyday social interactions in the City are constructed to include
and exclude different social actors. These scripts and strategies will be
the focus of chapters 5 to 8 in part II, where the parallels between
economic sociology and social interactionist approaches prove useful in
understanding what happens in banks; but I shall also demonstrate, in

the empirical analyses presented there, the parallels with both these approaches and feminist analyses of the construction of gender as a performance.

While geographers and economists are as yet less familiar with an emphasis on the micro-social practices in the workplace and tend to ignore the significance of issues of power, desire and embodiment at work, it is interesting that Bourdieu (1984) used the terms 'embeddedness' and 'embodiment' interchangeably. In this way, he also seems to straddle a sociological focus on the possession of capital culture by embodied actors and the more recent work on the body which I shall discuss below. As Bourdieu argued, the possession of cultural capital by high-status employees is evidenced not only in their educational and professional credentials and in the types of goods and possessions that they choose to purchase, but also in 'the embodied states, as mode of speech, accent, style, beauty and so forth' (Bourdieu, 1984, p. 243). Thus, I believe that it is crucial to connect the body, the individual and the organisation in attempting to understand the persistence of gender segregation.

GENDER SEGREGATION AT WORK

Before moving from the organisation to the body, however, I want to review briefly the history of approaches to the analysis of gender divisions of labour and occupational segregation by sex through to how the persistence of such a marked division in the labour market has been explained. Whether in times of economic stability or of marked change, such as those of the 1980s, it seems that women's concentration into a few sectors of the economy and certain types of occupations within them has remained a constant feature of the social division of labour (Crompton et al., 1996; Humphries and Rubery, 1995; Scott, 1994). In the face of this persistence, the unsexed worker, labour power unencumbered by a body or any other social attributes, has almost disappeared from all but the most blinkered of studies, as the lived experience of workers distinguished by, among other characteristics, their gender, ethnicity, age and family circumstances has become an important focus of research on work and organisations.

A growing body of work from the mid 1970s on women's exclusion from the workplace, gender segmentation, unequal power and low pay has demonstrated an evident continuity in patterns of gender segregation across time and space, illustrating how labour market institutions are significant loci of male power. Questions about gender relations at work, the social construction of gender identities in the workplace and the gendering of organisations themselves are now addressed in a range of disciplines, including anthropology, labour economics, geography, economic history, management studies, politics, psychology and sociology, as well as from various interdisciplinary positions (Amsden, 1980; Arber and Gilbert, 1992; Collinson et al., 1990; Crompton et al., 1996; Crompton and Sanderson, 1990; Gallie, 1988; Humphries and Rubery, 1995; Knights and Willmott, 1986; Reskin and Hartmann, 1986; Walby, 1986). Researchers in these disciplines draw on a wide range of theoretical perspectives, from cultural studies and discourse theory to organisational analysis and business studies, from feminist and gender analysis to postmodern legal studies, and have adopted a variety of methodological approaches including analyses of secondary sources, both historical and from the contemporary period, and quantitative and qualitative surveys and case studies of particular industries and workplaces. The net result has been a huge and exciting flowering of research on the gendering of work, stimulated not only by the intense theoretical interdisciplinary cross-fertilisation but also by the material changes in the structure of work in advanced industrial societies.

In the 1970s and 1980s the dominant perspective was a version of what might be termed the 'division of labour' approach (Frobel et al., 1980; Massey, 1984, 1994) in which workers entered the labour market with their gender attributes firmly established. In both the advanced and newly industrialising countries, women were theorised as a reserve of cheap labour, attractive to newly mobile capital in search of higher rates of profit. While the 'division of labour' approach implicitly drew on feminist analyses of how women's domestic responsibilities were part of the explanation for their construction as a reserve army, less attention was paid to the reasons for women being drawn into a narrow range of occupations even as the labour market became increasingly feminised. Women's occupational segregation was noted rather than explained. Feminist scholars working within a broad Marxist church, however, explained these patterns through theories of patriarchy, whether conceptualised as a separate system that parallels capitalism, drawing on Marxist notions of exploitation, or as an inseparable part of the capitalist mode of production (Beechey, 1977; Hartmann, 1979; Vogel, 1983; Walby, 1986, 1991b). This stream of explicitly feminist work has the closest links with the divisions of labour school in geography. Other theorists in other disciplines have worked within alternative frameworks (Dex, 1985). Economists, for example, have variously drawn on human capital theory (Mincer, 1962; Zellner, 1975) and dual and segmented labour market theory (Baron and Norris, 1976; Craig et al., 1982; Rubery, 1988) to posit women's responsibility for domestic labour as the major reason for their relegation to lowly positions in the labour market.

As well as abstract theorising and aggregate-scale analyses of women's labour market position, since the mid 1970s there have also been a number of smaller scale, qualitative analyses of women's subordinate position in the labour market. In the 1980s, these case studies, mainly but not exclusively in the manufacturing sector, began to shed light on a wide and varied range of social practices on the 'shop floor' that act as obstacles to women's advancement (Bradley, 1989; Cockburn, 1983, 1991; Game and Pringle, 1984; Milkman, 1987; Pringle, 1989; Westwood, 1984). While most of these case studies have been undertaken by scholars outside geography, geographers did not neglect women's occupational segregation in local labour market studies either. Their contribution to the growing literature has, not surprisingly, focused mainly on spatial issues in labour market behaviour, especially the significance of women's restricted journey-to-work patterns in comparison with men's as an important factor in reproducing women's inferior labour market position (Hanson and Johnston, 1985; Johnston-Anumonwo, 1992; Villeneuve and Rose, 1988). Hanson and Pratt's (1995) work has been particularly influential in drawing attention to geographical issues, extending the understanding of the role of residential location and gender differences in job search behaviour in the maintenance of occupational sex segregation. They developed a concept of spatial containment, consequent upon women's domestic responsibilities, to explain gender differences.

A second step in the explanation of gender segregation in the labour market came with the recognition that occupations and workers themselves are socially constructed through a variety of practices to conform to a particular set of gender attributes. Occupations are not empty slots to be filled, nor do workers enter the labour market and the workplace with fixed and immoveable gender attributes. Instead these features are negotiated and contested at work. As Scott (1988) recognised:

> if we write the history of women's work by gathering data that describe the activities, needs, interests, and culture of 'women workers', we leave in place the naturalised contrast and reify a fixed categorical difference between women and men. We start the story, in other words, too late, by uncritically accepting a gendered category (the 'woman worker') that itself needs investigation because its meaning is relative to its history. (p. 47)

The same observation is applicable to occupations and, thus, the processes of occupational sex-typing – or better, stereotyping – began to be analysed.

Jobs are not gender neutral – rather they are created as appropriate for either men or women, and the set of social practices that constitute and maintain them is constructed so as to embody socially sanctioned but *variable* characteristics of masculinity and femininity. This association seems self-evident in the analysis of classically 'masculine' occupations; consider, for example, the heroic struggle and camaraderie involved in heavy male manual labour (McDowell and Massey, 1984). The same belief now holds with respect to self-evidently female occupations such as secretarial work, but it is salutary to remember that the latter have changed their gender associations over the century (Bradley, 1989). Less obviously 'sexed' jobs and new occupations are struggled over and negotiated to establish their gender coding.

GENDERED ORGANISATIONS: SEXING AND RESEXING JOBS

In suggesting that the earlier studies of occupational segregation neglected the processes by which jobs become gendered, focusing on occupational segregation rather than occupational sex stereotyping, this is not to imply that the association of, for example, skill designation with gender or the embodiment of gender attributes in job definitions and workplace practices was ignored completely. This clearly is not so. There is a large body of work that has revealed how the supposedly natural attributes of femininity (be they docility, dexterity or 'caring') have been set up in opposition to masculine attributes in order to organise and reorganise labour processes and differentially reward workers on the basis of their gender (see, for example, Beechey, 1987; Beechey and Perkins, 1987; Cockburn, 1983; Crompton and Jones, 1984; Crompton and Sanderson, 1990; Milkman, 1987; Phillips and Taylor, 1980; Walby, 1986). But so far there has been less attention paid to the ways in which new jobs are stereotyped initially, and to the ways in which everyday social practices reaffirm or challenge these gender attributions over time. Formal organisational structures and informal workplace practices are not gender neutral but are saturated with gendered meanings and practices that construct both gendered subjectivities at work and different categories of work as congruent with particular gender identities. Interesting work is now being undertaken by sociologists (Leidner, 1993) and organisational theorists (Casey, 1995; Hearn and Parkin, 1987; Knights and Willmott, 1986) and increasingly by anthropologists interested in the multiple constructions of femininity and masculinity in different types of jobs and at different workplace sites (Wright, 1994). The ways in which 'resexing' jobs is a significant part or consequence of economic restructuring, often leading to loss of status, power or financial rewards, are also beginning to be investigated, linking the specificities of doing gender on the job to wider economic processes (Halford and Savage, 1995; Kerfoot and Knights, 1994; Morgan and Knights, 1991).

An important stimulus to my thinking about the construction and maintenance of gendered occupations in the financial services came from within organisation theory, especially from recent studies that have drawn attention to the ubiquity of sexuality in organisational processes and the ways in which it is related to the structures of power (Acker, 1990; Hearn and Parkin, 1987; Pringle, 1989). Within this literature, there has been a shift from what might be termed the 'gender-in-organisation model' – where organisations are seen as settings in which gendered actors behave, as gender-neutral places which affect men and women differently because of their different attributes – to theorising organisations themselves as embedded with gendered meanings and structured by the social relations of sexuality. In these studies, sexuality is defined as a socially constructed set of processes which includes patterns of desire, fantasy, pleasure and self-image. Hence, it is not restricted solely, nor indeed mainly, to sexual relations and the associated policy implications around the issue of sexual harassment. Rather the focus is on power and domination and the way in which assumptions about gender-appropriate behaviour and sexuality, as broadly defined, influence management practices, the organisational logic of job evaluations, promotion procedures and job specifications (Acker, 1990), and the everyday social relations between workers.

The growing recognition of the ways in which male sexuality structures organisational practices counters commonly held views that sexuality at work is a defining characteristic of *women* workers. As Acker (1990) has argued:

> their [organisations'] gendered nature is partly masked through obscuring the embodied nature of work. Abstract jobs and hierarchies [. . .] assume a disembodied and universal worker. This worker is actually a man: men's bodies, sexuality and relationships to procreation and waged work are subsumed in the image of the worker. Images of men's bodies and masculinity pervade organisational processes, marginalising women and contributing to the maintenance of gender segregation in organisations. (p. 139)

Part of the marginalisation is constructed through a particular discourse of sexuality that empowers men and positions women as subjects of masculine desire. Dominant notions of sexuality in contemporary western culture are based on a set of gendered power relations in which men's dominance over women is expressed and recreated. Images of hostility and domination, including fantasies of humiliation and revenge, have been shown to be a central part of masculine sexual identity. As Stoller (1979) has argued, a central element of the construction of sexuality in discourse, symbolism and social practice is an image of the phallus as 'aggressive, unfettered, unsympathetic, humiliating' (p. 74). Recent work on organisational structures in a range of industries has begun to demonstrate the centrality of this image in everyday social relations and interactions in many workplaces. It is a particularly significant image in the world of merchant banking, as I shall demonstrate in part II.

The earliest explorations of how organisations are saturated with male power and masculinist values, however, tended to take the social construction of masculinity for granted, instead uncovering in careful detailed work alternative versions of femininity (Kanter, 1977; Marshall, 1984). Although the centrality of a masculine model of employment, based on life-time, full-time and continuous employment, and the importance of waged work as a key element in the construction of a masculine identity were clear, the focus was on the ways in which these structures and assumptions exclude women rather than on the different ways in which alternative masculinities are constructed in the workplace. Pringle (1989), for example, in her study of the relationships between secretaries and bosses, noted that the association between masculinity and rationality allowed male sexuality to remain invisible yet dominant, positioning women as the inferior 'Other' at work, and yet she interviewed only women. In chapter 5, I draw on the vitality and insights of this approach to show how 'woman' is othered in the workplace. My focus will also be on women as a group, examining commonalities rather than differences between women. For a time, men will remain ungendered as the 'norm' against which women are found wanting.

The realisation that male embodiment and masculine sexuality must also be rendered visible and interrogated resulted in a significant shift in feminist analyses of the gendering of occupations. Men began to enter the analyses of feminist work and slowly more organisational sociology where the significance of gender previously had been ignored. But even so, as Scott (1994) has noted, 'The inclusion of men might seem obvious to many working in this field today, but we should remember that gender segregation is still popularly perceived as a "woman's problem"' (p. 3). Scott's book reports the results of the Social Change and Economic Life Initiative (SCELI), based on surveys carried out in the mid 1980s, and provides perhaps the first large-scale British comparison of men's and women's employment experiences.

If feminist scholars had tended to ignore men, with a few honourable exceptions including Cockburn's (1983) magnificent, path-breaking study of the print workers, male labour analysts had exhibited an even greater reluctance to take feminist analyses of gender relations seriously. According to Collinson and Hearn (1994), this resulted in an 'avoidance of theoretical and empirical analysis of men and masculinities, where analysis is reflexive and critique is turned upon ourselves' (p. 3). It was just too painful – and too threatening – for men to reveal the structures of power and oppression that maintain their privilege.

As Acker suggested, and Collinson and Hearn began to document, organisations reflect masculine values and power, permeating all aspects of the workplace in ways often taken for granted. Not only the formal structures of institutions, their recruitment, promotion and appraisal mechanisms and their working hours, but also informal structures of everyday interactions reinforce women's inferiority. Male power is implicitly reinforced in many of the micro-scale interactions in organisations: in workplace talk and jokes, for example, 'men see humour, teasing, camaraderie and strength . . . women often perceive crude, specifically masculine aggression, competition, harassment, intimidation and misogyny' (Collinson and Hearn, 1994, p. 3). There are numerous other ways in which particular workplace cultures in a range of occupations, in both the service and manufacturing sectors, appeal to 'highly masculine values of individualism, aggression, competition, sport and drinking' (Collinson and Hearn, 1994, p. 4).

The expansion of work about masculinity and organisations, about male power, masculine discourse and gendered social practices, is part of a wider move in feminist-influenced scholarship to understand the complexity of gendered subjectivities and the ways in which they are constructed in and vary between different sites – the home, the street and the workplace, for example. It coincided with attempts by feminists, particularly feminists of colour, to reveal the assumptions about 'woman' that lie behind the early feminist scholarship. Criticised for its implicit focus on a version of white, anglocentric and middle-class femininity, feminist scholars are increasingly working on the ways in which race, class and gender are mutually constituted. There has been a parallel rise of queer scholarship. Lesbian feminists, such as Butler (1990a, 1993), Fuss (1990) and Wittig (1992), have shown how the 'regulatory fiction' of heterosexuality (Rich, 1980; Rubin, 1975) reinforces a naturalised binary distinction between men and women. Similarly, in a remarkable growth of male gay scholarship from the mid 1980s, the construction and dominance of a hegemonic heterosexual masculinity which excludes other forms of masculinity has been revealed (Craig, 1992; Herdt, 1992; Kimmel, 1988; Metcalf and Humphries, 1985; Weeks, 1986).

In recent work on gender, therefore, in general as well as in the 'sociology of organisations' school, the notion of multiple masculinities has been developed to refer to the variety of forms of masculinity across space and time. There has been a rapid expansion of an exciting literature demonstrating the extent of historical and geographical variations (Gibson, 1994; Gilmore, 1990; Herzfeld, 1985; Kaufman, 1993; Klein, 1993; Mangan and Walvin, 1992; Messner, 1992; Nye, 1993; Roper and Tosh, 1991; Segal, 1990). Just as femininities are constructed in opposition to masculinity, so are alternative masculinities constructed in relation to a hegemonic version of masculinity (Connell, 1987; Donaldson, 1991, 1993). These masculinities are not fixed but shift over time; however in the same way that femininity is embedded within power relations, so too are versions of masculinity. Alternative or non-hegemonic masculinities are subordinate to the dominant version. Connell (1995) argued that new scholarship from history and anthropology has led to important research into the ways in which masculinities are produced as cultural forms. Institutional structures, individual agency and social struggles are involved in the production of hegemonic or exemplary versions of masculinity appropriate to a time and place. 'Definitions of masculinity are deeply enmeshed in the history of institutions and economic structures' (Connell, 1995, p. 29). To understand the diversity of forms and the transformations that occur, it is important to analyse masculinity in specific contexts and sets of organised social relations. Interesting work by, for example, Heward (1988) on a boys' public school in England in the inter-war period, by Grossberg (1990) on law firms in nineteenth century USA and the edited collection by anthropologists Cornwall and Lindisfarne (1994) began to reveal the ways in which institutional structures and social practices sustain particular versions of masculinity, excluding many men as well as women as a group. There are still surprisingly few recent studies, however, which directly compare men and women within the same organisation, even doing the same job, and which unravel the different ways in which non-hegemonic versions of femininity *and* masculinity are constricted and maintained as inferior. This is a reflection, of course, of the fact that so few men and women actually do the same job.

It is important, however, to undertake comparative work to uncover the ways in which versions of femininity and masculinity are constructed in particular social contexts and in different locations. As Giuffre and Williams (1994) have recognised, the sexualised workplace in contemporary Britain provides a context for the 'continued display and performance of heterosexuality' (p. 397). As I shall demonstrate, investment banks may be the site of the display and performance of multiple masculinities, but each revolves around hegemonic versions of a masculine heterosexuality. Cornwall and Lindisfarne have suggested that 'by looking in detail at everyday usage and the contexts in which people talk of masculinity, its complexity soon becomes apparent' (1994, p. 3). One of the aims of this study is to demonstrate something of this complexity and to show how, through language and everyday behaviour, certain types of heterosexual masculinity and particular versions of femininity are constructed in the different arenas of investment banking. This is the focus of chapters 6 to 8.

NORMALISING THE SELF

The focus on contructing the self at work led to a growing interest in the concept of 'normalisation' in Foucault's work. The narrow range of socially sanctioned gendered identities and ways of behaving are reinforced and policed through a set of structures that keep in place dominant and subordinate social relations. These structures or mechanisms include not only institutional force and sanctions from above but also self-surveillance and what Foucault termed 'capillary power'. This interest opened up a way to link analyses of institutional interests and power relations to micro-scale social practices (Foucault, 1979). Here the enormous expansion of interest in subjectivity and in the body by labour analysts and other social scientists is crucial.

New ways of thinking about theory, politics and the subject have developed in an interesting confrontation between feminism, postmodernism, and post-structuralism. Challenges to the supposed universalism of the rational subject of liberal theory have resulted in a new emphasis in a wide range of different disciplines on the positionality and situatedness of action and knowledge – concepts that are not unrelated to the notion of embeddedness in economic sociology. One of the central elements of these arguments is a challenge to the modernist confidence that individuality is grounded in a singular and unique subjectivity that is invariant. In contrast, it is now argued that the self is in a fragile process of construction throughout the life cycle and that a multiplicity of identities are constructed through the symbolic repertoires of everyday actions in institutional contexts (Chaney, 1993; Giddens, 1991, 1992; Lash and Friedman, 1992). In this sense, the significance of position or location has taken a new precedence in social theory. Further, 'these "positions" are not merely theoretical products, but fully embedded organizing principles of material practices and institutional arrangements, those matrices of power and discourse that produce me as a visible "subject"' (Butler, 1992, p. 9). Here then is a productive coincidence of the notions of embeddedness and embodiment.

The institutional arrangements and social practices within banks that produce subject positions are, of course, replete with taken-for-granted assumptions, many of which are inimical to women as well as class based, as I show later. A wide range of mechanisms are used to reproduce the culture of an organisation, including selective recruitment, training strategies, appraisal and promotion schemes as well as ensuring the adherence of agents or workers to organisational norms by subtle or less subtle means. Many of these strategies are examined in part II.

The theoretical focus on the body, sexualised performances and strategies of surveillance parallels material changes in the nature of work in service sector occupations. One of the key features of service sector work, compared with manufacturing jobs, is that the labour power and embodied performance of workers is part of the product in a way that was not the case in the production of manufactured goods. Services that are exchanged, sold, purchased, used up, be they producer or consumer service products – a pedicure, a lecture or a piece of legal advice – cannot be separated from the workers who are producing and exchanging them. Service occupations revolve around personal relationships or interactions between service providers and consumers, in the main unmediated by a set of exchange professionals as is more usual in the exchange of manufactured goods. In service interactions, the body of the worker – be it the 'managed heart' of care professionals or flight attendants (Hochschild, 1983), the uniform service of the fast food joint or personalised but scripted service of more upmarket restaurants (Crang, 1994; Gabriel, 1988; Leidner, 1991, 1993), the smiling charm of a bank teller or the professional advice of a besuited male manager (Kerfoot and Knights, 1994) – all demand an embodied and visible performance. Special clothing or uniforms may be required for the performance of particular tasks, and prohibitions, for example of facial hair or jewellery, are common in order to produce a specific, usually explicitly heterosexual self-image, both for men and for women. Leidner (1991, 1993) has termed these types of service occupations 'interactive work', where workers' looks, personalities and emotions, as well as their physical and intellectual capacities, are involved, sometimes forcing them to manipulate their identities more self-consciously than workers in other kinds of jobs. Interactive jobs are not new. It is salutary to recall Fromm's astute recognition of their significant characteristics almost 50 years ago:

> in order to have success it is not sufficient to have the skill and equipment for performing a given task but that one must also be able to 'put across' one's personality in competition with many others shapes that attitude toward oneself . . . since success depends largely on how one sells one's personality, one experiences oneself simultaneously as the seller and as the commodity to be sold. (Fromm, 1949, p. 12)

What, is new, however, is their economic dominance in advanced industrial nations.

Many current interactive occupations, especially those which have been studied in detail, are 'women's' work in various guises, reliant on that hegemonic version of heterosexual femininity that emphasises docility, passivity, servicing and generous attention to customers' needs, constructing women as unsuitable for positions of power and control in the higher echelons of organisations or for the type of professional work considered here. Where male subjects have been studied, the empirical focus remains on the bottom end of the service sector: restaurants are a particularly dominant location (Crang, 1994; Gabriel, 1988; Leidner, 1993). There have been almost no empirical studies of sexuality and the normalisation of bodies in professional service sector occupations, including the financial services sector, that expanded so rapidly in the 1980s, although Halford and Savage (1995) have examined retail banking and local authority administrative positions. In professional occupations, required bodily standards, acceptable clothing and a scripted performance in client/employee interactions are seldom made as explicit as they are in routine interactive service jobs. Instead, through a range of formal and informal procedures, including recruitment procedures and appraisal schemes, and through everyday social interactions between colleagues and between colleagues and clients, acceptable versions of professional workers are created, policed and maintained. But whether these occupations are professional or not, the importance of embodied performance is an increasing emphasis.

BODIES AT WORK

When I began this research, the texts on the body could be assembled on the corner of my desk. They now take up many shelves, although the specific focus on embodied performance in the workplace is a more recent focus of the expansion. The re-theorising of work as an embodied performance accords well with the realities of the restructured world of work with which this chapter began. One of the most significant aspects of the 1990s is the ways in which individuals' attachment to the labour force and to a particular job within it has changed. For increasing numbers of workers as we approach the end of the twentieth century, there is an expectation of a career that is discontinuous and interrupted, marked by successive contracts rather than the life-time tenure of a single occupation. Thus, as Petit (1995) has remarked, 'like actors, we will spend our working lives being hired and fired . . . with each new job demanding we take on a new part' (p. 5). Work, once regarded as a (relative) certainty and a central aspect of personal identity, especially for men, has itself become a fluid, multiple and uncertain performance.

Despite these uncertainties, however, and women's greater visibility in the workplace, the most dominant image that continues to structure the world of work in contemporary Britain is that it is a public arena, associated with men and masculinity. As feminist scholars have argued, in western enlightenment societies, embodied social structures, and the physical locations in which they take place, construct acceptable ways of being and 'reasonable' behaviour on the basis of a set of binaries. As Bourdieu (1984) noted:

> The network of oppositions between high (sublime, elevated, pure) and low (vulgar, low, modest), spiritual and material, fine (refined, elegant) and coarse (heavy, fat, crude, brutal), light (subtle, lively, sharp, adroit) and heavy (slow, thick, blunt, laborious, clumsy), free and forced, broad and narrow, or in another dimension, between unique (rare, different, distinguished, exceptional, singular, novel) and common (ordinary, banal, common place, trivial, routine), brilliant (intelligent) and dull (obscure, grey, mediocre) is the matrix of all the commonplaces which find such ready acceptance because behind them lies the whole social order. (p. 468)

And, he continued, they 'derive their ideological strength from the fact that they refer back to the most fundamental oppositions between the dominant and the dominated, which is *inscribed in the division of labour*' (p. 469, my emphasis).

In contemporary western societies, therefore, these binaries structure the embodiment of waged labour. They act to define woman as inferior, separating her purportedly natural and private world from the public world of men (Benhabib and Cornell, 1987; Pateman and Grosz, 1986) which, as a public arena, is portrayed as being as distant from the natural world as it is possible to be. Abstract symbols of power, particularly money, are the markers of status and culture. Whereas the natural world is associated with animality, the cultural and cultured world of work is distinguished by its humanity. It is constructed as a rational, objective world in which behaviour and decisions are ruled by accepted and conventional norms. In modern industrial societies, the workplace is distinguished by its rational and bureaucratic social order, an arena supposedly unmarked by emotion or by personal characteristics or attributes, one that above all is associated with all that is culturally valued as masculine. Thus, women are literally out of place at work for, as many commentators have pointed out – some approvingly, others critically – woman is to nature as man is to culture. Women, like nature, are viewed as fecund and unreliable, part of the natural order of things, the body rather than the mind, and so unfit for the cool rationality of the public arena. This gendered distinction is not, however, unambiguous, as the widespread notion of women's 'civilising influence' (she who soothes the savage breast) makes clear. There is an important tradition in the social and biological sciences that regards the cultural world of humanity as a constraint on the natural world of animality. Thus, there is a link here between man's 'natural' aggression and dominance (which, as we shall see, is a significant metaphor on the trading floor) to the construction of male sexuality as rampant and unfettered. As Freud argued, the successful establishment of social life requires prohibitions and taboos, the restraint of in-stinctual behaviour which, if incorrectly repressed, may lead to mental illness. Christianity has also been an important influence on the con-struction of the body as a fleshy evil that needs control as well as a vessel to worship. Thus, there is a love–hate relationship with the body and a set of dualistic contradictions between mind and body, body and soul, sexuality and civilisation, which are ambiguously gendered.

But women are out of place in the embodied social structures of the workplace precisely because they are unable to acquire the cultural markers associated with the attributes valued in the workplace, or perhaps to qualify this, those associated with the rational and bureaucratic workplace. As Young has pointed out, the idealisation of a particular notion of (dis)embodiment in the workplace means that 'women suffer workplace disadvantage ... because many men regard women in inappropriate sexual terms and because women's clothes, comportment, voices and so on disrupt the disembodied ideal of masculinist bureaucracy' (Young, 1990a, p. 176). Embodiment is, in Young's view, one of five key elements which construct hierarchies of unequally placed groups in contemporary capitalist societies. She labelled the politics of embodiment 'cultural im-perialism', drawing attention to the violence done to the self-image of those who deviate from the contemporary hegemonic version of an ide-alised body – not only male but also slim and light-skinned. This ideali-sation establishes as the 'Other' not only women but also people of colour and those who are not an approximation of the perfect shape or size. Young emphasised the significance of lived social experience in the maintenance of oppression through cultural imperialism, arguing that much of the oppressive experience of cultural imperialism occurs in mundane contexts of interaction – in the gestures, speech, tone of voice, movement and reactions of others. 'Pulses of attraction and aversion modulate all interactions, with specific consequences for experience of the body. When the dominant culture defines some groups as different, as the Other, the members of those groups are imprisoned in their bodies. Dominant discourse defines them in terms of bodily characteris-tics, and constructs those bodies as ugly, dirty, defiled, impure, contami-nated or sick' (p. 123). The net result is what Young referred to as 'epidermalising the world' or the 'scaling of bodies'.

Tseelon (1995) suggested that women's embodiment is based on a number of paradoxes. Her work seems to usefully extend Young's notion of the scaling of bodies, at least in consideration of femininity. Four of her paradoxes were particularly helpful in thinking through the inter-views I undertook with women bankers. The first is the modesty paradox in which the woman is constructed as seduction – to be ever punished for it. The second is the duplicity paradox: the woman is constructed as artifice, and marginalised for lacking essence and authenticity. The third is the visibility paradox: the woman is constructed as spectacle while being culturally invisible. The final paradox is the beauty paradox: the woman embodies ugliness while signifying beauty. These paradoxes help to explain why women challenge the assumptions that construct an ideal worker as rational, unemotional, disembodied but authoritative.

It might be argued, however, that the cultural assumptions of late capitalist society have made the focus on the body and its appearance a more general one, rather than a specific 'female' concern. A large number of postmodern theorists of the body (among them Bauman, 1992; Featherstone et al., 1991; Shilling, 1993), or, as Giddens (1991) would prefer, sociologists of late modernity, have argued that in a consumer culture obsessed with appearance, the status of the body has been transformed from a fixed and natural given to a malleable cultural product, perhaps the last frontier of control in a world marked by uncertainty. Anxiety about the body and its control through punishing regimes of dietary and exercise management, sculpting and reshaping the body through exercise and surgery, as well as obsessive interests in clothing and other forms of bodily adornment, are no longer the sole preserve of women but are associated with a more general desire to construct a body-beautiful, to fashion and refashion personal identity (Bordo, 1993; Tseelon, 1995). The body matters increasingly for men and for women, although it is important to note that, as Tseelon emphasised, 'a concern with carrying off a performance does not necessarily imply a deep and abiding identification with that appearance' (p. 5). As I demonstrate later, this has resonances with Butler's theorisation of gender as a bodily performance or masquerade and also helps us to understand the unease that many of my respondents felt with their workplace personas.

But there is little doubt about the increasing centrality of the body at work at the end of the twentieth century. As Fiske (1993) has argued:

> The body is the primary site of social experience. It is where social life is turned into lived experience. To understand the body we have to know who controls it as it moves through the spaces and times of our daily routines, who shapes its sensuous experiences, its sexualities, its pleasures in eating and exercise, *who controls its performance at work,* its behaviour at home and school and also influences how it is dressed and made to appear in its function of presenting us to others. The body is the core of our social experience. (p. 57, my emphasis)

And, as Featherstone (1991b) has noted: 'the tendency towards narcissism, the negotiating, performing self is . . . most noticeable in the professional-managerial middle-class who have both the time and money to engage in lifestyle activities and the cultivation of the persona' (p. 192).

As I argued earlier, merchant bankers are a classic example of the newly dominant professional-managerial middle class and, as I show in chapters 6 to 8, bodily appearance at work is of predominant concern to both the men and the women among them. Featherstone unfortunately restricted his analysis of embodied performance to the realm of consumption and leisure and ignored the workplace. The social spaces inhabited by the middle-class performers he identified are the 'new shopping centres, the beach, the modern pub' (1991a, p. 192). However, in acquiring the time and money that facilitate new lifestyle activities, the professional-managerial class that he singled out are also likely to be involved in occupations that demand a performance by an aesthetically pleasing body. Thus, body image and maintenance is not solely a consumption-based or leisure activity but an integral part of workplace performance.

Indeed, in interactive service work, it has been suggested that the traditional separation of production and consumption that was characteristic in an era when manufacturing employment was dominant is no longer relevant. Thus, in a study of work and identity in the retail sector, Du Gay (1996) has argued that 'the inherently "social" nature of much of service work could involve a distinct change in the cultural relations of the workplace, and the production of novel, "hybrid", work-based subjects' (p. 4) in which, he suggested, 'new modes of organisational conduct have blurred the traditional differences between production and consumption' (p. 5). In the specific context of the rise of new types of work in the City of London, Budd and Whimster (1992) have argued along similar lines, suggesting that work in the City has become constructed as fun with the result that there is a growing 'interpenetration of previously separate spheres of life' (p. 3). In the final part of this chapter, I want to extend this line of argument, turning away from identity *per se*, however, to look at ways of thinking about the significance of the location of work and the built environment within which it takes place. While this chapter is restricted to theoretical approaches, in the next chapter I shall turn to material changes in the City's built environment in the Big Bang years.

THE PLACES AND SPACES OF WORK

Despite the incisiveness of these various sets of literatures about gender, work, power and organisations, they all seem to have a remarkable blindness to the significance of location. What is happening in the new forms of organisational structures and workplaces has been emphasised to the neglect of where new forms of behaviour occur. Yet, as geographers, urban theorists and semioticians have argued, workplace behaviour is both shaped by and shapes the design of the workplace environment at the scale of the city itself, of spaces and localities within it and of individual buildings. The meanings given to different social behaviours, to the characteristics that distinguish femininity and masculinity, are grounded in and accordingly judged more or less appropriate to particular physical spaces.

Lash and Urry (1994) have argued that radical economic changes are paralleled by shifts in the location and structure of industrial spaces. The production and exchange of manufactured products in industrial economies resulted in the production of specialised industrial spaces, the manufacturing heartlands of the industrial nations. Similarly, the production and exchange of commodified signs − the cultural industries and advertising are their example, but financial products such as futures and derivatives are even clearer examples − result in the emergence of post-industrial spaces, even though the goods and services of the late twentieth century economy are less place-bound in the sense of being reliant on a spatially bound set of raw materials or a local market. As the delivery of services becomes more important and the quality of the interaction between producers and consumers becomes part of the product, the availability both of the right type of labour (often young and personable as well as highly educated for high-status services) and of the *location* of the interaction in an appropriate environment that reinforces the meaning of the commodified signs increases in importance. Indeed, in post-industrial economies, architecture and urban design themselves are a key part of cultural production, both of the products and of performing selves. 'The image-projecting and consciousness-transforming industries, all . . . contribute to the constitution, confirmation or reconstitution of human subjectivity and cultural identity' (King, 1990a, p. 398). It might be stretching the point to include merchant banking as part of the cultural industries, but, as I show in chapter 6, images of banking are now part of the entertainment industry which, in turn, affects the self-images of merchant bankers.

The significance of the built form in the social construction of place is now a key aspect of contemporary analyses of the production and selling of spectacular place images in capitalist societies (Harvey, 1989a; Kearns and Philo, 1993). In the 1990s, analyses of the production of the built environment have moved from a predominantly political economy perspective, concerned with the relations between capital, the state and class fractions, towards a set of theories drawn from urban architectural studies, art, film and literary criticism, and cultural studies. Perspectives drawn largely from the humanities have begun to complement or even replace the essentially structuralist analyses, although there have been notable attempts to hold together 'capital and culture' (Zukin, 1988). Drawing in particular on the work of Lefebvre (1991) and on a range of social semioticians, including Saussure and Barthes (Duncan and Duncan, 1988), a group of social and cultural geographers as well as urban and cultural theorists (Barnes and Duncan, 1992; Duncan, 1990; Duncan and Ley, 1993; Gottdiener, 1995; Harvey, 1989a; King, 1990a, c, 1996; Shields, 1991, 1996; Zukin, 1992, 1995) have begun to theorise the city as a representation, reading the city as a text (Duncan, 1990) or a discursive construction, analysing the images and symbols that give meaning to urban living. City buildings, parks, open spaces, statues as well as urban novels, films, art and poetry have become as significant for current urban theorists as the class and ethnic movements were for earlier urban theorists. So dominant has this shift become that recent commentators have even suggested that the imaginary city is beginning to hide urban 'reality', arguing, for example, that 'the boundary between social reality and representations of that reality has collapsed' (Jacobs, 1993, p. 827). It might be argued, however, paralleling the dual changes in the materiality and approaches to work, that this refocusing also reflects changes in the material basis of city economies. As I briefly note in the introduction, cultural industries are increasingly dominating the economies of large cities (King, 1996; Robson, 1994; Sassen, 1990; Zukin, 1995). As well as the expansion of financial services in the 1980s and 1990s, global cities became important locations for cultural ventures, from museums and universities to the advertising industry. These industries are part of that 'aestheticisation' of urban life identified earlier, and Zukin (1995) has shown how, in New York at least, the physical reconstruction of urban spaces for workplace and leisure activities for the new middle class is part of the redefinition and reclaiming of inner-city areas. Through the form of the buildings themselves and the nature of interstitial spaces, as well as through mechanisms of physical surveillance and electronic control, undesirable or 'dangerous classes' are excluded.

Despite the apparent shift to emphasise representations, the best new work on urban landscapes is distinguished by its determination to link together the material production of the built environment, symbolic meanings and forms of representation and the sets of material and social practices facilitated or constrained by both physical and symbolic forms. Landscapes are, after all, but the concrete expression of a society, especially its institutions of class and power. Buildings 'represent, transmit and transform institutionally embedded power relations' (Zukin, 1991, p. 21). They are not only symbolic representations of discourse, ideologies and relations of power but also constitute and affect these same attitudes, beliefs, social relations and structures, and so the very distinction between representations and reality falls to the ground. As I argue later, in a parallel discussion of images in text and film rather than the built environment, the same distinction is also misleading. Representations of fictional bankers influence the behaviour and attitudes of 'real' bankers, and vice versa.

While the relations of power and class have been emphasised in this new 'school' of urban scholarship, the way in which the built environment reflects and affects gender relations has been given relatively less attention, at least until the early '90s (Colomina, 1992; Bell and Valentine, 1995). The links between masculine power in city politics and the economy and its reflection in the built environment have, however, been noted. Lefebvre (1991) briefly commented on the 'phallic verticality' of business districts and Sassen noted the inscription of central area land use with the values of corporate culture. Drawing on Sennett (1992), she suggested that corporate culture is dominated by notions of precision and expertise, imposing its authority on the central area though high-rise corporate towers. 'The vertical grid of the corporate tower is imbued with the same neutrality and rationality attributed to the horizontal grid of American cities' (Sassen, 1996, p. 191). The neutrality and rationality she identified are the same characteristics that construct the female body as out of place in the workplace, as I have argued above. Rather surprisingly, Sassen did not explicitly connect the representation of corporate culture as neutral, rational, efficient, technologically advanced and authoritative with masculinity, but rather contrasted these corporate spaces and places with the more disordered use of urban space by small businesses, old manufacturing operations and ethnic enterprises. Neglecting the representation of woman and femininity as Other, she instead noted that 'the corporate economy evicts these other economies and workers from economic representation, and the corporate culture represents them as the other. It evicts other ways of being in the city and in the economy' (Sassen, 1996, p. 193). Like Allen and Pryke (1994), Sassen correctly recognised that the dominant representations and the physical spaces of corporate culture exclude the fact that many of the people working in corporate organisations by day are low-paid secretaries and messengers, and by night even more low-paid cleaners who inscribe the spaces with a wholly different culture of work. Here, gender as well as class differences deserve to be explored. But, further, as I demonstrate later, there are also important differences within corporate culture both between different sectors and industries and between their high-status 'corporate' workers.

In an interesting collection of essays (Colomina, 1992), several contributors established provocative but provisional links between sexuality and space. Wigley (1992), for example, drew attention to the ways in which the 'exclusion of sexuality is itself sexual' (p. 328). He took as an example the 'neutral' spaces of the university, 'an elaborate system of representation, a mechanism that sustains a system of spaces, an architecture, by masking the particular construction of sexuality that makes those spaces possible' (p. 328). In these neutral spaces from which sexuality is theoretically excluded, male dominance permits a degree of sexual harassment of women by men, of inferiors by superiors, that is doubly shocking in the spaces of work and learning. As I show later, this occurs to an extent in the 'rational' spaces of corporate finance, but I also demonstrate how other workplaces within merchant banks are inscribed with apparently transgressive behaviours, threatening the notional rationality of work. In the same collection, Grosz (1992) linked bodies to cities in an attempt to demonstrate how the sexual specificity of corporeality is, in part, a material consequence of a body's location. Her aim was to explore 'the ways in which the body is psychically, socially, sexually, and discursively or representationally produced, and the ways, in turn, bodies reinscribe and project themselves onto their sociocultural environment so that this environment both produces and reflects the form and interests of the body' (p. 242). She sketched in the links between the body and the body-politic in cities (see also Sennett, 1994) and discussed the ways in which residence in different parts of cities orients and organises family, sexual and social relations by dividing 'cultural life into public and private domains, [and by] geographically dividing and defining the particular social positions and locations occupied by individuals and groups . . . these spaces, divisions and interconnections are the roles and means by which bodies are individuated to become subjects' (Grosz, 1992, p. 250). As I show at the end of the next chapter, the layout of new corporate buildings in the financial sector, the public and private spaces they define, enclose and control, and their internal divisions of space construct some bodies as appropriate occupants and exclude others as inappropriate. Despite the collapse of space into time and the instantaneous transformation of information, even in this most global of industries, the location of work as a specific space in the city means that the sexed body still matters.

CONCLUSIONS

In this chapter, I have set the scene in both a theoretical and an empirical sense, demonstrating women's entry into the labour force and the ways in which it has been explained. I have argued that the sociology and culture of work literatures, especially those that focus on the gendering of organisational structures and practices, may profitably be brought into juxtaposition with the literatures from urban studies, architecture, geography, cultural studies and urban sociology, which focus on the built environment not only as a container for the social practices and everyday

2

City Work/Places: The Old and New City

There was no question that it [the new corporate and individual wealth] transformed the City of London, whose skyline proclaimed it the financial capital of Europe. Its geography, language, ease of dealing and freedom from controls all attracted Americans and Japanese as well as Europeans. Young dealers or fund managers earned salaries which opened up extravagant lifestyles, and the flow of money spilled out of the Square Mile into Docklands and the West End. It was a heady change. The British were reasserting their traditional metier as world traders sensitive to every distant market.

A. Sampson, 1992, p. 11

The City of London is a tale of two cities. The one was traditional and stuffy, with codes of conduct reflecting a close-bound world of long-established firms and personal relationships built on trust. . . . The financial revolution of the eighties marked the emergence of the new city. . . . Previously one had gone into the City because one was rich, whereas now the attraction for new entrants was to become rich.

L. Budd and S. Whimster, 1992, p. 4

The City's reputation is now irredeemably compromised. 'My word is my bond' has been exploded as cant.

Guardian, 6 March 1995

INTRODUCTION

The City of London is the focus of this chapter. Here I examine arguments about recent patterns of growth and change, drawing out their consequences for class and, in particular, gender divisions, as the context for the detailed empirical study of patterns of employment, recruitment and workplace interactions that follows. I want to lay out arguments about the supposed transformation from an 'old' to a 'new' City in the course of the radical changes in both employment practices and the structure of the physical environment that occurred in the late 1980s as London moved from an international to a global city (Pryke, 1991).

In these years, and into the 1990s, there has been a remarkable restructuring within the banking sector that has transformed the pattern of labour demand and terms of employment that had characterised the industry for decades. Old assumptions about a career for life and inevitable progression were undermined. While these changes were most marked in the retail banking sector, merchant banking was not immune to change. In the City, new forms of tiered entry systems and the development of specialist units led to new patterns of work, especially after the Financial Services Act 1986. Entry was increasingly based on merit and depended on credentials, and internal labour markets within banks disappeared. It has been argued that one of the consequences has been the abolition of old social and class barriers, with 'the effect of accelerating social class change in the City of London' (Leyshon et al., 1987, p. 54). I believe that this comment was premature. The actual extent of the imagined transformation could not possibly have been clear in 1987, so soon after deregulation, although Leyshon et al. suggested that the arrival of meritocratic American banks and the entry of working-class foreign exchange dealers into City institutions had been apparent from the 1960s onwards. In the late 1980s, however, a dualistic narrative became dominant, relying on the notion of metamorphosis from a stuffy old City, parodied in images of bowler hats and umbrellas, to the world of fast money and smooth operators. This binary story is too simple. It neglects differences between 'firms' – in this case merchant banks, which are distinctive entities. Both between and within the merchant banks that have offices in the City, there are considerable differences in attitudes, behaviour, recruitment policies and ways of operating that affect the culture of each organisation. The history and character of merchant banks, their national origins and familial loyalties, their specialisms and their market position all affect and reflect the ways of working that become acceptable and reinforce particular patterns of behaviour in different parts of a bank and within a bank as a whole. These differentiated cultures also affect who is recruited to different occupations within merchant banking and the ways in which class and gender attributes interconnect in the construction of an employee who 'fits' into the culture of a particular organisation or part of an organisation. Before I examine differences, however, the overall class, gender and physical characteristics of the 'old' and 'new' City are outlined.

A BRIEF HISTORY OF OLD MONEY

There are many fine histories of the City and its position in Greater London (Michie, 1992; Porter, 1994), as well as histories of the role of important banks within it. My aim is neither to replicate nor supplant them, but rather to outline the main features of the social organisation of the 'old' world of merchant banking, that is as it was before the mid 1980s.

According to Porter (1994) in his history of London, London was the world's greatest city and financial centre 'between the two Elizabeths, between 1570 and 1986 to be precise' (p. 1). It is interesting that he located the decline of London from the date at which the concerns of this book begin. The introduction of the Financial Services Act in 1986 brought the deregulation of many financial activities and set the scene for a decade's changes. It ushered in a period of financial instability at the end of the decade and into the early 1990s, as I began to interview City workers. These years were a paradoxical period in which the growth and expansion of the financial sector, the rapid rise in salaries for the richest and the huge increase in house prices all seemed to mark the apotheosis of Thatcherite success. But the late 1980s was also a period marked by financial scandals, tarnishing the City's reputation, and 1986 saw the end of a democratically elected metropolitan government as the Greater London Council was abolished. According to Porter, 'late twentieth-century administrations prefer to avert their eyes from the deteriorating megalopolis and let nature, or international financiers and the multinationals, take their course' (p. 1). While imminent decline may be an unduly pessimistic analysis, there is little doubt that London's future is inextricably bound up within international finance and is less amenable to national control than at perhaps any period in its recent history (Allen, 1992; Hutton, 1995a).

The history of London as a financial centre is a familiar one. Its dominance in the international financial system is bound up with Britain's long imperial past. The modern City began to emerge from the Restoration period when, based on international trade, the development of an important financial sector brought London immense wealth and extensive employment through a nexus of institutions that handled banking, investment and currency dealing. The physical development of the City as a financial centre dates from the mid-seventeenth century, when an interconnected network of dealers, stockbrokers and insurance agents established the exchanges, and a national bank was founded in 1694 by the Company of the Bank of England. In 1723 the Bank of England moved to a building in Threadneedle Street, which remains its present site although in a more recent building. By 1750 there were 40 banks in London, and almost twice as many at the start of the nineteenth century.

It was in the nineteenth century that the City perhaps reached its peak. The first established merchant bank was Barings, founded in 1763. This bank will play an important part in this book as its demise in 1995 provided an interesting insight into class and gender attitudes in the City today. A further 11 merchant banks were founded between 1804 and 1839, of which Rothschilds became the most successful. Growing numbers of the merchant banking houses were of foreign origin – George Peabody from Baltimore (later to become J. S. Morgan and Co.), Hambros from Copenhagen and Speyers from New York also established houses in London, increasing the international significance of the City. Later in the century, imperial and continental banks opened London branches, including the Ottoman Bank (1863), Comptoir d'Escompte de Paris (1867), Crédit Lyonnais (1870), Société Générale (1871), the Swiss Bank Corporation (1898) and major German, Italian, Belgian and Russian banks, as well as the Bank of Japan in 1898. These were followed by American banks – Chase Manhattan (1887), Morgan Garanty (1892) and Citibank (1902). The nineteenth century was not a completely unalloyed story of success however, as in 1890 Barings had to be rescued from over-exposure in South American stocks. A credit squeeze at home caused a crisis as the bank was unable to meet its immediate liabilities. In 1890 the Bank of England came to Barings' aid; it was a different story in 1995.

The first half of the twentieth century was initially one of decline in the fortunes of investment bankers. The First World War had a serious effect on the City as German banks left and the London money market was 'utterly disrupted' (McRae and Cairncross, 1991, p. 14). Income from overseas investments, on which the country depended to pay for its trade deficit, virtually vanished, although government debt issues during the war were important. In the inter-war period, domestic companies provided the main source of City activity as the international depression virtually killed foreign lending. The Second World War saw a repeat withdrawal of foreign banks from the City, although in the 1940s it was Italian and Japanese banks who closed their branches.

There was something of a resurgence, however, in London's fortunes from 1958 onwards, following the relaxation of controls and the development of the Eurobond and Eurocurrency markets in the 1960s. By this time the City's role had changed to become a financial entrepôt and a centre of international markets and their support services, rather than a net exporter of funds and an international banking reserve centre. It was in this period that London moved from its place at the centre of international banking to become one of the small number of global cities – New York and Tokyo are the most significant others – which are at the nodes of a complex interlocking network of markets, each the key player in a different time zone. With a sophisticated and stable banking system and a geographical position conveniently midway between Asia and North America, London became the world's largest single borrowing source in the 1960s, attracting increasing numbers of foreign banks. Between 1960 and 1980, the number of foreign banks or representative offices increased fourfold, from 100 to more than 400, and by end of the 1980s to 450, employing more than 50,000 people. As the 1990s opened, London accounted for 20 per cent of total world international banking and 43 per cent of foreign currency dealing. In 1989 the largest contingent of foreign banks were from Europe – 235 out of a total of 450 – compared with earlier periods when Japanese and US banks were more numerous. These countries' banks were still significant, however: thus, for example, *The Banker* in 1990 dubbed London the Japanese capital of Europe.

In securing this pre-eminence in the period from the 1960s until the mid to late 1980s, the Bank of England played an important role, largely by interfering as little as possible but being a symbol of strength and insisting on a minimal level of regulation. The 1980s success was built on the continuing belief in deregulation. It was a decade of free-market economics as Conservative administrations placed increasing reliance on the financial services sector as an engine of national growth.

> The hope was that a booming financial sector would energize the capital, creating a new enterprise culture, buzzing with dynamic business people eager to seize golden opportunities to make their fortunes. City prosperity, the theory ran, would have knock on effects, generating investment and property development, new businesses great and small, extensive service employment and a consumer boom among an affluent yuppie generation – barrow boy capitalists making big money in and around the Square Mile. (Porter, 1994, p. 373)

A desire to establish exactly who these new recruits were – whether putative yuppies, barrow boys or still the representatives of an older bourgeois middle class – was part of the impetus for this study. As Budd and Whimster (1992) also noted, detailed research was needed to establish whether 'the newly wealthy of the international City salariat [are the] old middle class or upwardly mobile from lower down the class hierarchy', and whether 'a process of differentiation in the formation and transmission of cultural and material capital may be occurring' (p. 25).

It is clear, however, that an image of a new, more dynamic and less hidebound city captured the discursive construction of City employees in the late 1980s in numerous comparisons of the 'old' and 'new' City. The basic features of the social organisation of the 'old' city have been well documented (Cassis et al., 1995; Lisle-Williams, 1984a, b; Michie, 1992; Pryke, 1991). Throughout the nineteenth and most of the twentieth century, the City was dominated by a small number of banking families, who were among the most powerful of the English bourgeoisie although many of them were not English in origin. These families and their employees dominated the City until the mid 1980s, if not in actual number then in the establishment of a particular moral order. This moral order was based around a particular version of 'a gentleman and his word' which, in the nineteenth century, fused the traditions of the English landed gentry with those of the public school system. This 'old society' was structured by 'the twin principles of elitism and patriarchy . . . an hierarchical society which revolved round a group of "gentlemen", . . . who justified their position as leaders of society on the grounds of their "natural" God-given authority' (Scott, 1991, p. 44). While the landed aristocracy played a key role in the structures of power and patronage, larger capitalists and City merchants developed increasing power through-out the nineteenth and early twentieth centuries, in part through their close and growing business and personal links with the gentry. Personal-ised chains of attachment, commonly described in terms of friendship, were a key feature of this elite, and a strong horizontal sense of identity bound the powerful together with 'expectations of reciprocity, common outlook, identification of interest and sheer coercion in the name of a social ideal' (Scott, 1991, p. 53).

The latter part of the nineteenth century saw the rise of 'family capi-talism'. It was an era in which entrepreneurs managed their firms as an extension of themselves, when kinship, ownership and control were syn-onymous and dynastic marriage was a means of corporate merger. Swift ascent in the corporate hierarchy was assured for those of proper de-scent. Although the great manufacturing families developed in part as an alternative power bloc to the landed aristocracy, much closer links were forged between the *rentiers* and the capitalist class based in finance and commerce. And according to Unseem (1990):

> In Britain the move of the aristocracy into commerce, necessitated by political and financial reality, was not initially at the price of assimilation. The upper class moved to rule business with the same self assured sense of mission with which it had long overseen land, politics and the empire. Capitalism was its new mission, but the primary role of the family re-mained intact. (pp. 282–3)

In Britain, '[t]he solidarity [of this class] is underpinned by a unique lattice work of old school ties, exclusive urban haunts, and aristocratic traditions that are without real counterpart in American life' (p. 265). 'A common background and pattern of socialisation, reinforced through inter-marriage, club memberships etc. generated a community feeling among members of the propertied class and this feeling could be articu-lated into a class awareness by the most active members of the class' (Scott, 1991, pp. 125–6). Indeed, this tradition of 'gentlemanly capital-ism' and its class awareness has been seen as one of the reasons for Britain's relatively poor industrial performance in the twentieth century and the 'short-termism' of lending institutions: 'The kind of economic activity the elite acclaimed was not industrial; it was financial, commercial or mercantile' (Hutton, 1995b, p. 119). At the core of this power bloc was:

> [the] group which came to be termed the 'establishment' . . . an exclusive upper circle of the status hierarchy, a group rooted in their common education in the public schools and their commitment to the maintenance of the established traditions of old England. This establishment dominated political power within the national and local state apparatus, and its power and influence stretched out to all the salient institutions of British society. The establishment was a tightly interknit group of intermarried families who monopolised the exercise of political power in Britain. (Scott, 1991, pp. 61–2)

However, in the twentieth century, the real power of family capitalism was gradually displaced by corporate capital. In the economy as a whole, there was a slow but steady displacement of upper-class dominance by corporate interests, as evidenced by the emergence of large firms, multidivisional structures and new forms of administrative control. A network of overlapping directorships developed among finance capital-ists, resulting in an 'inner circle' (Unseem, 1984) of company directors who may have relatively insignificant personal stakes in the enterprises they represent 'but they have accumulated large numbers of directorships and represent the interests of the controlling institutions on the boards' (Scott, 1991, p. 69) on which they sit. These men, and a few women, are usually non-executive directors. Scott examined the links between finance and corporate capital and argued that the size of the 'inner circle' re-mained small. In 1988 there were 290 multiple directors on the boards of the top 250 companies, of which only five were women. As Scott showed:

> over two-thirds of these leading finance capitalists held a directorship on a bank or insurance company, and half of these were bank or insurance executives. Through their directorships, they tied the financial institutions into an extensive network which extended to include the major financial and commercial enterprises. The institutions are hegemonic in the mobi-lization of capital, and the members of the inner circle represent the interests of the hegemonic institutions on the various boards on which they are members. (p. 79)

He also noted that entrepreneurial control remains particularly signifi-cant in a number of industries, including merchant banking. Further, family dynasties have remained important in merchant banking. At the end of the 1980s, a considerable number of the largest companies were still in entrepreneurial rather than institutional control, including Kleinwort, Benson Lonsdale, Robert Fleming Holdings, Schroders, N. M. Rothschild and Barings (Beresford, 1990).

The significance of an elite education also appears to have retained a tenacious grip. In an investigation of the backgrounds of 97 senior partners or chief executives of top City firms (banks, stockbrokers, life insurance companies, investment trust managers, solicitors and accountants) in 1992, Bowen (1992) found that ten went to Eton, nine to Winchester and 37 to other public schools. While 30 of the 97 had no university degree at all, confirming the continuing significance of family background and experience in the banking world, only 12 of the 52 British graduates had attended a redbrick university. The rest were Oxbridge products. As Bowen (1992) pointed out, given that 'an 18 year old Etonian who had joined a stock broker in 1962, would after all only be in his late forties now' (p. 14), the influence of these men (only 2 per cent were women) will persist well into the twenty-first century.

THE MONEY CULTURE: CHANGES IN THE 'NEW' CITY

Despite these continuities, however, change is a dominant emphasis in City narratives since 1986. One of the most prevalent themes is the idea of a shift towards what have been termed 'American practices'. The class-bound structures of the 'old' City are frequently compared with new and more democratic methods of organisation. Professional management structures have become more dominant and, as daily and final decision-making power is transferred from family members to trained managers, new bureaucratic career structures within firms have opened up. Often the members of this executive class are less secure in their membership than the old bourgeoisie, and their class privileges and advantaged lifestyle are dependent on their success within an organisation rather than on familial and inherited status. High pay and good benefits are crucial to their chances of maintaining this lifestyle for their children and into their own retirement. For these people, the acquisition of cultural capital through education and the elite universities is a crucial method of securing their place in the 'establishment'. One of the results of the changing order, it is suggested, is the development of a new set of business financiers and associated networks of professionals, without any legitimacy other than that based on technical expertise. 'Good manners and social connections lost their importance in favour of technical competence' (Dezalay, 1990, p. 287) and, although Dezalay was describing the legal profession, his comment is perhaps equally applicable to investment bankers: 'the law comes to resemble less and less a club for "gentlemen", and more and more a business like any other' (p. 287).

Many of my respondents, and others (in the oral histories collected by the City Lives Project (1991) for example) spoke of the growing penetration of American practices in the London financial market. An extreme version of these practices is Lewis's hilarious, exaggerated accounts of new ways of working on Wall Street and in the City, where fast talking and cut-throat action by corporate raiders and traders who saw themselves as 'romantic guerrillas in the corporate jungle' (Lewis, 1991, p. 10), challenged the earlier reliance on 'a gentleman's word'. According to Lewis, 'the drift of European financiers towards the American value system undermined the established class pretensions . . . American investment bankers may have been a force of positive social change in the Old World' (p. 155), although Dezalay (1990) noted a less positive impact of post-Big Bang changes on the City:

> The renewal of the financial establishment, and the arrival on the scene of new kinds of players who both profit from and intensify the new situation, increases international deregulation and disequilibrium. Corporate raiders and 'white knights' who buy up organisations courtesy of junk bonds, and then carve them up, do not have the same scruples as heirs of paternalistic capitalism (p. 283).

Certainly, in Britain from the mid 1980s, there have been many signs of 'new standards', including a range of unacceptable behaviours from the ungentlemanly, to put it at its mildest, to corruption and fraud in the City. One financial scandal after another hit the pages of the financial press in the late 1980s and early 1990s – Barlow Clowes, Blue Arrow, Guinness, BCCI, Barings – and the days seem long past when the then chairman of Lazards, Lord Poole, could proudly proclaim, after the 1974 crash, that: ' "I never lost any money, because I never lent any money to anyone I didn't go to school with" ' (cited in Charman, 1989, p. 3). Some of my respondents, however, disagreed that 'Americanisation' and cultural changes had, in fact, altered ethical standards.

> The ethics of the City? No, I don't believe that the ethics of people have changed. ... What has changed is the perception of what is ethical. In the '50s, the thought that people would use information about their deals for their benefit wouldn't be regarded as a crime. ... It was part of the practice that people went and dealt in things because they knew the results. So you can't say they were less ethical than the people who wouldn't dream of doing insider dealing now. I'd say the ethics of the people are exactly the same – what is perceived to be right and wrong has changed. (male director, Northbank)[1]

It is also salutary to remember that banking scandals are not the prerogative of the late twentieth century. McRae and Cairncross (1991) agreed that 'it is not clear that there has been any long-term change in City ethics at all. Looking back over its history, the pattern seems much more of sporadic splurges, in which a few people become very rich and a lot of the City's customers are defrauded, interspersed on periods when regulation is tightened and standards are lifted' (p. xi). The casino capitalism (Strange, 1986) of the present had its forerunners in the global markets of previous centuries. Greed, credulity and venality are constant features of financial markets and, as Marquand (1995) suggested, rather than witnessing the emergence of a 'new' City, 'we have returned to an all too-familiar old one whose history we have perversely chosen to forget. We have gone back to the untamed, unregulated, anxiety-haunted, socially destructive and economically wasteful capitalism which the Keynesian-corporatist social democrats of the mid-twentieth century eventually saved from itself' (p. 22).

In the increasingly technocratic – and perhaps egalitarian – City, however, it seems clear that more recent City employees are convinced that they owe their position to their qualifications and to both their technical and their personal competences (their energy or dynamism for example). Their view of the world is different from that of older and older-style bankers; action rather than family connections are valorised. While these changes may be breaking the class boundaries of the City, there has been no investigation of the impact on gender divisions. An ethos and culture that demands fast talk and fast action may be as inimical to women as the older gentlemanly paternalism. In work on the changing class composition and class attitudes of business leaders and civil servants in France, Bourdieu (1984) designated the younger new bourgeoisie 'the new masters of the economy' and emphasised that the new culture in France – one of action, business and power – is reserved for men (p. 315). So while the class composition of the new 'masters' may have changed, gender dominance may not have been affected.

Before I turn, however, to an examination of gendered differences in recruitment and patterns of employment and to a comparison of men's and women's career histories in succeeding chapters, I want to complete the comparison of the old and new City by looking at the built environment. As I argued earlier, the built environment is more than a container for social interaction; it also constitutes the gendered subjectivities of the men and women who work in the 'new' City and affects their sense of self and belonging. Here too a new City is being built, challenging the old assumptions of a particular class-based masculinist power that was reflected in its physical form.

THE LANDSCAPE OF MONEY: CITY SPACES

One of the greatest paradoxes of money is that although it permits the separation of buying and selling and of the actors involved in these exchanges in space, challenging and ultimately eliminating the absolute nature of a place, it also 'creates an enormous capacity to concentrate social power in space, for . . . it can be accumulated at a particular place without restraint. And these immense concentrations of social power can be put to work to realise massive transformations of nature, the construction of built environments' (Harvey, 1989b, p. 176). This paradox explains the continuing significance of a particular place – the Square Mile of the City of London (and its recent extensions) – in the global system of financial exchange. Despite the placelessness of information moving around the globe almost instantaneously, the Square Mile of the City of London remains the visible heart of London's financial landscape, its concentration established by formal and informal rules of proximity between Stock Exchange members and between foreign bank offices and the Bank of England (Thrift, 1994). Out of the total of 58 members of the British Merchant Banking and Securities Houses Association, 56 are based in the capital. About half of all the foreign and UK banks have headquarters right in the heart of the City around the Bank of England. Similarly, a large proportion of insurance broking, underwriting and reinsurance forms are located in EC3 near Lloyds and the Institute of London Underwriters. Although there has been an expansion, for example over Liverpool Street Station and into the West End, when certain US institutions (Salomon Brothers and the First Bank of Boston for example) moved there because of high rents and space shortages in the City proper, the traditional core of the City remains dominant (see maps 2.1 and 2.2). The planned expansion of Canary Wharf in the London docklands has yet to take off although some financial institutions, including part of Barclays Bank, have moved there.

As I argued in chapter 1, the social meaning of the urban landscapes varies, although clearly it is the most powerful groups in a society who have the capacity to impose their views, or systems of meaning, on the landscape. Thus, hegemonic notions of class, gender and ethnicity are expressed in the landscapes of finance capital in capital cities. These notions, however, have to be continuously recreated and reinscribed in a process of creative destruction, as the associations of merchant and financial capital with a particular social elite are fractured and remade. The built environment of the City may therefore be seen as a series of

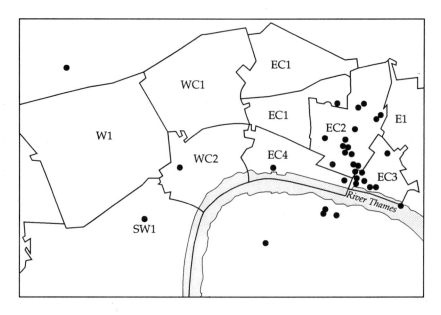

Map 2.1 UK banks and other finance houses in the City, 1994
Source: The Times 1000, 1994

overlapping texts in which previous layers of meaning are overlain with new meanings which strengthen, succeed or disrupt earlier meanings. Reading the new spaces of power in the City reveals a challenge to traditional images of the City.

In the heart of the City, the dominant images are still those established by Victorian architects and builders whose predominant motif was a classical façade, behind which lay a domed hall, often with an elaborate mosaic floor. These buildings – the headquarters of the major banking dynasties – were designed to reflect an image of banking that was rather closer to the temples of God than the temples of Mammon, of justice and equality rather than greed and power, counting houses good enough for a king as well as for the legions of bourgeois males who daily entered their portals.

The City also contains a second set of important spaces. These are the market places or exchanges, of which some have a physical expression or location in a symbolic place or building and others do not. Thus, for example, the LIFFE (the London International Financial Futures and Options Exchange), the London Metal Exchange, the Baltic Exchange, the International Petroleum Exchange, and the London Commodity Exchange have physical meeting places in the City or nearby (the latter

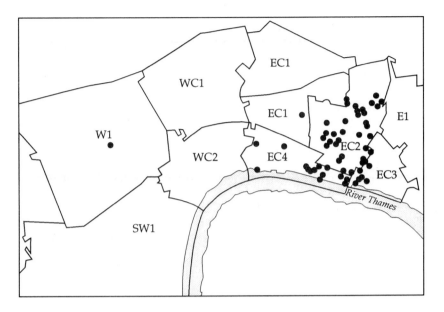

Map 2.2 Foreign banks in the City, 1993
Source: The Banker, November 1993

two are based at St Katherine's Dock, near the Tower of London). Lloyds of London and the Institute of London Underwriters also have their own buildings. Other, more recent exchanges, however, have no specific physical meeting place but instead dealing is carried out electronically via computer screens and over the telephone network. These markets include the Foreign Exchange or Forex market, the Eurobond market, the Stocks and Shares market and the Derivatives market.

The physical exchanges reflect their origin in market places where trade was highly visible on an open floor to increase circulation and the probability of encounters between traders. These buildings, and banks, are united in their spatial form – 'external closure, controlled access, internal open but sheltered space for transactions and private offices' (Marcus, 1993, p. 310). The second Royal Exchange, built after the 1666 Fire of London, was designed by Jerman; the central court and the peripheral arcades were divided into 'walks', each the domain of merchants specialising in either a trade or a type of good, such as silk, or a geographical area. In addition, insurance (or ship) brokers had their own spots. Upstairs, although originally planned as shops, the Royal Exchange and other companies had their offices. Around the site were coffee houses and clubs and the dealing in stocks and shares which had originally started in the 'walks' was transferred into the coffee house until Peacock's Stock Exchange was built in Capel Court in 1801–2. The famous origins of Lloyds of London in a coffee house are well known.

Coffee houses, according to Marcus (1993, p. 157), had their origins in Oxford and not London but soon spread there in great numbers, only to be destroyed by the Fire, but later rebuilt. By the mid-eighteenth century, the City of London was thick with them.

> As the *habitués* formed more tight knit groups, disseminating privileged information by word of mouth, printed handbills, newspapers and pamphlets, they created partitioned boxes to mark their identity. Increased entrance charges gave greater selectivity until finally some groups clubbed together and bought up entire coffee houses for their exclusive use. This was the birth of the club as well as of famous business houses such as Lloyds and the Stock Exchange. The close association with the professions, the military, politics and business inevitably made coffee houses a male preserve, a tradition carried through into clubs. (Marcus, 1993, p. 158)

And, of course, the world of the City of Lloyds and the Stock Exchange was always assumed to be connected with that of gentleman's clubs where, in previous centuries at least, men were able to make money, through personal contacts, and lose money, through gambling. This image of the City as a series of gentleman's clubs is one which is current today and informs the interior decor and the expected social behaviour, as I show in later chapters. It is an image, and a reality, that militates against the easy acceptance of women, as their very physical being is out of place in this world.

The growing significance of exchange relations, especially in the nineteenth century, of symbolic as well as real goods, is marked in the ways in which exchange buildings became more ornate.

> The increasing power represented by these buildings is clear not only in their functional and spatial orientation but also in the formal features of clocks, bell cupolas, balconies both for public ceremony and for surveying the open market square – and ceremonial staircases, heraldic emblems, flags and iconography relating to the town's history. Stylistically the plain vernacular gradually gave way to self-conscious early Renaissance, then Palladian and eventually neo-Classical forms. (Marcus, 1993, p. 159)

At the beginning of the twentieth century the City presented a sober yet elegant façade. Sennett (1994) imagined the feelings of an American businessman who:

> walking through London on the eve of the First World War might be pardoned the conviction that his country should never have rebelled.

Edwardian London displayed its imperial magnificence in ribbons of magnificent buildings running mile after mile, vast government offices in the
centre flanked by the dense economic cells of the banker's and trader's city
to the east, . . . all slathered block after block in ornate stucco. . . . London
displayed the spoils of a global reach unknown since the Roman Empire.
(p. 317)

But as the twentieth century advanced, and as changes in the division
of labour altered the ways in which banks were occupied, the physical
structures and internal layouts became less useful, although the symbolic
meaning of the location and façades of these buildings remained as
important as ever. By the mid 1970s, the communications revolution was
making these buildings less suitable for modern use. Trading, in large
part, became limited to static screens at an individual's desk and many of
the enclosed open spaces of the old exchanges became redundant, as did
the small and individual offices surrounding them. New areas where
large numbers of individuals might sit in serried ranks were required,
and the phenomenon of the dealing floor appeared from 1986, where
buildings with a large central space, usually with double height ceiling
and a minimum of columns giving uninterrupted 20,000 square-feet
floors, became a common requirement. The spaces in the old buildings
were too small and often were insufficiently ventilated for modern technologies. As a result, the late 1970s and the 1980s, especially after Big
Bang in 1986, were a particularly important period of landscape reconstruction in the City, although the early 1990s recession meant that the
City property market suffered badly.

The urban surface for the 1980s reconstruction was no 'tabula rasa of
capital accumulation' (Zukin, 1991, p. 19). Rather, traces and elements,
the old meanings sedimented into the landscape, and listed buildings,
gave rise to contested visions of the future by innumerable actors and
interested parties. City residents and workers, national conservation groups
and Royal Princes all had opinions on an appropriate visual form for the
new City (Jacobs, 1994b). However, as in other capital cities, the views
and attitudes of local and even national groups were increasingly subor-
dinated to the interests of international capital (Fainstein, 1994; Knox,
1993) as a landscape of global money was imposed on the older City.

One of the first ways in which the old city landscape began to change
was through 'infilling' rather than redevelopment. The best-known example and challenge to the established urban iconography of money is
the new Lloyds building which was started in 1982. The intrusion of
Richard Rogers' modernist Lloyds building into the sober frontages is a
visual shock that dismays as well as pleases many critics and visitors
(plate 2.1). The internal divisions of the building, however, combine the

Plate 2.1 The new Lloyds building juxtaposed to Victorian solidarity
Source: photo by Emma Hallett

old with the new, tradition with innovation, as well as an incongruous element of pastiche. Thus, the old tradition of the boxes that were provided in the old coffee houses remains, with broking firms renting curious wooden boxy desks inside the high-tech shell. On the open floor in the basement, above which a towering atrium floats, is the old rostrum, by which red-coated waiters are positioned, and the original register of shipping losses, still kept up to date, is nearby. As in all office space, status and hierarchy are made visible by height and the director's office is at the top of the building, where marble floors and dark woodwork replace the modernist decor of lower floors, reinforcing the old associations of the City with a gentleman's club. Thus, the very spaces of the City, both outside and inside, remind women of a history that excluded them.

Throughout the 1980s, City sites were assembled for redevelopment. Although there was a good deal of 'façadism', where new offices were built behind old façades, many of the younger buildings of the City, especially the post-war high-rise offices, were cheaper to demolish and rebuild than to adapt to the demands of new technology (Williams, 1992). Between 1985 and the end of 1993, the equivalent of one half of the entire stock of office buildings in and around the City of London were built and rebuilt (Burdett, 1992). A large part of this construction was the replacement of out-of-date buildings and, despite a large increase in the permitted floor space in the City between 1986 and 1991 in particular, the overall increase in the total stock of offices was only 12 per cent. The newly built urban landscape of the City of London is internationalist in form, with its key buildings designed and built by architects and engineers with world-wide reputations and practices for clients who are national and international investors. Thus, while the landscape of the 'old' City reflects Britain's earlier imperial dominance in an earlier international division of production and financial power, the new landscapes mirror increasing interconnections between a set of global cities that have as many links between them as with their national urban hierarchy (Sassen, 1990). This internationalisation is exhibited in a new form of global architecture – termed by Zukin (1992) a 'landscape of power' – where Japanese investors may recruit British architects to design buildings in the USA or Australia. The 1980s also saw the first instance of an architects' firm being listed on the London securities market (King, 1990a).

Old or new, the spaces of power constructed by capital in the City of London reflect the dominance of London in the international financial arena. As Allen and Pryke (1994) have demonstrated, these abstract spaces of financial power are bound up with the practices of power. Through daily and longer-term social interactions, the dominant meanings or codings of City spaces are reinforced. 'The ability to endow a site with meaning is an expression of power in the spatial practices of the City, their repetition (or rhythm as Lefebvre (1991) emphasises) and variety, which signifies what may and may not take place in and around the various institutions that make up the City and who is "out of place" and, indeed, time' (Allen and Pryke, 1994, p. 455). For the majority of its temporal existence it has been the ebb and flow of men who have given meaning to these abstract spaces. Throughout history it has been men who filled the coffee houses, men who shouted and screamed on the floors of the exchanges and men in serious sober suiting (except, of course, at the splendid City functions such as the Lord Mayor's procession and banquet when they were allowed to dress up) who proffered financial advice in the inner sanctums of the marble-floored Victorian buildings.

Although the new City landscapes of power reflect a revolution in workplace technologies and in their glass and steel towers distil the new screen-based trading into a singular image of international dominance, remnants of past socio-spatial practices remain in internal spaces. In anomalous boardrooms and private dining rooms, oak-panelled and beamed, often a careful pastiche constructed from fragments saved in the demolition of older structures, and in more 'modern' rooms, the portraits of whiskery patriarchs stare sternly down on their descendants at the levers of financial power. Women are seldom among these portraits, other than images of the Queen.

These new spaces of power also differ in another way from the previous built environment. They reflect and affect the changing social construction and meaning of work in the new service-based economy. Making money became in the 1980s the quintessence of the economic form identified by Lash and Urry (1994) as one of 'signs and space'. Instead of money-making being serious work undertaken by men in specialised and exclusive spaces, service sector work was redefined as fun. This redefinition and its reflection in the built environment is significant as the new types of workplace landscape have trangressed the boundaries between what is serious and what is fun, which had in nineteenth and twentieth century cities been associated with functionally and spatially segregated urban landscapes, although the money exchanges had always had parallels with markets and carnivals. But the sites of these markets, carnivals and other spectacular activities had increasingly become private or moved inside in the Victorian era, and work had been segregated from leisure, public from private and men from women. Charlotte Brontë in *Villette* captured the spatial separation of these activities and the association of each with particular parts of London:

> I got into the heart of City life. I saw and felt London at last: I got into the Strand; I went into Cornhill; I mixed with life passing along; I dared the peril of crossings. To do this, and to do it utterly alone gave me, perhaps an irrational, but a real pleasure. Since those days I have seen the West-end, the parks, the fine squares; but I love the city far better. The City seems so much more in earnest, its rush, its roar are such serious things, sights, sound. The City is getting its living – the West-end but enjoying its pleasures. At the West-end, you may be amused, but in the City you are excited. (Brontë, 1992, p. 183; originally published 1853)

As I shall argue in later chapters, the blurring of the boundaries between work and leisure challenges the links between masculinity ('suits') and the

Plate 2.2 Broadgate façade
Source: Broadgate and Liverpool Street Station, 1991
(Rosehaugh Stanhope), p. 94

workplace and may be beneficial for women, but it may also reinforce their image as 'not serious'.

I want to pursue for the moment, however, this argument about the blurring of boundaries in terms of the built environment by taking a specific example. In the 1980s the most significant expansion of the Square Mile was in the development of the Broadgate Centre, built on 29 acres of disused railway land and a car park surrounding Liverpool Street Station. I examine this development in particular as it was here that one of the case study banks was located. The site was developed by a consortium, Rosehaugh Stanhope, formed by Stuart Lipton, the chief executive of Stanhope Properties, and Godfrey Bradman of Rosehaugh – in partnership with the British Rail Property Board. The first four phases were designed and built by Arup Associates and the rest by Skidmore, Owings and Merrill. Here, rather than the overtly modernist designs of Rogers, we return to more classical or monumental forms with regular façades. Vertical power, sleek steel and glass, iron ribs echoing the rails below in a rebuilt Liverpool Street Station are mixed with massive granite cladding of monumental buildings, with a mix of styles sufficient to be labelled pastiche. The continuous stretch of buildings along Bishopsgate, for example, exemplify the classical monumentalism of Skidmore, Owings and Merrill's Chicago-style 'warmed-up Beaux Arts style' with 'Italianate stone arcades on the ground, granite cladding in the smooth-edge aesthetic of the Modernists, Victorian glass-coffered atria, Chicago "cast-iron" corners, monumental New York 1930s granite and wood treatments to the entrance halls and lift cars, and grand boulevard treatment for Bishopsgate itself, complete with Hawkesmoor-style street furniture' (Williams, 1992, p. 256) (plate 2.2).

On the site, the architects and developers have constructed not only offices that meet the technological requirements of international finance but also dreamscapes for visual and actual consumption, stages on which work and consumption may take place. In the new built environments for financial services, work and leisure activities were elided with 'the interpenetration of areas of life previously separated by hierarchies and boundaries' (Budd and Whimster, 1992, pp. 2–3). In the Broadgate Centre the physical layout of the buildings and the spaces between them results in the interconnection of work and leisure spaces. New office buildings enclose squares and greens, where cafés and open spaces for performance abut the office entrances (see plate 2.3). And inside these entrances, the common use of soaring, planted atria not only brings the outside inside but the similarities between contemporary hotels and offices confuse the unsuspecting visitor. These spaces are not the old pattern of buildings lining the streets where workers are strictly separated from passers-by, but new enclosed spaces of work and play for the exclusive use of the financial sector middle class. And to further reinforce this confusion between work and leisure, statues and planting are an important part of the construction of a particular image for these new financial spaces. Are they public or private, a park, café or workspace?

Harvey (1989a) and others (for example, Kearns and Philo, 1993; Knox, 1993) have drawn on Debord's (1983, 1990) notion of the development of a 'society of the spectacle' in the late modern period in their analyses of the changing nature of the built form. In an era when time–space compression leads to cultural homogenisation, to achieve distinctiveness within a particular city or urban development increasing emphasis is placed on surface appearance, on the distinctive look of buildings and their surrounding spaces. They suggested that symbolism and meaning

Plate 2.3 Bankers at play
Source: Guardian; photo by Gary Weaver

rather than the functional features of buildings have achieved heightened significance in the selling of urban spaces. Style and design, textures and finish, open space and statuary, the opportunity to purchase or consume a range of aestheticised commodities in the new City spaces are all important. Thus, the surroundings of City buildings, as well as the individual buildings themselves, are now part of the design in a way that was not the case in the Edwardian City discussed by Sennett. Victorian and Edwardian bankers may have spent some of their leisure time in the clubs of the period but they would not have expected to be able to sit at open cafés in piazzas, as do increasing numbers of City workers in the late twentieth century. In addition, these new service-class workers are able to maintain their aestheticised bodies in a health club with a pool and three squash courts, and to care for them in the medical centre.

The spectacular nature of the Broadgate development and the blurring of public and private space is also achieved through the commissioning of artistic events and festivals and through the more permanent display of a range of contemporary sculpture. These include Richard Serra's 'Fulcrum' (a propped set of rusting iron plates – see plate 2.4),

Plate 2.4 Serra's 'Fulcrum'
Source: Broadgate Visitors' Guide, p. 12

George Segal's 'Rush Hour', Xavier Corbero's 'Broad Family' (a conventional heterosexual group of dad, mum and two children complete with concrete dog and ball) and Fernando Botero's spectacular 'Reclining Figure' or 'Broadgate Venus' (plate 2.5), as well as a number of other pieces based on animal themes. The female figure of the 'Broadgate Venus' is quite unlike other female allegorical forms associated with the world of banking, such as the images of womanhood on Victorian and later banknotes. Instead of the virtuous woman, the warlike images of Britannia and her ilk or the regal images of royal women and other heads of state (Hewitt, 1994), this statue revels in her ample body, which is black too. There is no voluminous cloak or draped garment, not even the modest peeping of a bare shoulder and breast common in banknote design to symbolise a 'native' land being civilised by an imperial power;

Plate 2.5 Botero's 'Broadgate Venus'
Source: photo by L. McDowell

instead the 'Broadgate Venus' is absolutely stark naked. Nor is she a sweet-faced, smiling young woman, but instead a large and threatening personification of voluptuous, ripe womanhood. It is hard to assess the intention of the developers or the effects on the men and women who lean against this statue during summer lunchtimes. For women, however, the intrusion of leisure into workplace scenes may make it even more difficult to avoid the associations of the female body with pleasure and fun. I explore these associations in part II.

Areas of redevelopment and new building like the Broadgate Centre have been termed 'scenographic enclaves' by Crilley (1993) – each of them a 'self-enclosed architectural tableau, each designed as relatively autonomous entities with contextual concern only for what is immediately adjacent or directly contributive to value' (p. 247). A spurious diversity is created by the introduction of dislocated scenes from other times and places – African festivals, for example, or medieval players at Broadgate but more elaborate and permanent references elsewhere. Thus, in the Southbank redevelopment, a mock Venice has been produced, and in the redevelopment planned for the unpopular concrete modernism of Paternoster Square hard by St Paul's Cathedral, a pastiche of the old medieval street pattern is proposed, also incorporating references to the classic City buildings of the nineteenth century Bank of England and twentieth century buildings such as Lutyens' Midland Bank.

Harvey has argued that the scenographic enclaves and postmodern buildings and spaces resemble a 'carnival mask that diverts and entertains, leaving the social problems that lie behind the mask unseen and uncared for . . . the formula smacks of a constructed fetishism in which every aesthetic power is mobilised to mask the intensifying class, racial and ethnic polarisation going on beneath' (Harvey, 1989a, p. 21). This metaphor of carnival and mask is a common one in the literature about the (re)construction and marketing of postmodern places (Kearns and Philo, 1993) and, as we shall see in a later chapter, it is also a significant metaphor in the production of embodied performances in City workspaces, the selling of self rather than place. The two are linked because, as I argued earlier, social meanings are inscribed both on the body and in physical spaces which not only reflect but affect the evaluation of feminine and masculine attributes.

Debord also argued that the spectacular society 'which eliminates geographical distance reproduces distance internally as spectacular division' (1990, p. 167). In Broadgate, this division is apparent in the spatial separation of the complex from the neighbouring streets and communities in one of the poorest areas of London. The walls of shops and office façades create and shelter a segregated and protected interior space with few and concealed entrances. While the segregation is less savage than the fortified landscape of the financial district in Los Angeles (Davis, 1990), the effect is similar. As in Los Angeles, a private security firm patrols the boundaries and ensures access is prohibited for the socially and economically undesirable. Although the design briefs and publicity material for the Broadgate development trumpeted the creation of new public leisure and shopping spaces, the spaces and facilities are best used in the business lunch hour and the shops and types of entertainment available are securely aimed at a middle-class market rather than the local residents of the adjacent inner-city community.

Across Bishopsgate, a busy street which reinforces the separation of the 'spaces of redevelopment and those of underdevelopment' (Crilley, 1993, p. 249), there is a different landscape. The terraces of small Victorian houses built in the last century for Jews and other immigrants, interspersed in a few places with an earlier landscape of houses for Flemish weavers and more commonly by inter-war and post-war municipal developments, attest to a still significant residential population on the edge of the financial City. Here, more recent immigrants, in the main from Bangladesh, are evidence of the continuing importance of the area as an initial settlement for immigrants. A Muslim temple, that in earlier rounds of immigration was successively a Huguenot church, a synagogue and a Methodist mission, stands on the corner of a street where discount clothing stores, Bengali butchers and greengrocers jostle against the

'Indian' restaurants that cater for the daily influx of office workers from the Broadgate centre, seeking an 'exotic' lunch. There can be few more spectacular internal divisions in London than these, where people from rural parts of South Asia rub shoulders on a daily basis with the 'masters of the universe'.

The building boom of the mid 1980s also led to new office developments elsewhere in the City, the most notorious being the development of Canary Wharf in the docklands which, despite difficulties in letting, now houses a number of American banks, Morgan Stanley and American Express. But there have also been major office developments in the West End of London and on the south bank of the Thames, and with plans to develop the area around King's Cross, it has been suggested that the historic division between the City and central London is disappearing (Diamond, 1991, King, 1993). Like the story of Spitalfields, this is not the place to discuss the rise and fall of Canary Wharf or other developments which have been recounted elsewhere in detail (Crilley, 1993; Fainstein, 1994; Thornley, 1992). I did not interview in Canary Wharf or the West End but in the Square Mile and its extension. Of the three banks in which the in-depth interviews were carried out, one was located in the City proper, one in the Broadgate Centre and one on the main artery connecting the two areas.

CONCLUSIONS

It is clear that the expansion of the financial services sector in the 1980s was crucial for the British economy as a whole and for the continued dominance of London as a global city. Associated with technological change and changes in the national regulatory framework in Britain, there was a considerable growth of employment in the financial services sector as a whole and in particular in Greater London, of which investment banking was a major element. What is open to question, however, is how many women gained positions of power compared with the growing numbers of young men also entering merchant banking. For these young women, the climate of the workplace was changing. It might be that the new landscapes of power in the City, with their interconnected spaces of pleasure and leisure as well as workspaces, present a less masculinised and intimidating environment for women. Alternatively, the intrusion of spaces of leisure into the workplace may act to re-place women as objects of pleasure and so paradoxically reconfirm rather than challenge their exclusion from the 'serious' spaces of serious money.

In the chapters that follow, a range of different ways of exploring the patterns of gender segregation and gendered social relations in merchant banking are explored in turn. In chapters 3 and 4, what might be termed liberal analyses of gender segregation are presented, in which an assumption that workers are individuals who merit equal treatment lies behind the empirical illustrations. Chapters 5 to 8 present analyses that depend on the notion of employees as members of diverse social groups who are subject to unequal treatment on the basis of their distinctive embodied characteristics.

NOTE

1   In presenting evidence from the transcripts I have used the usual conventions adopted by sociolinguists. Three dots separated by spaces (. . .) show that something has been omitted, but three unspaced dots (...) indicate a slight pause. The words have been written as the speaker spoke them, without correcting for written 'grammar'.

3

Gendered Work Patterns

'I mean there's any number of – a mass of – masses of very, very, good young ladies working in the market. And they will come through, they will get elected to the committee in time and – if they stick with the business, you know. . . . I hope they do. Because it's an awful pity to go through a major training exercise and then to lose somebody very good, for the understandable reason, perfectly understandable reason, they want to look after a family. So it's a difficult one.'

City Lives Project, 1991

All in all, despite marginal changes within specific occupations, there is much less evidence of desegregation than might have been expected given the extent of social and economic change in the 1980s. . . . this is mainly due to enduring inequalities in the domestic division of labour and deeply-held beliefs about the nature of gender itself.

Scott, 1994, p. 35

INTRODUCTION

In this chapter, I want to begin the analysis of gendered patterns of work and recruitment and the mechanisms that construct and maintain gender segregation in merchant banks. As we saw in chapter 2, the City remains an elitist and masculinist environment. In this and the following chapters, I draw on information collected through a questionnaire survey of all investment banks in the City of London and its immediate environs, an analysis of the personnel data for one bank and detailed interviews with a sample of the employees in this bank and two others, which I have called Merbank, Bluebros and Northbank to maintain confidentiality. Further details of the field work are to be found in the appendix.

In these chapters, I begin to unpack gender differences in patterns of employment in the early 1990s, as well as showing how recruitment strategies in 1992 and 1993 reproduced class and gender biases among the high-status, professional employees of merchant banks. Because I interviewed men and women in similar occupations, I am also able to compare their career paths. These are the subject of chapter 4.

GENDER AND EMPLOYMENT GROWTH
FROM BIG BANG

Although the significance of the City for London's economic fortunes is indisputable, the extent of growth is difficult to assess accurately because of the lack of reliable and comparative data for the sector at a sufficiently disaggregated scale. Overall employment figures, let alone details of class and gender composition, are barely adequate.

The main source of figures for overall growth is the decennial Census of Employment. Figure 3.1 and table 3.1 show respectively the total employment in Greater London in each of the categories that make up the financial services sector and London's share of national employment totals in financial services, from 1981 to 1991. In 1991 – as I began my survey work – employment in banking, insurance and other financial services was 15 per cent higher than a decade earlier. If law, accountancy and business services – those professions that had expanded to service the growing business of international and domestic banking – are added in, employment in the financial and related services had risen by 33 per cent over a decade, accounting for almost one in five of Greater London's employees in 1991. The significance of the financial services sector to Greater London's prosperity is hard to over-estimate.

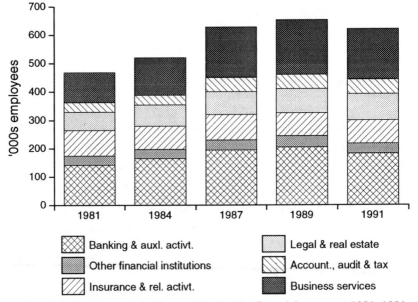

Figure 3.1 Employment in Greater London by financial category, 1981–1991
Source: Census of Employment

Table 3.1 Employment in financial services in Greater London by financial category as a percentage of total UK employment, 1981–1991

	1981	1984	1987	1989	1991
Banking and auxiliary services	38.7	38.1	41.4	40.4	39.1
Other financial institutions	27.4	25.4	24.6	21.0	19.4
Insurance and related activities	29.8	29.1	27.1	23.5	22.4

Source: Census of Employment, Office of Population Censuses and Surveys (OPCS), London

The financial services sector, especially merchant banking, is not only over-represented in Greater London, but it is also concentrated in the City of London. Table 3.2 shows the total employment in the City in 1991 and its dominance of London.

There is no doubt that the remarkable boom in financial and related services opened up employment for women. Two thirds of the total national employment growth was captured by women. However, the City exhibited a noticeably different pattern. Here indeed, banking employment for men expanded at the same rate as for women, and for both sexes the employment increase was predominantly in full-time work. This reflects the significance of career or professional positions in the City, with its overwhelming concentration of male-dominated high-profile jobs.

For a number of reasons, however, women might have been expected to gain more ground in the 1980s. In the first place, recruitment procedures seemed to become more systematic and promotion more meritocratic in the face of competition for good recruits in an expanding market,

Table 3.2 Employment in financial services in the City of London by category, 1991

	'000s employees	as % of total employment in Greater London
Banking and auxiliary services	83.2	45.5
Other financial institutions	6.3	18.0
Insurance and related activities	121.0	40.2

Source: Census of Employment, OPCS, London

perhaps benefiting women with the requisite credentials. Second, the restructuring which followed Big Bang created larger firms which may have found it difficult to recruit exclusively upper-class graduates. Third, the wider competition for Oxbridge graduates from the growing subsidiary but related sectors, as well as elsewhere in the expanding economy of the mid to late 1980s, meant that City firms were forced to look to other sources for recruits. While the Oxbridge domination remains, and indeed, as I shall argue later, may have become even more significant in the 1990s as recruitment levels fell, what is clear is that the possession of credentials by aspiring City workers became more important. Research by Rajan et al. (1990) demonstrated that the demand for 'knowledge workers' in City banking and other financial institutions increased after 1988. This increased emphasis on credentialism, and perhaps the tendency still to look to Oxbridge for recruits (the proportion of women in the undergraduate body in these universities is now more than 40 per cent compared with 12 per cent at the end of the 1960s), should have created a window of opportunity for women to enter the ranks of the City elite. Rajan et al. (1990, pp. 34, 39) did present, on the basis of detailed survey evidence, a slightly more optimistic picture than Census data revealed. They suggested that the number of women in City banks had increased somewhat more quickly than the number of men if the period between 1984 and 1990, rather than 1981 and 1991, is examined. However, their optimistic prediction of continued female expansion in the 1990–5 period was, in the event, countered by very low rates of recruitment between 1990 and 1993. As I completed interviewing in 1994, prospects had begun to look more optimistic again.

GENDER SEGREGATION IN THE CITY

From my survey of City banks, I found that 41 per cent of all their employees in early 1992 were women. Although the majority of them worked in a clerical capacity, some had succeeded in obtaining managerial positions (table 3.3).

More than 70 per cent of women were classified as clerical workers and just 3 per cent as strategic or operational managers and directors. The situation for men was very different: 32 per cent were in clerical occupations and 17 per cent were in managerial positions. Overall, women accounted for 12 per cent of managers and 61 per cent of clerical workers (figure 3.2). The only other occupational group with a higher proportion of women than the average was, perhaps predictably, 'other support staff', a category which includes personnel, marketing and public relations. On a more optimistic note, however, 48 per cent of trainees were women in 1992.

Table 3.3 Occupational distribution of women and men in the City of London's investment banks, 1992

	Men (%)	Women (%)
Directors and operational/strategic managers	17	3
Treasury and investment specialists	17	5
Business specialists	13	6
IT specialists	8	5
Other support specialists	4	7
Other professionals (lawyers etc.)	3	1
Graduate and other trainees	2	2
Clerical staff	32	70
Other (catering staff, messengers etc.)	4	1
Total (number)	13,212	9,283

Source: author's survey, 1992

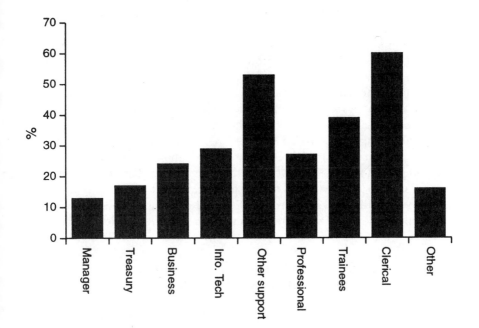

Figure 3.2 Women as a percentage of all employees in investment banks in the City, 1992

These data, while giving some indication of the distribution of men and women across the occupations in investment banks, are a rather crude measure of men's and women's experiences of segregation at work. In an investigation of six local labour markets (known as the SCELI projects), the economists and sociologists involved (Penn et al., 1994; Rubery and Wilkinson, 1994; Scott, 1994) used a subjective measure of segregation, asking their respondents whether or not they worked mainly with men or with women. Although individual perceptions may vary, even between respondents doing exactly the same job, and differences in the wording of questions tend to limit comparability between different studies, it has been demonstrated that there is a high correlation between objective and subjective measures. In merchant banking, however, the correlation may be considerably lower because for many professionals involved in the field, a large part of their work involves interacting with clients who are almost invariably male. Such interactions often tend to deepen measures of segregation that are based on employee data only. For this reason all interviewees were asked whether their total daily employment-related interactions were predominantly with men or with women. This wording may somewhat under-estimate segregation for other categories of workers as, for example, secretaries, who are usually women, interact with their bosses and other professional workers who, in merchant banks, are predominantly men.

In the interviews I carried out in three banks, I asked all my respondents with whom they interacted on a daily basis – mainly men, mainly women or mixed groups. Table 3.4 confirms my expectations.

Although the temporal basis of these comparisons is not satisfactory as the SCELI surveys were originally undertaken in the mid 1980s, the data provide an interesting indication of the extreme degree of segregation in merchant banking compared with private services in general. A much higher percentage of the 'three banks' sample thought that there was a high degree of gender segregation in their occupation than in the private services sector as a whole. This is partly explained by the bias in the sample from the banks towards professional occupations but also gives an accurate picture of the extremely masculine nature of the three banks.

GENDER SEGREGATION IN MERBANK: PIPELINE OR GLASS CEILING?

While the static picture of segregation in occupations is revealing, a more interesting and revealing comparison is of the career progressions of women and men. To assess the extent to which men and women with similar credentials and experience moved up the occupational

Table 3.4 Perceived job segregation by economic sector (%)

	Degree of gender segregation (%)			
	High	*Medium*	*Low*	*Other**
SCELI data (Private services)				
Men	29	47	22	3
Women	19	44	31	6
Three banks data				
Men	57	43	–	–
Women	62	33	4	–

Source: SCELI data from Scott, 1994, p. 12, Table 1.5
*Other = the residuals or 'cross-sex' jobs

hierarchies with the same degree of success, detailed employee data from one of the three merchant banks I examined was analysed. Merbank is a wholly owned subsidiary of a major clearing bank which in 1992 employed more than 1,400 people carrying out a range of financial activities including share dealing, corporate finance, venture capital services and investment management. Its employees are divided into two major categories – those on executive level grades and those on clerical grades. The latter include secretarial staff, transactions settlement staff

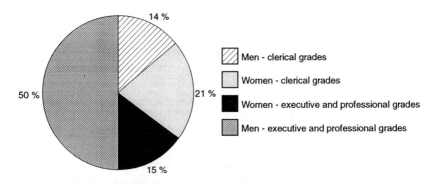

Figure 3.3 Employment in Merbank by gender and status
Source: Merbank employment records, 1992

and security staff and account for 35 per cent of total employees (see figure 3.3).

The analyses in the rest of the chapter are based on the progress of women and men on executive grades (the remaining two thirds of the workforce) – more than 900 employees – to evaluate arguments about both credentials and career progression. It is often argued that, as women entered the banking world at a later date than men, their current position reflects circumstances that will change over time. Women will eventually reach senior positions merely through the passage of time. This argument might be termed the 'pipeline' theory in contrast to the notion that women are restricted to junior positions by an invisible 'glass ceiling' which ensures that they never reach the giddy heights of seniority nor grasp the levers of power. The analysis of Merbank's personnel data enabled a partial evaluation of the 'pipeline' theory. Further examination of the comparative career paths of men and women is also possible as, in the detailed survey work, a number of interviews with matched samples of men and women at the same level in the occupational hierarchies of the three banks were undertaken. I shall turn to career paths and work histories in the next chapter.

Merbank is divided into four main departments – Investment Banking (which includes corporate finance, corporate banking and venture capital), Equities (trading in and brokering of shares), Investment Management (pension and other fund management activities) and Central Services (personnel, public relations, financial control and planning etc.). Equities is the largest department by a considerable margin, accounting for almost half of executive grade employees. Investment Banking and Investment Management together employ an additional third of the workforce at this level, with Central Services accounting for the remaining fifth. There is a marked difference in significance between Central Services and the first three departments, which are business areas directly responsible for income generation. Central Services essentially supports the business areas in their fee-earning activities and is perceived to have a more indirect influence on the bank's income. It is also the only area of the bank in which women outnumber men. There are corresponding differences in status and prestige between the business areas and Central Services, the former being seen as more prestigious, associated with higher-profile, higher-status activities. Within the three business areas themselves, there is a further differential. Corporate finance is seen as the most 'blue-blooded' area of the bank's operations. Although this does not necessarily translate into a clear-cut and consistent claim to higher status, it has an impact on recruitment policy and on financial remuneration, as well as on everyday social relations, as chapters 7 and 8 will show.

Within the executive grades at Merbank, there are nine categories of employee – Graduate Trainee, Executive Trainee, Executive, Assistant Manager, Manager, Assistant Director, Associate Director, Status Director and Legal Director. Just under one fifth of executive grade staff are full directors with a further 29 per cent in the associate and assistant director categories. The two manager grades account for an additional 29 per cent of employees and the remaining 23 per cent are either executives (one fifth) or trainees (3 per cent). The executive grade workforce is relatively young, with an average age of 33, and highly qualified; 43 per cent of these employees have degree-level qualifications and an additional 15 per cent have either postgraduate degrees or professional qualifications.

GENDER AND EMPLOYMENT IN MERBANK

The first major division between employees at Merbank is that between clerical and executive grade staff. This is itself a gendered division with women dominating the non-executive grades and men taking the bulk of executive positions. Of the 1,400 employees in the bank, 37 per cent are women and yet they account for more than 60 per cent of non-executive grade staff and only 24 per cent of those on executive grades. Men, on the other hand, constitute 63 per cent of the total workforce, accounting for more than three quarters of those in executive grades and just 40 per cent of clerical workers. Thus, while almost four fifths of male employees are in executive grades, only two fifths of women are at the same level.

Even within the executive grades, however, gender differences are marked (figure 3.4). In the first place, relative to men, a disproportionate number of women are employed in Central Services activities. This department accounts for almost 33 per cent of executive grade women and less than 14 per cent of men. As a result, more than two fifths of employees in the department are women. This means that correspondingly fewer female executives are employed in the more prestigious business area departments and confirms the argument that the gendered traits of support and 'back office' functions are typically associated with the supposed attributes of femininity. This compares with the masculinised areas of Equities and Investment Banking where women account for only 17 per cent of employees. The situation is somewhat more equal in Investment Management, where a third of employees are women, but this department accounts for only 13 per cent of executive grade employment. In contrast, the other two business areas (Equities and Investment Banking) together employ 69 per cent of the total.

At Merbank the distribution of female executive employees by grade also differs from that of male employees (figure 3.5). A higher proportion

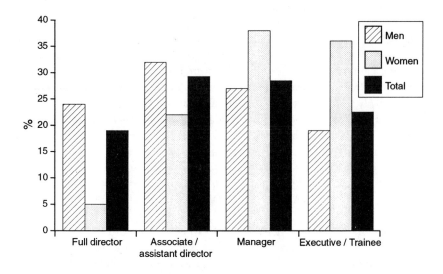

Figure 3.4 Distribution of professional men and women
by department in Merbank
Source: Merbank employment records, 1992

of women is found in the lower grades than is the case for men. The executive and trainee grades, for example, employ 36 per cent of women and only 19 per cent of men. At the other end of the scale, almost a quarter of men have directorial status, a category which includes just 5 per cent of women. These differences are broadly mirrored in each of the four departments where the differences between men and women in terms of grade reached is marked.[1] In each of the three business areas, women account for less than 10 per cent of directors and less than 20 per cent of associate and assistant directors. In Central Services a somewhat higher percentage of directors are women (21 per cent). It is, however, noticeable that in the one division where women numerically do well relative to men, fewer employees are promoted to high-status positions. Men are particularly dominant in the more prestigious, high-profile departments.

An individual's progress through the grading structure of Merbank is closely related to their age (table 3.5). More than two-thirds of those in the under-25 age group, for example, are classified as either executives or trainees and just over 5 per cent are assistant or associate directors. For those aged 40 and over, on the other hand, just 14 per cent are executives and more than one half are full directors. This suggests that if

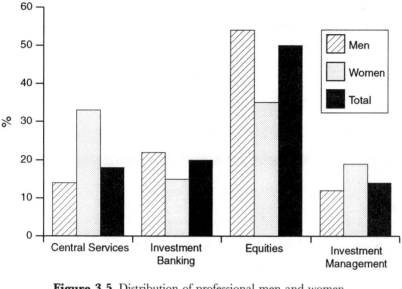

Figure 3.5 Distribution of professional men and women
by grade in Merbank
Source: Merbank personnel data

women and men in Merbank have different age profiles, their status
within the organisation in terms of grade would also be expected to
differ. On average, executive grade women at Merbank are about one
and a half years younger than their male counterparts (the mean age for
women is 32.4 years and for men 33.8 years). However, when comparing
women and men by grade, differences remain even after age has been
taken into account. This is the case for each five-year age group between
25 and 40+. For those under 25 years, the differences between women
and men in terms of the grade they have reached are not so marked.[2]
Nevertheless, even here some evidence of divergence is apparent: 35 per
cent of men are in grades above executive and only 20 per cent of
women. For those in the older age groups, however, a clear difference in
the grade status of men and women emerges. In each of the five-year age
bands, a higher proportion of women are found in the lower grades than
is the case for men. For example, in the 30–34 age group more than a
quarter of women and less than a tenth of men are classified as either
executives or trainees. Higher up the scale, 43 per cent of men and 36
per cent of women are associate and assistant directors, and a fifth of
men and just 3 per cent of women are full directors.

Using cross-sectional data of this type makes it difficult to establish
whether these differences are due to women's relatively recent entry into

Table 3.5 Women and men by age and grade in Merbank, expressed as a percentage of each grade

	Director	Associate/ assistant director	Manager	Executive/ trainee	No.
Women < 25	0	0	20.0	80.0	15
Men < 25	0	6.1	28.8	65.1	66
Women 25–29	1.3	12.8	46.2	39.7	78
Men 25–29	6.4	28.2	38.8	26.6	188
Women 30–34	3.2	35.5	35.5	25.8	62
Men 30–34	21.0	42.5	27.5	9.0	200
Women 35–39	11.4	28.6	34.3	25.7	35
Men 35–39	36.4	42.4	13.4	3.0	99
Women 40+	14.3	21.4	32.2	32.1	28
Men 40+	53.2	24.8	11.4	10.6	141

Source: Merbank personnel data

merchant banking professions (those in the youngest age group have more similar experiences to men because the practices which have produced the differences evident in those aged 25+ have been eliminated) or to a continuing process of differentiation between men and women in all age groups. The emergence of differences even among those under 25 years suggests, however, that while women and men begin their careers in similar circumstances, their career paths begin to diverge at a relatively early age. Women have been increasing their representation in the City workforce since the early 1980s with a particularly large increase in the late 1980s. Most of these women will now be in their late 20s and at Merbank it is in precisely this age group that women account for the highest proportion (29 per cent) of employees. Their careers over the past five years suggest that women and men are continuing to follow very different trajectories – in the 25–29 age group more than a third of men have reached directorial status compared to just 14 per cent of women.

As I argued above, Crompton and Sanderson's (1990, 1994) work on women in a number of different professions, including retail banking, suggested that one of the reasons for men's superior performance in the labour market at present relates to their higher overall level of qualifications. They argued, however, that as women are now achieving degree-level and occupational and professional qualifications in similar numbers to men, they will be able to use the 'qualifications lever' successfully to gain access to positions and to careers from which they have previously been excluded. This argument places a great deal of weight on the importance of qualifications in differentiating employees in the workplace and implies that if women achieve parity with men in this respect, one of the major obstacles to career progression and the realisation of career aspirations will have been removed.

The data on women in executive grades at Merbank provide some support for this argument but suggest that equality of qualifications constitutes only one dimension of the changes required for women and men to gain parity in the workplace. As noted above, employees at Merbank are highly qualified relative to the population as a whole. More than two fifths of both men and women have degrees, 5 per cent have professional qualifications and 10 per cent have postgraduate degrees. The Merbank data also show that there are some differences between men's and women's qualifications – a slightly higher proportion of women than men have no listed qualifications (27 per cent compared with 23 per cent) and more men than women have postgraduate qualifications (12 per cent compared to 5 per cent). On the other hand, very similar proportions of women and men have first degrees and more women than men have professional qualifications (6 per cent compared to 4 per cent).[3]

In terms of qualifications, then, the main difference between men and women is in their acquisition of postgraduate degrees and professional certification. This in itself is clearly related to age, and the proportion of employees with such qualifications reaches a peak in the 35–39 age group (22 per cent). A smaller proportion of women than men is in this group, which may account for some of the variation. More important, however, is the finding that while women are consistently concentrated in lower grades than men throughout all age groups, there is no such consistency with regard to qualifications. Women under 30 actually have *higher* qualifications than their male counterparts: 13 per cent of women in this age group have postgraduate or professional qualifications compared with 9 per cent of men. This advantage is lost in the early 30s, but thereafter, although a higher proportion of men have professional and postgraduate qualifications than is the case for women, the differences become less marked (and they cease to be statistically significant).

This suggests that new women entrants to merchant banking are very highly qualified, more so than those currently in their 30s and 40s. Women in the older age groups have been slower to acquire postgraduate qualifications than men. This perhaps reflects the nature of the qualifications in question, as well as the relative proportions of men and women in the postgraduate population at the time at which these degrees were acquired. Many of the postgraduate degrees obtained by Merbank employees are MBAs and related degrees – and nationwide three quarters of those gaining higher degrees in business and administration studies are men (Government Statistical Service, 1992).

CONCLUSIONS

The Merbank analysis suggests that there is no linear relationship between level of qualification and career success. While both men and women in the higher grades at Merbank tend to be more highly qualified than those at the lower end of the grading scale, differences between the career progression of women and men exist (to the disadvantage of women) even when the former have a higher level of qualifications than their male colleagues. This analysis shows that just as getting into the workplace has proved a necessary but insufficient step towards undermining male power structures, obtaining credentials may be a necessary but insufficient step towards gaining access to power within the workplace and influencing organisational culture. In a later chapter, I shall examine this question of organisational culture, in the specific context of recruitment. First, however, I want to move from the aggregate analysis of Merbank data to compare career patterns of some of the women and men who were working in the City in the early 1990s.

NOTES

1 Statistically significant at the 5 per cent level for all and at 1 per cent in Equities and Investment Management.
2 Neither are they statistically significant using the chi square test.
3 These differences are not statistically significant at the 5 per cent level, however.

4

Gendered Career Paths

===

For men, childbirth has little impact upon their worklife occupational mobility.
Elias, 1994, p. 90

'Let's face it. Most women don't want careers. They don't want to be the same as men.'
Scientist in the oil industry, quoted in Davidson, 1985, p. 2

INTRODUCTION

The analysis of personnel data from Merbank revealed differences between men's and women's status in that bank, showing that successful male and female applicants seem to end up in different positions, both in terms of the department they work in and their level of seniority. What cross-sectional data cannot reveal, however, is differences in the respective paths taken by men and women in attaining a particular position. This is where the analysis of work histories is useful. In this chapter, the career paths of a number of women and men working in the three sample banks are investigated. I move away from aggregate statistical analysis to a detailed assessment of the narratives presented by the employees who were interviewed in depth.

The material collected through interviews cannot be regarded as representative in a statistical sense. Rather, a 'sample' of employees was selected in order to reveal processes of gender segregation and discrimination. For this reason it was crucial to include women at all levels in the banks' hierarchies to compare with men in similar positions. Because there are so few senior women in merchant banks, in some cases virtually all, or even all, the women working at a particular level had to be included. Thus, the women in the 'director's sample' are the entire field rather than a sample. Overall 50 respondents in professional occupations were interviewed − 31 women and 19 men. Within each occupational group, a small number of matched pairs of respondents – a woman and a man in identical occupations at the same level in the hierarchy – were included in order to compare their work histories prior to their current job, their qualifications and their salaries. To maintain confidentiality, all the respondents are referred to here by pseudonyms.

WORK HISTORIES

The collection of life histories has a long tradition in urban sociology and anthropology and may be traced back to the Chicago school of urban sociology. The origins of recent work, according to Dex (1991), are to be found in the publication of Hareven's (1978) and Elder's (1978) work on the concept of life course analysis. This approach focuses on 'the overlap between individuals' experiences and those coincidental in chronological time, be they other individuals, family members, structural changes, policy changes or whatever' (Dex, 1991, p. 4). Perhaps the most typical use of life course analysis has been in the investigation of intra-generational mobility and the class structure. The approach is less familiar in the context of workplace studies but a number of labour market analysts and feminist economists and sociologists have begun to use work histories in their investigations of gender differences in career paths (Burchell, 1993; Dex, 1987; Marsh and Gershuny in Dex, 1991; Payne and Abbott, 1990; Scott and Burchell, 1994; Walby, 1991a), often linking this work with class analysis (Dex, 1987; Payne and Abbott, 1990). The approach is perhaps particularly appropriate for understanding women's lives and employment patterns, as 'life' and 'work' decisions are so interconnected. A life history approach also provides insight into some of the structural factors which impinge on women's work histories, constraining or facilitating their choices. For the older women in the sample, the circumstances in the City in the 1960s and 1970s led to different options than for the younger women who entered merchant banks from the mid 1980s onwards. Similarly, a wider set of socio-economic, familial and legal changes are important influences on the choices available to women of different generations. A whole range of factors operating at various geographic scales – from location of the home to the deregulation of the international financial system – are reflected in individual career paths.

Collecting retrospective information raises, of course, the difficult questions of relying on personal memories, of how to deal with selective recall and of assessing how an individual's recollection of the past is affected by current circumstances. In collecting work histories by recall, errors increase the further back the respondent is required to go, but as the majority of my respondents were relatively young and many of them were at the beginning of their working lives and well educated, I decided that I could justify ignoring these problems and accept the details given to me by my interviewees. Reassurance was found in Dex's (1987) argument that key events such as first entering the labour market are usually remembered accurately, although events which are more detailed in nature or shorter in duration (such as short periods of unemployment) are subject to greater error. Very few of my respondents, however, had experienced even short periods of unemployment, despite the City being hit by recession and a jobs shakeout in the early years of the 1990s. The very fact that they were in employment in 1993 and 1994 meant that they were among the most successful – or lucky – City employees.

It has long been established that, even in professional occupations, women in general follow a different path from men, marked by discontinuous labour market attachment and downward mobility after childbirth (Brannen, 1989; Brannen and Moss, 1991; Dex, 1987; Elias, 1983; Hanson and Pratt, 1995; McRae, 1991; Stewart and Greenhalgh, 1982, 1984). Many analyses of women's employment histories have demonstrated the significance of their domestic and childcare responsibilities, as well as the consequences of decisions by other household members, for women's attachment to the labour market, for their job search behaviour and occupational choices, and for patterns of gender segregation in general. It is important to note, however, Walby's (1991a) pertinent criticism. She suggested that this 'familial' emphasis overstates the significance of biological events at the expense of the significance of other factors structuring women's lives.

> There is a problematic tendency to use a 'job model' to explain men's work patterns and a different one, a 'gender model' in order to explain women's work patterns. That is, labour market and industrial structures are used to explain patterns in men's work and domestic events used to explain patterns in women's work. The greater tendency to the life history method in the analysis of women's as opposed to men's labour force experience, may thus push our understanding of women's employment in a different direction from that of men to a greater extent than is warranted. (Walby, 1991a, p. 167)

As both men's and women's career patterns have been collected in the present study, I hope to avoid this danger. Indeed, my work is atypical in including both men and women. The comparative experiences of men and women in same industries and, especially, in same occupations are not well established. 'We know relatively little about how *men's* work history patterns link with occupational segregation [as] recent explorations of these issues have mainly focused on women' (Scott and Burchell

Table 4.1 Marital and familial status and age of women and men in professional occupations in the 'three banks' sample

Age/status	Women		Men	
	No.	%	No.	%
Under 25	3	6	1	2
25–29	11	22	7	14
30–34	11	22	8	16
35–39	3	6	2	4
40–44	1	2	-	-
45–49	1	2	-	-
50 and over	1	2	1	2
Single/widowed/divorced	16	32	7	14
Married*/no children	10	20	5	10
Married*/children	5	10	7	14

*Includes *de facto* married

1994, p. 123, their emphasis). In this chapter, my aim is to partially remedy this neglect.

A predominantly familial explanation or a gender model is also inappropriate here as women who are employed in a professional capacity in merchant banks are an atypical segment of the female labour force as a whole. Just over half of the women in my sample were unmarried (*de jure* or *de facto*) and very few of them were mothers (see table 4.1), a reflection of their relative youth and the particular demands of their jobs, especially the excessively long hours habitually spent in the workplace by my respondents. Only five of the 31 women had children and three of this five were older women (over 35) of whom two had had their children before they entered merchant banking. Thus, 84 per cent of the women who were interviewed were childless, although a single respondent was pregnant, compared with less than a quarter of all women of working age. This makes their working life histories very different from most women's and more similar to a male model, not only because of the absence of children but also because of their professional status.

Table 4.2 shows the gender breakdown of my respondents in each of the professional categories, their ages, qualifications, length of working life and, where information was given, their salary. The salary information is not reliable as bankers receive significant annual bonuses which vary and so are difficult to estimate. Further, some respondents were

Table 4.2 The characteristics of the 'three banks' sample of professional employees (total = 50)

Job category	Sex	Age	Highest qualification	Salary (£000 p.a.)	Working life Total	Working life This bank
Trainee						
	f	23	A levels	17.5	4	4.5
	m	23	A levels	17.5	4.75	5
Executive						
	f	23	BA	26	1.5	1.5
	f	25	BA	40	2.5	2.5
	f	26	BA + acc.	–	1.5	5
	f	26	BA	22	2	2.5
	f	34	A levels	50	3	15
	m	26	BA	30	1	4
	m	30	B.Sc. + acc.	44	2	9
	m	30	BA	28	2	8
	m	33	B.Sc.	75	3.5	12
Assistant manager						
	f	29	O levels + fin. sch.	28	10	10
Manager						
	f	24	MA	45	2.5	2.5
	f	26	A levels	35	3	8
	f	27	BA	–	5	5
	f	27	BA	35	0.5	5
	f	27	BA	53	3	6
	f	30	MA	35	1.5	8
	f	30	LL M	58	4	9
	f	32	Dip. Econ.	38	2	10
	f	32	BA	44.5	6	10
	f	33	B.Sc.	55	7	11
	f	37	MA	–	6.5	15
	m	27	MA	33	1.5	4
	m	28	BA	56.5	6	6
	m	29	B.Sc. + acc.	45	5	8
	m	30	BA	50	2	2
	m	30	O levels	–	8	12
	m	32	LL M	70	3	8

Table continued on next page

Job category	Sex	Age	Highest qualification	Salary (£000 p.a.)	Working life Total	This bank
Assistant director						
	f	28	MBA	60	5	6
	f	29	BA	40	6	6
	f	29	BA	43	8	8
	f	30	BA	50	2	9
	f	34	BA	34	5	13
	f	35	MA	25	1	13
	m	27	BA	–	5	5
	m	28	B.Sc.	80	5	6.5
	m	29	BA	60	6	6
	m	32	BA + acc.	70	6	11
	m	35	MA	25	1	13
Associate director						
	f	33	BA	–	5	11
	f	36	BA	–	3	14
	m	34	BA	–	6	12
Director						
	f	32	MBA	120	2	10
	f	37	MBA	160	7	16
	f	42	B.Sc.	–	16	20
	f	49	MA	–	5	26
	f	51	LLM	–	10	29
	m	37	BA + acc.	170	81	5
Board director						
	m	52	banking exams	–	35	35

more forthcoming than others about the exact size of their most recent bonus. Also, a range of additional elements are included in the overall remuneration package for most respondents, including health insurance, a car, free parking and low interest loans, especially for house purchase. It was difficult to collect accurate details of these items, let alone work out an imputed value. Thus, the salary information is indicative of a possible range rather than an accurate reflection of pecuniary rewards in this part of the financial services sector.

Not surprisingly, given the way the sample was composed, no clear pattern of gender differentiation is revealed by this table. I included men and women in each occupational category, and, although there is some relationship between position in the hierarchy and age, it is evident that promotion at a relatively young age is not uncommon. Both men and women are able to reach the directorial level in their early 30s, and even younger in the assistant director grade. While the majority of respondents have degree-level qualifications and some of them are also professionally qualified as either accountants or solicitors, it is apparently still possible for people with only school-leaving qualifications to obtain professional positions in the world of merchant banking. It is significant, however, that the trainees, the executive and the manager with A levels only are all employed in the trading and dealing areas of merchant banking, substantiating stereotypical views of this side of banking – that is, quick thinking youngsters straight from the East End of London or Essex. Employment in this area also brings the largest salaries. The

Table 4.3 Comparison of salary levels in investment banking in 1992

	Day Associates (£000s)	Three banks (£000s)
Foreign exchange money		
Forex and money manager	325.6	—
Forex currency dealer	57.3	35.0
Corporate finance		
Corporate finance manager	158.3*	70.0
Investment manager	113.4	105.0
Lending		
Credit manager	117.1	67.5
Project manager	50.5	34.0
Accounts, operations and administration		
Financial controller	77.8	77.0
Data processing manager	62.5	51.0
Personnel manager	42.4	44.5

Source: Day Associates data taken from City Research Project, 1995, table 7.11.

*The two people whom I interviewed in corporate finance who earned around £170k in 1992 were assistant directors rather than managers. I selected for comparison the highest paid individual in each category.

differentials within each category are explained in the main by the high annual salaries of traders and dealers. Thus, among the executives, for example, the highest-paid respondent is a gilts salesman, as is the highest-paid woman at this rank. However, as employees rise through the hierarchy, salaries in the corporate finance division begin to match these levels. So, for example, the highest-paid man and woman at the level of manager are both in corporate finance departments, and both, incidentally, have a legal background, although it is unclear whether their LL M automatically qualifies them for a high salary.

In table 4.3, salary data for different occupations in merchant banks from a survey by Day Associates (City Research Project, 1995) is compared with the information my respondents offered. It is possible that the Day Associates data are more accurate and reliable as their survey was anonymous, whereas I was asking people face to face what they earned and the notable British reticence about their pay hindered my investigations. It is impossible to tell, however, how old and experienced the Day Associates' respondents were and so the figures are only indications of salary levels in the City in 1992 as I began to interview.

Turning from current salaries to career paths, it was noticeable how few of the respondents had spent their entire working life in the bank in which they were currently employed – only eight of the total sample and two of these were relatively junior staff in the executive grade. The employee with the longest-standing record of employment with a single employer, however, was the most senior person of those interviewed – a male director and member of the board who had been with the same bank almost all his working life of 35 years – albeit as the bank went through several phases of reincarnation and more than one change of ownership. The career of this man more accurately mirrors a previous era in the City, when young men entered a bank, often through personal connections, and progressed steadily through the hierarchy, gaining qualifications 'on the job' as it were, as indeed this respondent had done. These patterns of intra-firm mobility seem to have disappeared.

The majority of respondents working in professional occupations are now much more likely to have started their careers with university qualifications. Although nine of the 50 respondents had not been to university – three of the dealers among them – all the others had and many of them to prestigious institutions (and see chapter 5). The majority of the sample also differed from an earlier pattern in that they were highly likely to have worked for more than one bank. There is, however, high attachment to the banking sector among a majority of employees: 52 per cent of the sample had been previously employed only in merchant banking, and a further 32 per cent in the related areas of accounting, insurance broking and business services, compared with a minority (16 per cent) who had worked in a range of occupations in different sectors.

OCCUPATIONAL MOBILITY AMONG WOMEN IN PROFESSIONAL OCCUPATIONS: SOME COMPARATIVE EVIDENCE

In an interesting re-analysis of a national survey of women's employment (Martin and Roberts, 1984), Dex (1987) has produced perhaps the fullest available evidence of the experiences of British women in professional occupations, providing a useful basis for comparison with women in professional employment in banking. Dex was, however, extremely cautious about generalisation because not only were there very small numbers of women in the sample who had experienced a professional job during their work history, but also their experiences were varied, difficult to describe and much more unstable and unpredictable than the careers of women in other occupational profiles.

A successful professional profile was considered to be one in which a woman had a succession of professional jobs, retaining occupational attachment over the whole or most of her work history. This pattern was found only in the cases where women were continuously employed, either because they were single or childless or because they took maternity leave instead of having more permanent breaks from work for childbirth. Interestingly, Dex's data established a highly mobile pattern between professional jobs, lending little support to the continuity found by Felmlee (1982) in the US, but more consistent with my findings described below.

Entry into a professional profile usually occurred right at the beginning of a woman's work history as her first job or occasionally after a very short and often temporary job in a semi-skilled occupation, or less commonly in a clerical job of short duration with the subsequent changes being between professional jobs. With the increased emphasis on the importance of credentials in the British labour market (Crompton, 1992; Crompton and Sanderson, 1990), movement from a non-professional to a professional profile became even more exceptional during the 1980s. A third route into a professional job, but not to a professional profile, was from either clerical work or intermediate non-manual work after a long and continued attachment to the same employer. This was rare among the women surveyed in 1980 and has probably become rarer still since that date.

As a group, Dex found that women with professional profiles were older than average when they started work, more highly educated and more likely to be married at the start of their work history, but they were also more often under 40 years of age when they were surveyed. Many of those who started out in professional jobs at the beginning of their work histories did not continue in them for long. The main reason for a disruption was 'moving because of husband's job' and it was experienced frequently during the initial work period. Loss of professional status for the female partner was common after such a disruption and these women then moved into teaching, other intermediate non-manual jobs and clerical jobs – a clear example of downward occupational mobility. Dex found that redundancy from professional jobs was rare and had occurred only in one case in her sample. Other causes of a disrupted career path included illness, perhaps because of the strain of 'dual roles', and voluntary job change because of dissatisfaction, to take up education opportunities or because of a temporary professional job coming to an end. Dex suggested that these disruptions 'occurred often enough to illustrate that women who set out in professional jobs are less conventional in occupational attachment than other women and possibly more flexible with a wider set of options. They are also more used to temporary jobs and less disrupted by them' (p. 44). Some of this flexibility is evident among the women in my sample, as I demonstrate below.

CAREER PROGRESSION IN MERCHANT BANKING

Merchant banking, as table 4.1 shows, is very much a young people's world. The majority of the 50 professional workers who were interviewed at length were in their 20s and 30s. The trading, dealing and sales side of merchant banking, in particular, is the terrain of the young where mental agility and physical stamina are the essential prerequisites of money-making. But all occupations in merchant banking seem to require stamina to survive the long hours that are expected. As Lewis remarked about the best analysts in his portrait of the City in the 1980s, they 'lost the will to live. They gave themselves entirely over to their employers and worked round the clock. They rarely slept and often looked ill; the better they became at the job, the nearer they appeared to death' (Lewis, 1989, p. 41).

My own respondents recognised that the demands of many of the professional occupations in banking led to a limited career span. Trading was most commonly referred to as the shortest-lived occupation:

Trading is a means to an end. You do 15 or 20 years, get out at 35, 40, whatever, and then hopefully progress somewhere else, into management perhaps. (male forex dealer, 30)

The average age of the dealers, traders and salespeople whom I interviewed was 26.8 years, compared with a comparatively elderly average of 31.6 for professionals employed on the corporate finance side of the business and 34.0 for those in central services functions. Even the most senior person I interviewed was a mere 52 years old.

There was, however, still almost 30 years between the youngest and the oldest respondent, and it is clear that the particular circumstances of the City at the time of entry – in terms of social background, educational requirements and the sheer availability of jobs (or not) – makes a difference to who is recruited at particular times. For many of the respondents in my sample, their initial employment in the City had been linked to the mid 1980s expansion, especially the time of Big Bang in 1986. As several respondents remarked, this was when City portals were flung open and the exclusivity of the City was most vulnerable to challenge. A Glasgow-born-and-bred grammar school boy, reflecting on his own entry to the capital markets division of Northbank in the mid 1980s, said:

With the growth of financial services in the mid 1980s it was very easy to get a job; it was a piece of cake. I came back [from working abroad] without a job and within two weeks I'd had four or five offers – it was an absolute doddle. The thing was expanding so quickly and no one had any idea how to manage those things, so they were literally recruiting right, left and centre, thinking that would solve their problems. (man, 32)

But, he added, 'it all went sour pretty quickly' and by the early 1990s many banks in the City had had to reduce recruitment and several were forced to make redundancies to survive the period of recession before relative expansion again at the end of 1992 and into 1993.

I shall explore recruitment in more detail in the next chapter. Here, in order to compare the diverse experiences of people recruited to the City at different periods, as well as to compare women with men as they move through the occupational hierarchy of merchant banking, I want to present in detail the class and educational backgrounds and the work histories of four pairs of women and men. They include a young male and female trainee dealer, a similar pair of dealers who had progressed into the managerial grade, a pair of managers in the corporate finance division and the most senior man and woman in the sample who were both directors. I then conclude with a comparison of two other women – of different ages – who had also reached the status of director. In this way the relative effects of gender, class and age will be revealed. In each case the pair worked in the same bank, including all three women at director level who are employed by Northbank which perhaps indicates the relative open-mindedness of this bank compared with the other two. Again, I shall look at the similarities and differences in the cultures of the three banks in the next chapter.

STARTING OUT – TRAINEE DEALERS

Tim and Jo were both 23 and single. Tim lived with his parents in Southend in Essex on the eastern fringes of London but was looking for a flat to buy closer to the City, and Jo had just bought a small house, coincidentally quite close to where Tim's parents lived. Both resented the time spent travelling to work as the early morning start often meant that they had to leave at 6.30 a.m. They had been with the same bank as trainee dealers for four years in the case of Jo and about six months longer in Tim's case. They both left school with A levels and went straight to work in the City in 1987 – just as the period of huge expansion was coming to an end.

I thought of going to university but basically I wanted to go straight into work, so ... (Tim)

This was a common path for traders when degree-level qualifications were not required but, as Tim explained later, it has become less usual in recent years.

Tim had worked for 12 weeks as an insurance clerk for Barclays – 'my Dad was a salesman so he said like get involved in that sort of thing' – but Tim was then too young for selling and he found clerical work tedious. He joined Northbank in October 1987, almost on the eve of the crash, and went into a back office position as a settlements clerk. It was not until almost two years later that Tim's potential was recognised and he moved into the dealing room – and into another world.

I was 18 and a junior clerk working in a room with maybe 70 people in. The people who ran each section were sort of middle-aged assistant managers who you had a lot of respect for 'cos they'd been here 20 years, so it was quite a well-run place. When I moved and went into the dealing room my supervisor was, well, a year older than me, and there was sort of like 35–40 people on the floor, and the atmosphere was electric. It was a complete change; it was great, it really was, just what I wanted.

    . . .

I got into the dealing room in a job on positions. I'd made it clear that was what I wanted and then eight months later a job came up as a trainee dealer and I got it.

On being asked whether his experience was a typical way of entering a dealing room, Tim explained:

It is and it isn't. I think a lot of it now ... well, it depends. A lot of adverts for trainee dealers tend to be for graduates, they're just basically all graduates, but then the actual level of all employment ... I think you need better qualifications now, 'cos there are just so many people walking round with better qualifications, . . . but the trouble is, it's the sort of atmosphere where you've got to be reasonably intelligent to get on there but you've also got to have a bit of basic instinct for it. You know, you can have someone who is superbly intelligent, got an IQ of 180 but no common sense. They won't be able to do it, but then you might get the other person who, you know, might not have ... it's not like the old days when they used to see people with white socks screaming and shouting at each other, it's not quite like that, but there's still an element of that there ...

Jo, too, had entered the bank as a settlements clerk. Like Tim she had been clear about what she did not want to do in the financial sector but less certain about her move into dealing.

I chose to work in the City because I knew I didn't want to work in Southend High Street behind Barclays, cashing cheques and that. . . . I started here in settlements on like a training scheme – three years. I did more or less every section and they asked if I wanted to be a supervisor and I said yes. The next day the dealing room phoned down and offered me the dealing job so I thought 'it's easier to get back into the settlements area if I don't like the dealing room than to stay in settlements and to try to get into dealing again if I don't like being a supervisor'. I didn't start thinking I wanted to be a dealer, it just sort of happened. It wasn't something I'd always aimed at or anything. But I had earlier applied for a job on the money market dealing desk and I didn't get it – a bloke that I worked with downstairs got it.

Jo also had similar views about the need for graduate-level qualifications for her job.

The two directors of the dealing room told me it goes more on personality than on paper qualifications. You did have to do a test – quick maths questions – a minute to answer 30 multiple choice questions – a couple of those.

If Tim and Jo had relatively similar experiences in entry and recruitment to the dealing room, if not in their own motivation, what about their experiences working as trainee dealers?

Jo had found the atmosphere of the dealing room to be very masculine and believed that initially she had not got the money markets position she had wanted because she was a woman. Her current position was on the corporate money market desk and involved 'managing other people's funds rather than purely trading. It's trading for other people, looking after their money' – a position about which the director who had interviewed her remarked, rather elliptically according to Jo, 'there's a lot less involved in this type of dealing. It's not as noisy as the dealing room.'

In fact the foreign exchange desk, the money markets and the corporate desk were all in the same room, although slightly separated. Jo was quite clear, however, that an informal policy of gender segregation was in operation: she was the only woman working as a trainee dealer and had been directed to a specific area.

I get the feeling they wanted a bloke for the money markets. I also get the feeling they wanted a woman for this job ... I think it's sort of seen as, erm ... I don't know how to explain it ... it's as though the woman would be more approachable and ... sort of like a sales assistant in a shop is more or less going to be a woman. The money market dealers are all men ... I think that was probably the main reason. You know, they'd be thinking how a woman would fit in, I would think. The corporate desk is a bit more on its own and there's a lot of sort of taking customers out to lunch and in the evening. They obviously thought I would be more suited to that than to actual trading.

Both trainees believed that their careers as dealers would be short – although for different reasons. Tim thought he would be burned out by his mid 30s:

It's basically a young man's game; up to, up to 40 probably. But then, it's your own personal choice. I think 32, 33. It depends how well you are going. ... The money will be very good soon but remember it's not forever, not for 20 years even; you've got to be looking at ten maximum and then look for another job.

Jo, on the other hand, despite still being single and unattached, considered that her job would be short lived because of its incompatibility with family life. It already imposed restrictions on her social life.

All my friends at home work quite locally so I'm always 'the tired one'. It would be difficult to do this job if I had a serious relationship or children. ... If I had children I think I would probably give up work, at least for a couple of years, and then I would probably not go back into something quite so demanding.

Like many women in semi-professional occupations, Jo clearly expected to have to trade off career prospects and family commitments later in her working life. But although she intended to return to an occupation other than banking if she had a break, it was Jo rather than Tim who was studying for the Institute of Bankers exams in her leisure time.

The constraints experienced by a man and woman slightly further up the corporate ladder are explored next.

HITTING THE BIG(GER) TIME

Jeremy and Vanessa were also dealers, but with a few more years' experience in their trade; they had reached the managerial grade at the time I interviewed them. Vanessa was in her mid 20s, whereas Jeremy had just reached his 30th birthday.

These two also seemed to embody the stereotypical view of dealers as East End or Essex barrow boy (and girl). Both had gained their current position without a university education. Vanessa had three A levels, Jeremy only O levels. Both had been with their current bank for eight years and both were foreign exchange dealers. Their paths to the present had also been similar, despite Jeremy's four additional years of experience which is reflected in his somewhat higher earnings. Vanessa had achieved a position in a dealing room after two years' back office experience, whereas Jeremy took only nine months. Both of them had been ambitious from the start and determined to move into dealing.

I wanted to be a dealer. I just decided that was the sort of thing I wanted to do. ... I am not very good with people, and dealing was just something I really wanted to do. I really like the environment. (Vanessa)

While their working lives were similar – characterised by long hours and high pressure – the domestic circumstances of this pair were completely different. Vanessa was single and accepted that the job was difficult to combine with having a family – not only because of the demanding hours but also because of common attitudes in the financial sector, at least in the world of dealing.

Going for jobs, it does make a big difference being a girl[1] – in the way that you always get asked 'Are you married, are you seeing someone and are you thinking of having children?' It really annoys me. I've always been asked things like that every time I have been for an interview. ... If you went for an interview and you had kids, I don't think you'd get it. Most of the girls I know are roughly the same age as me and none of them have thought of having children. ... I did have a row with the guys at work because a couple of them said 'Well, if she's got children, she shouldn't be allowed to work because it's going to affect her job.' And I said 'How can you say that, it's so ridiculous?' And that is quite the feeling – what the guys said – even the young guys in my work.

Vanessa intended to remain single and childless but her options were quite clearly constrained by the attitudes she found in her workplace. Jeremy, on the other hand, was a family man – married with a two-year-old daughter. His wife initially had returned to work on a part-time basis but recently she had increased her hours by working from home. Jeremy expressed 'traditional' attitudes to men's and women's respective domestic obligations:

Childcare and housework obviously falls very heavily on my wife ... it all boils down to the money factor. I happen to earn a lot more money than my wife does obviously, so you know, at the end of the day, we've got a mortgage to pay for, and my job has to be put first on that basis, a purely financial thing ... although we do clash quite often.

Perhaps what seemed so 'obvious' to Jeremy was not so clear cut to his wife. His major complaint, at least as voiced to me, was about the responsibility for overnight childcare – a responsibility that appeared to happen only once a year.

Er, ... well the biggest thing is like in the instance of my wife ... they had their yearly directors' meeting; she had to attend that, which in this case means staying overnight at an hotel and working late, being out of the house and ... so, I have to leave early in the evenings and get in late in the mornings ... I won't get in 'til 9 o'clock, which is the best part of nearly two hours late for me.

On being questioned about whether or not his employer might make the odd exception, Jeremy's reply was both defensive and revealing:

There's no way I would like to do that every other week ... I don't ... at this bank it probably would be acceptable, but it wouldn't necessarily be, you know ... I personally wouldn't like it anyhow.

Perhaps the institutional obstacles perceived by both Jo and Vanessa are as much to do with the attitudes of individual men in positions of responsibility as with the way the job is structured. Vanessa made it plain that she felt entirely within her rights to leave at 5 p.m. if the work was done, despite most of her male colleagues staying later.

I always get comments when I leave at 5 – half day sort of stuff – but I make sure no one is floundering and I've agreed the deals. If you make money, you can do what you like.

Like Tim and Jo, Jeremy and Vanessa accepted the limited prospects of a dealer; however, not only were their plans different from each other's but Vanessa also spurned the conventional female path of childcare and the associated downward mobility that Jo apparently accepted for her own future. Vanessa had clear and entrepreneurial plans for the future:

I love my job but I am only going to do it for another three years and then I am going to be out of it. I really want to set up my own company. I've started looking round. I am mad on sailing and a couple of chandleries have just come up in my way, very cheaply. I am about to turn 27 and if you stay in this market too long it is really hire and fire and you are going to end up ... it's going to happen to quite a few people and at 35 to 40 they're looking over their shoulder, waiting for redundancy basically. Then you're just not qualified for anything else, you've got no skills in anything and I just thought I really don't want to end up like that.

Jeremy was also clear about his limited prospects in dealing but expected to be able to move through to the management hierarchy within the financial world – a prospect that Vanessa felt was still denied to her because of institutional discrimination and individual sexist attitudes. This was Jeremy's view of his current job and future career:

A trading room is means to an end, perhaps to get quick money. When you've made enough money you just sell up and move elsewhere ... hopefully progress somewhere in senior management ... perhaps in another bank or in a broking house elsewhere. I'd basically stay in the City.

So in the four case studies here, there are similarities and differences, not always based on gendered choices and opportunities. All four of the dealers – and indeed the other seven who were included among the 50 professional workers interviewed in depth – accepted the limited life of a career as a dealer. When it came to future plans though, neither the two men nor Vanessa had any intention of accepting downward mobility. For Jo, however, the conventional female path of career break and lower earnings seemed inevitable.

In the next two sets of male/female comparisons, the respondents are further up the occupational hierarchy and employed in corporate finance, where the currency is advice rather than direct money-making. First, the career patterns of two young, well-paid assistant directors are examined before the careers of a man and woman who have scaled the giddy heights to become directors and board members become the focus.

SERIOUS MONEY – ASSISTANT DIRECTORS IN CORPORATE FINANCE

Kit and Suzi embody the social characteristics of 'the other side' of merchant banking, the more exclusive world of corporate finance – exclusive, that is, in terms of the social and educational background of the majority of employees. Here, a degree, preferably from one of the 'better' universities – Oxbridge, Bristol and Durham were mentioned not only by the senior personnel officers of the three participating banks but also by many respondents – is a desirable, if not absolutely essential, passport to entry. Suzi had an Oxford BA in modern languages, whereas Kit had graduated from Exeter with a BA in economics and statistics, having tried but failed to read law at Cambridge. Both had joined their current bank in 1986, straight from university. Suzi was recruited into the graduate training programme whereas Kit, who had had experience working in a venture capital house during his university summer vacations, was employed to work in capital markets. His view of this area paralleled that expressed by the dealers above, and it was Kit who felt uncomfortable:

I decided to try and move over. I felt out of place. At the time I just thought that that sort of area was a bit sort of 'Essex man' and lots of affairs and I thought I'd never really get anywhere basically. I thought that I would get to a stage by the time I was 30 and I probably may not move on much further.

. . .

   I was the only person there with a degree then [in 1986], but it's developed now. The bank has realised that that's an area where you can lose a hell of a lot of money or make a hell of a lot of money, and so they've changed their policy as to who they recruit there and therefore, while there are natural traders, there are also people who ... sort of rocket scientist types, guys who sit alongside each other and one sits with the theory and one sits with the gut feel and between them they work out the answer.

Kit recognised that his move may have cost him immediate financial recompense: 'to be honest they get paid a lot of money which I don't, but still'. In fact Kit's annual salary in 1992 with bonus had been £60,000. The initial decision to move sideways into the corporate finance division had also caused him anxiety as the work initially had seemed boring.

There were times when I found it tedious and then I suppose after about ... after about a year, it just suddenly clicked and I realised what it was all about and I started taking responsibility for doing things myself, on my own initiative.

   After a few months, early in 1989, Kit had then had what he referred to as 'the biggest break in my life, or in my working life' when the bank created a special team as an autonomous unit to focus specifically on smaller companies. It was a team of nine and Kit was appointed as an assistant director, responsible for the day-to-day running of the team and managing the transactions under two directors. Kit spoke about what he called his 'luck' in a deprecating manner, under-estimating the success of the unit:

It's been very successful, well, relatively successful I should say. What we have been very lucky with is that at the smaller end people's selectivity, as it were, is not so great, smaller clients don't expect to get 'the best' as it were and therefore, while I do think we are very good, it is a lot easier to win business.

It is interesting that Kit referred to his career in terms of luck as it is often argued that this is a typically female way of constructing a career (Bateson, 1990), whereas men tend to construct, partly through *post hoc* rationalisation, a more purposeful path to their current position. It was clear, however, that Kit enjoyed his present work and felt committed to it – 'At the moment I actually love what I am doing' – and, despite his protestations of luck, he expected to make it to the director level within five years.

Suzi, who entered the bank at the same time as Kit, had also risen to the level of assistant director by 1993. She too was in her late 20s and had been continuously employed by the same bank for six years – exactly the same period as Kit. Her path to assistant director though had been different and slower than Kit's. When Kit was first promoted to assistant director level in early 1989, Suzi had just been promoted to the managerial grade. Like Kit she had had a period in capital markets, although only six months in her case in between two periods in corporate finance. For Suzi, a mentoring relationship rather than luck (talent and sheer hard work too, no doubt) had been the key to her promotion. On her return to the corporate finance division she had worked very closely in a specialist area with one of the directors and although reorganisation of the department meant she had moved into generalist rather than specialist work, she had kept a watching brief for that area. In spring 1992 she had been promoted to the assistant director level and the next step would be to head up a team of her own.

Suzi's initial decision to enter merchant banking had not been through personal contacts or previous experience. Rather, 'at the time we were graduating it was rather the "in thing" to do. An awful lot of people were applying to investment banks.' She regarded her rate of progress through the bank as somewhat better than average, suggesting that 'it's a very meritocratic environment – if you are thought of well, you'll progress but there's no automatic promotion'. A detailed appraisal system was in place in the bank, covering areas such as technical knowledge and computer literacy, as well as personal attributes. These included, according to Suzi, 'skills of persuasion, self-confidence, being well organised, analytical skills, attention to detail, ability to take an overview, working as a team member and working with people generally'. She felt that the scheme itself was gender neutral in the sense that it was based on a mixture of attributes, some of which were seen as masculine and others as feminine, although she remarked that initially in her career she had experienced some difficulty with both clients and colleagues who tended to disregard her views, mainly, she believed, because she was a young woman:

There's a greater inclination on the part of people to dismiss or not take seriously somebody who's both young and female. . . . I think young and male clients can just about cope with. As you grow older you become a bit more credible, I suppose. But I've never had any overt discrimination, nobody refusing to deal with me or being rude, that sort of thing.

Suzi felt that her career progression had not suffered from age or gender and she fully expected to be promoted to the director level within two years or so. But then in the course of the interview she began to express doubts about her prospects:

At my level and above, this is where I think there really does start to be a difference between men and women. I feel very strongly now that women do come to a point where you've got to decide whether you want a family or a career or whether you're prepared to try and juggle the two – which is potentially very stressful and demanding. If I have children I would not want to do the job I'm doing, I know that ... I'd probably look for some part-time work but it's quite difficult to do our job on a part-time basis.
. . .
I think that when I have children I will start to look for a different career. I think your aspirations change – I was very ambitious when I was younger, but now I think I want a life where I can spend time with my family.

Suzi was 29 when she was interviewed. Like Kit she was married, and neither had children, despite Suzi's comments above. The comparability of their current situations provides an opportunity to explore the significance of partners' views on the career path of a man and woman. It is often argued that women's promotion prospects are restricted and their careers cut short because they are more likely to make decisions that are a consequence of their male partner's career choice rather than their own. This tends to operate regardless of whether or not a woman has children. Both Kit and Suzi spoke openly about their partners and their home lives. Kit, in particular, was extremely frank about the priority of his job in the partnership with his wife.

My wife works locally [i.e. near their home in Clapham in south west London] for a firm, erm ... to just bring in some money, and she does as few hours as possible as it were, she just does it to get pocket money as it were. ... She just does 9 to 5, but she'll hate me for saying this, but it's not particularly taxing. I don't think. It's secretarial for an estate agent. I don't imagine them doing a great deal.
. . .

She does the bulk of the housework. I hate to admit it but she does the bulk of it, which is why, partly, she's got the job she has, so it will allow her to do that and she will typically do, sort of, an hour and a half a night and that's enough to keep it ticking over – and I do the washing up.

Kit helped with the weekend shopping, although his motives were hardly selfless: 'we both might do the shopping because she might not get the nice things that I want'.

When questioned about how his life might change if they had children, Kit was defensive, suggesting that the pattern of his working life would be difficult to change. Indeed, he argued, 'I'll have to work that much harder', and added:

It's not realistic or fair for a woman to tell her husband that, because they have got children, he's got to change, to be home at such and such a time when he's trying to hold down a job that's reasonably sort of dynamic and at the forefront of whatever it is.

Compare these views with those expressed by Suzi who at the current time was in a more equal partnership in terms of both comparable careers and domestic responsibilities:

We try to share things; if there's a delivery or we've got someone coming round whoever is less busy stays at home for them. We do have quite a good arrangement but – and this is true of most couples I know – the woman still has main responsibility for thinking about what shopping you're going to get, the planning side, what needs to be done about the house and I take the main responsibility for that.

. . .

My husband is a lawyer in the City and his work is fairly unpredictable as well. He works late into the evening. That's why going back to the family type issue, because he doesn't have predictable working hours either it would be difficult for the two of us to balance these jobs with children. I'm keener to give up than he is. He makes jokes about being a house-husband but he enjoys his job and he's doing quite well so I don't think he'd want to give it up.

It is interesting that Suzi, who was recruited at the same time as Kit, was not in a similar position of responsibility within the bank, although she was an assistant director. It is hard to know whether this is because of Kit's early 'luck' in being in the right place at the time of an internal organisation, because of differences in their abilities and – the bottom line in a bank – in bringing in profitable deals, or because of Suzi's admitted weakening of ambition as she began to think about having a family.

I interviewed another woman in the professional sample who was doing exactly the same job as Kit. Harriet too was 29 and had entered the bank as a trainee like Suzi, although a year earlier than Kit and Suzi. In many ways Harriet's career paralleled Suzi's. She too was moved back and forth from corporate finance; she was promoted to a manager in 1989 and to an assistant director in 1992, although Harriet, unlike Suzi, was also a team leader at the time of interview. The major difference between their careers, however, was that Harriet had taken a six-month break from October 1990, during which she had travelled to Australia, because she had become disillusioned with the City lifestyle. This move 'affected my pay, but it hasn't hindered my career. People saw it as something interesting rather than a skive.' Unlike Suzi, Harriet saw her youth and femininity as an advantage in relating to clients (an aspect of the job that will be discussed in greater detail in a later chapter) and was clearly a more adventurous and extrovert character than Suzi, who herself was not lacking in possession and self-confidence.

At the time of interview, the two women assistant directors earned the same amount, despite Harriet's break, and Kit earned about £15,000 more per annum (although these figures are not completely reliable because of variations in how bonuses and fringe benefits were reported, as explained earlier). This case study supports the general finding from the personnel data analysis that there appears to be a gendered discrepancy in levels of pay, responsibilities and promotion. But perhaps this discrepancy does reflect a calculation by senior management about the relative commitment of men and women to life in the City. Like Suzi, Harriet could not see herself staying in the City – or at least in merchant banking – for many more years.

It's very difficult to lead a sort of normal life doing this job and the more senior you get the harder it gets, so I mean, I think inevitably, I will probably leave and go and do something that finishes at 5 o'clock in the evening. . . . at the moment with the culture and attitudes of the people in the department at the moment you can't reconcile a normal life with doing the job that's to be done.

The question of the extent to which the culture and the 'abnormal' life of banking reflect an extreme and particular masculinist version of work will be addressed in the next part of the book.

The matched pairs of bankers whose careers have been examined so far have had, partly because of their youth, a relatively uncomplicated and straightforward pattern of progression, predominantly within a single bank. They neither substantiate nor challenge the arguments about gender differences in career paths established through the examination of large-scale survey analyses and outlined earlier, although there does seem to be a difference in the rate at which women progress up the career ladder in the banks compared with men. I now turn to employees who are older and further up the hierarchy, to compare the career patterns of men and women who have had successful professional careers. The 'top' careers outlined first are those of a male and female director, both of whom were in their early 50s and were, in fact, the oldest people I interviewed.

GETTING TO THE TOP

Peter and Ruth were both full directors of Northbank, although Ruth had a non-executive position. It is here that we begin to see the different patterns in the careers of the men and the exceptional women who have made it to the very highest position in the world of merchant banking. Whereas Peter had spent all his working life in banking and the great majority of it within the confines of this same bank, Ruth had had a markedly different career pattern, one characterised by bold moves into different fields, often necessitated, however, by that most female of constraints – a move with a male partner.

Peter's career typifies what we might now regard as an old-style or traditional banking career in which a man entered the bank at a tender age – between 16 and 19 years old but usually towards the upper end of the teenage years – starting as a trainee who would be moved between departments to gain an all-round experience, but with the expectation of early and rapid promotion. Many of these young men who joined banks and broking houses in the 1950s had personal contacts in the City, through family and friends or through school networks.

Peter – who was in his early 50s in 1992 – exemplifies this career trajectory. He joined a small family-owned bank as an office boy of 17 – a bank which, as he explained to me, would have been termed a merchant bank by some and a bill brokers by others. In the early stages of Peter's career the bank was 'really run by Victorians' and consisted of six directors and about 20 employees. As the bank began to expand in the 1960s, Peter, who had been studying at night school to take banking exams, rose rapidly through the firm as he gained invaluable expertise when the bank moved into investment management and other corporate finance transactions. For a number of years he 'did the donkey work for two or three directors' and in 1969, at the age of 29, he became a director himself. As Peter explained:

I think with me you are looking at a different generation. That could happen in those years. Talking to directors of other banks of my age, none of us went to university, most of us went directly from school, often into accountancy at the age of 18. A number would have done national service, a number would have just missed it. . . . A director of another bank said to me 'we've now got two groups of people as directors – people who have got firsts at Oxford and people like us'. Before the mid to late '60s being in the right place at the right time was what mattered, though some merchant banks have always recruited from university – Rothschilds for example.

Peter's career, after its early high-flying start, marked time somewhat in the 1970s, partly as a consequence of the bank's involvement in the volatile property market which crashed in 1973/4. Business for the bank was slack throughout the remainder of the 1970s, but with a profitable merger in 1980, business, according to Peter, 'gradually got back on an even keel' in the 1980s. During the 1970s Peter stayed where he was in the corporate finance department and as a member of the board. He became an extremely important symbol of continuity with the past, as well as a mine of information about changing City practices over three decades and a lynchpin in long-standing business arrangements, as the bank expanded rapidly again during the 1980s.

Peter compared his long career within what has basically been a single organisation, despite its metamorphoses, with the current career path of young men and women joining a particular organisation at the trainee or executive level:

People move around much more now. They are aggressive and pushy and you are no good if you are not pushy. There's no problem now about going from one merchant bank to another; there used to be. All that changed in the late '60s and '70s. We'll have a man [*sic*] here from virtually all the other banks.

Peter tried to keep his home life – which was very important to him – separate from his work life. Despite continuing to work the crazy hours of more junior members of his division, Peter disliked the intense round of socialising that was a necessary part of his working life, avoiding it whenever he could. He was actively involved in a range of voluntary activities, both in the City and in his home area, and he seemed to me to have achieved a more satisfactory balance in his life than his younger colleagues. This balance, perhaps, is a privilege of a long career in the bank.

Ruth, on the other hand, Peter's partner in my sample, seemed to positively relish the frantic pace of City life. She was a high-powered, high-energy woman in her 50s who entered the City in 1982. Disenchanted with her position as a senior civil servant in a department which the Conservatives were, in her view, emasculating, she was seconded to the bank at director level by her department. She later became a permanent bank employee and had more recently added a number of non-executive directorships within the financial services sector to her portfolio. Her current position within the bank was on a part-time basis.

Ruth's career pattern is a classic example of making do and succeeding – a pattern that perhaps typifies educated women of her generation (Bateson, 1990). She came from an established middle-class family and entered Cambridge at 18 as the third generation of women in her family to do so. After graduating with a degree in law, she did her articles with a firm of solicitors and began practising before an early marriage to an academic took her to the USA where she made do with a number of different jobs which she clearly felt were unsatisfactory. Her first marriage was a casualty of this dissatisfaction with life in the US.

Ruth returned to England and:

I had a couple of years messing around and then I thought I must stop that and I went into the Civil Service.

She married for a second time when she was 31 and wanted to have a family immediately, despite recognising that 'it was an extremely inconvenient moment – careerwise – to have a child'. She went ahead nevertheless and accepted the compromises necessary to keep her job as a career civil servant and her home life in a reasonable, if not ideal, balance.

I think women now are more able to get near to having all that they want. They let those decisions, those life decisions, override anything that's happening in a career. For me it was all wrong and I never had the confidence to have three or four years out because I thought if I did nobody would ever have me back. But I did take proper amounts of maternity leave and I did work part-time when it was necessary.

In 1982 Ruth came into the bank which capitalised on her good social and working connections with the government, the Civil Service and business. Indeed, she obtained her current position in the bank through a personal contact: 'one of my fellow directors had trained with me as a young solicitor and we'd always stayed in touch'. After initial work on privatisation buyouts, Ruth began to play more of a personal-contact/client-relationship role for Northbank than a technical one. Her aim was to bring into the bank clients or friends, who were often indistinguishable: 'my life is totally mixed up ... I actually would be pushed to tell you which are clients and which are friends'. And as she explained:

I've now got a bit grand for actually doing the work. I mean a bit old ... at my age my friends are very senior and usually ..., if I'm sent out to bring in a client or bring in a friend, another director is promptly hung round my neck to do the work.

On occasion, as she talked, Ruth seemed to me to be slightly defensive about her work, although she emphasised how 'steamingly hard' every-body, including her, had to work, especially during an important deal. But she also confessed that 'I think they [her colleagues] think they've got a part-time butterfly here', but, she continued, 'on the other hand it's well worth it to them. Personal contacts are absolutely key. That's what they keep me for.'

Earlier in the conversation – it would be hard to suggest that I had actually interviewed this formidable woman – Ruth suggested that senior women in the City seldom either did the technical work or had their hands on the real levers of power but were more usually to be found in regulatory or advisory positions. While her role in the bank was more of an interactive, facilitatory one, it seems to substantiate her argument about a gender division of responsibilities. However, she also suggested that younger women were to be found in growing numbers in the retail broking end of banking:

In the last ten years in particular the number of women in selling stocks and shares, selling brokerage services is growing. You'll find women there and good ones, and as analysts in merchant banks which is not the boring back-room job you think it sounds like ... quite a lot of the really authoritative analysts who really know your industry are women.

Reflecting on her overall career pattern, Ruth suggested that 'my car-eer's an absolute rogue one'. Rather, I would suggest that it mirrors quite closely the career paths of those women of her age and social back-ground who had a great determination to succeed. The biographies and autobiographies of a number of successful women in higher education, especially in administrative areas or in the Civil Service and business, reveal that for them too an atypical pattern is common, at least when compared with the career paths of men who are also successful. These women too have followed a 'rogue' route. As Mary Catherine Bateson (1990) argued in her portrait of six successful North American women, women tend to 'compose a life' out of the various options that come their way, rather than plan a career. The younger women whom I interviewed also recognised differences between the career paths of senior men and women. As one said:

The women seem to come in at the top, not work their way up. Look at corporate finance ... in the main it's so paternalistic, nearly all men and there's very few people who didn't join Northbank as a junior. (analyst, 30, Northbank)

WOMEN DIRECTORS

A final comparison is presented as a way of unpacking what is often termed the cohort effect in studies of women's occupational mobility. The circumstances in the economy as a whole and in banking in particular, as well as the social circumstances and ideological attitudes about women's lives and workplace opportunities, all have a significant effect on the choices made by women of different generations. This comparison, therefore, focuses on the lives of two younger women – in their early 40s and early 30s respectively – who had also reached the level of director. Here we will be able to assess Ruth's claim that younger women are more likely to be able to 'have it all' or whether these younger women have a more conventional 'masculine' career path.

Mary was 42 and a director in the credit control division in Northbank when she was interviewed. She had been working in merchant banking for 20 years since leaving university in 1972. Her unprompted opening comment seemed immediately to substantiate arguments about the chance element in women's careers:

I think it is quite fair to say that I ended up in the City by accident ... I literally fell into a job at a merchant bank. It just happened that I was in the right place at the right time with the right sort of qualifications ... and it was ... it wasn't a graduate training type post, because in those days, I think almost all banks didn't take women for graduate training posts. This would be in 1972 ... before sex discrimination and everything else, you know that doesn't come until 1976, ... so blatant discrimination was practised before then.

When women were appointed in the 1970s, it was mainly to fill gender-stereotyped positions.

I think they were looking for women because it was a job where you had to go round and talk to a lot of marketing executives and write reports on what they were doing and they looked for women because these chaps really resented having to give information to anyone. So if you were female, preferably with a short skirt, they thought it would be more ... advantageous at getting information.

Mary's section disbanded within a year as her male boss 'fell from favour'. She then moved into the credit analysis department where her economics degree was regarded as a suitable qualification. She worked in this position for three and a half years until 'I could do the job standing on my head, doing the *Times* crossword at the same time'. She went to the personnel director to request a move:

I said to him 'Look, you know I feel I've got the ability to do other things. What can you do?' And he said to me 'Well, you know we value your services very highly in the back room, but uhm ... I mean, we couldn't let you go and see our customers. What would they think?' So I got the hint there and started to look for employment elsewhere and I came to this bank, ostensibly as a credit analyst, but to take charge of a section, and I succeeded at that fairly successfully, moved onto the business front, where – surprise surprise – their customers actually quite liked meeting a woman.

But Mary's front office role was not to last. She joined Northbank in 1976 and a merger four years later resulted in a large, cumbersome and disorganised credit area which Mary was asked to reorganise.

I was fairly reluctant, I mean it's a back-room job and you do get paid accordingly. But I worked at that time for a boss who was very fair and not remotely sexist and I went back and did it, and I suppose because of doing it and being successful at it that really led to my promotion, both to assistant director and director and I've been doing it ever since.

So Mary was persuaded by appeals to her professionalism and notions of equality, which actually had an adverse financial impact on her and led to a different career path from the one she might have had in the front end of the bank. It is hard to know what difference this move had, though, as Mary then decided to have children.

I now have two children so it suits me to have a job where I can regulate my hours, because there's a lot of routine work and you don't get involved in any deal that you've got to work through the night on, it's not that sort of job. I'd find that very restricting because I don't see the point of having children if I'm not going to see them at all. So to that extent I'm not pushed to move out of this type of environment.

Whereas Mary's career pattern is unusual among women of her age in that she had remained in a professional occupation all her life, it typifies a 'female' path in that her career choices were related to decisions about motherhood and familial obligations. Her steady progress through the firm contrasts with Ruth's pattern of entering at directorial level after moving in and out of a number of occupations. The next example – Louise who was a decade younger than Mary and two decades younger than Ruth – reveals yet another route to a directorship. In this case, ruthless ambition and judicious, rather than unplanned, job mobility distinguishes Louise from the older two women. Louise seemed to typify the 'new career woman' of the 1980s, whose path to the top more nearly mirrors a masculine model of planned unilinear direction rather than chance or self-sacrifice. But whether Louise 'has it all' is uncertain.

Louise was 32 at the time I interviewed her. She was a graduate of a North American University and a qualified accountant, and she had an MBA from a prestigious European institution. She embodies Rajan's arguments about enhanced educational capital among the younger professional workers in the City (Rajan et al., 1990). After an initial hiccup that involved a change of course during her first degree, Louise seemed to have had a remarkably clear-sighted and goal-oriented view of her prospective career – or so she presented it to me.

I wanted to work for a big accountancy firm in the tax department but they only took people with a law degree or with audit experience and I didn't want to do audit work. So I went to work for the Internal Revenue Service which is the equivalent of the British Inland Revenue. I thought I could prove to the firm I was really serious and I had something special that would make it possible to differentiate. So I did that and I was hired in 1981. I wanted to work abroad right from the start and I asked at every evaluation. Finally, I guess I'd only been there about a year and a half but I thought I knew everything and I thought I was, you know, superwoman, and I went in and told my boss I was annoyed with him. This was the head of the tax practice. Here I was threatening and everything but he found me a position in London. That was a Friday and I had to be there on the Monday. So I packed up my apartment and came to London. That was in February 1983.

Louise's career was to be marked by a recurring pattern – a strong belief in her own worth and the ability to make demands.

Anything I wanted I went in and demanded. I didn't ask quietly or politely. I just said I want this or I want that. They definitely weren't used to that but I got everything I wanted. Girls used to come and work for them and they'd sit down at their desks and do whatever they were told, and stay shy and quiet and silent and all that sort of thing. Then here comes this lunatic demanding things that even the guys weren't demanding. I guess they thought, why not? I did work very hard too and I did perform very well.

But Louise also recognised that circumstances were in her favour.

I think at that time too the accounting firms were aware they hadn't promoted any women much at all. And if they had someone they were happy with, they were prepared to put up with a little more than they might have otherwise and they were also willing to promote relatively quickly.

There then followed two more moves in London, but in ultimately unsatisfactory positions. In both cases, 'I resigned'. The next two years included successful entry onto a European MBA course, preceded by travel and living in France to improve her language skills and to study art. In 1986, Louise was ready to re-enter the job market, and this time:

I'd set my heart on merchant banking. I really wanted to do mergers and acquisitions. I'm not quite sure why. I don't think I even knew what it was. . . . I decided to do some research and pick the company I wanted to go and work for and go and speak to them. And I did that. I got in touch with them, interviewed with them and eventually went to work for them. But it took ages.

Louise explained her remarkable confidence and belief in her own worth as a consequence of her upbringing:

I think it was the way my father brought us up. . . . [He] always, always told me you can do whatever you want to do. It's a question of whether you want to or not. There's no limitations – none.

Louise also recognised the significance of her siblings:

I had three sisters and a brother – but my brother was much younger and I was only ever compared with my older sister, a year older. It did make a difference.

Oakley (1985) has suggested that many successful women come from families where they were one of a number of sisters, and also often attended single-sex schools. She suggests that these women, who were never directly compared with men, seldom thought that they were second-rate or that they were incapable of doing anything.

Louise attributed her success in merchant banking to two important figures in her first position in mergers and acquisitions – a senior woman vice-president who, after Louise's first few months in the bank, said:

'Has anybody sat you down and told you what the basic guidelines are or anything like that?' She spent about half a day talking me through it. It was pretty simple, not rocket science, but you need somebody to tell you. You can't just work it out for yourself. I think she would have done that for anyone. Definitely. But I think she and I had some of the same difficulties because we were both women.

The other mentor or sponsor was a male senior vice-president who was a significant figure in Louise's future career progress as, in 1990, she followed him from a US bank in London to Northbank. Louise took a step down to assistant director on her move but at the time of interview had been promoted to the director level, albeit against some resistance. She felt that part of the reason was to do with the different cultures of US and British banks.

My previous bank was the sort of organisation where it didn't make any difference how long you'd worked there; all they cared about was how good a job you did. . . . So you had older people working for younger people and you had different

nationalities and you had women and men. It just didn't make any difference who you were. All that counted was how you did. I'd done very well in that environment. I'd had something to prove, I guess, and they'd given me the opportunity and I'd proved it, and they'd rewarded me for it.
. . .

I thought I should come over here as a director and to me that was very important but I have always felt, and I don't know it from experience, that the opportunities for women in English merchant banks are very limited. And also for someone young. It's very much a hierarchy and you move up based on time, not on performance. It's not to say that is the way it is here, but it's what I feared from the outside.

Louise had been persuaded, however, to come in as an assistant director. Her remarks indicate the significance of the culture of different organisations and the expectations of what an ideal and senior employee might be like – that Louise mentions her youth, nationality and gender illustrates the importance of the interaction of gender with other social characteristics. Differences between women may be as significant as the supposed characteristics of an idealised femininity which unite them. The burden of her comment, of course, is that senior bankers, in British banks at least (and the three banks under investigation here are all British owned – or at least were so in 1992) should be male, British and not young, although it is important to remember that Louise had actually 'made it' to the top by the age of 32. These assumptions about the characteristics of employees and the culture of an organisation may, however, affect the relative career patterns and progression of both men and women. Something about either the expected characteristics of the people who do particular kinds of work or the general culture of organisations may be inimical to the progress of all but the few exceptional women who were in the highest-status positions in these banks.

CONCLUSIONS

In more recent work on gender stereotyping and occupational segregation, it has become common to argue that workplace tasks and jobs themselves are gendered. The social character of work is itself inscribed with a set of gendered attributes which carry with them assumptions about the appropriate gender of the worker recruited to do the task. Although these gendered attributes are not fixed and all work may be reinterpreted or reinscribed with gendered characteristics that are congruent with the gender of the person carrying out the task (Leidner, 1991), certain associations are harder to shift than others. Evidence from the legal profession (Epstein, 1980), the armed forces (Barkalow, 1990) and the police (McElhinny, 1994), for example, shows how difficult it is for women to succeed in areas that are among the most masculinised of professions. Merchant banking, too, is associated with a set of heavily masculinised and classed images which have an important effect on the ways in which work is represented, given meaning and organised on a daily basis. These meanings themselves therefore influence the ways in which workers 'do gender' in the workplace. For men and women do not come to work every day with their gendered attributes fully in place. Instead, the workplace itself is a site for the inscription of sexual difference. Expectations about the specific meanings of different types of work and their association with embodied workers affects how these workers invest in themselves particular ways of being a man or a woman. These expectations and investments are the subject of part II.

But it seems that it is more than gender, albeit gender as constructed on the job rather than as an essential attribute associated with embodied men and women, that is at work. A number of key questions arise from the comparisons of the career patterns of successful women bankers. Turning first to Ruth, Mary and Louise, perhaps the main factor that unites these three women is, paradoxically, the singularity of their career paths. Ruth and Louise had a similar pattern of movement between occupations and employers, although Louise's career was more consistent in the sense of its restriction to the financial services sector. In this feature, however, Louise's pattern is more comparable with Mary's career – which was also within a sector but with fewer movements between employers and a far less aggressive sense of her own value. What the comparison does illustrate is the extent to which aggregate statistical analyses of career paths hide the particularities of individuals' careers. These three women were all in the same position within the same industry and yet they reached it by significantly different paths – different from each other and from their male comparator – Peter. They are also marked by large age differences – 20 years between Louise and Ruth – thus seeming to disprove Louise's belief about the significance of hierarchy and time-serving in British investment banks. But all of them mentioned the significance of being women and the ways in which they decided how, in Louise's words, 'to get by as a woman'. It is these ways of 'doing femininity' that will be addressed in the rest of the book.

Of course it is not possible to generalise from a small number of case studies, and detailed qualitative studies of the type described here indicate the sorts of processes and decisions that have been important for particular men and women at different moments in their lives. But qualitative explorations of job histories enable the complexities of gendered career paths to be investigated. In this way the specificities of particular sectors in local labour markets at a single moment in time may be unravelled, and the generalisations from aggregate statistical analyses revealed as just that – inappropriate or inapplicable in certain ways to particular cases. This is not to deny the validity of the large-scale survey: indeed it is an essential starting point in many investigations – as in this one. Without the building bricks contained in the work of many scholars on patterns of occupational segregation and mobility – based on national and local surveys and on case studies of particular industries and local labour markets – this study would have been impossible. Further, the statistical analyses of Merbank's personnel data, the subject of the first half of this chapter, provided the general outlines of the gendered career patterns in that bank, against which the particular cases presented in detail here might be compared to show the continuities and discontinuities between aggregate patterns and the singular example. As Sayer and Morgan (1985, 1988) have so adequately demonstrated in their own empirical work, quantitative and qualitative methods are complementary rather than alternatives. Qualitative or intensive methods are essential to unpick the processes and particular sets of decisions, choices and con-straints that lie behind the general patterns that quantitative analyses so elegantly and efficiently reveal (Brannen, 1992).

It seems from these qualitative case studies that some women are successful in the world of banking – and here age does not seem to be the significant factor, thus disputing the 'pipeline model' of women in or-ganisations (the argument that women are only now entering in sufficient numbers for their representation to become apparent at senior levels in the future). It may be, however, that these women are exceptional in certain ways, able to escape from the glass ceiling that traps other women. Certainly the senior women whom I interviewed – and not only the three considered in detail in this chapter – were remarkably self-confident, albeit in different ways. They all had degrees, many of them also had professional qualifications in law or accountancy and they all came from solidly middle-class backgrounds with fathers who were, *inter alia*, law-yers, academics or businessmen. Sadly the professional backgrounds of their mothers were not mentioned as significant influences. They seem, like Athena, to be daughters only of the male. So are these women exceptional in some way – not representative of their sex? Certainly key individuals, like Louise's father, or particular choices, sometimes en-forced, like Ruth's move to the US, seem important in the explanation of these women's career paths. It may be, however, the peculiar con-juncture of the world of merchant banking and the particular character-istics of its employees – be they class, gender or other characteristics – that explains some women's success and others' (relative) failure. The culture of British merchant banks and the ways in which they select their

5

The Culture of Banking:
Reproducing Class and
Gender Divisions

The basic actor in a market economy is the firm. . . . the firm is not only at the heart of the economy; it is at the heart of society. It is where people work and define their lives; it delivers wages, occupations and status. It is corporate citizen, economic actor and social institution.

Hutton, 1995b, p. 110

I still think it's very much the old boy network. I went for an interview at another merchant bank and one of the interviewers had been to the same school as me. He asked if I knew so and so and I said, no, no, no and was promptly whisked out. I obviously didn't know the right people in this case. And at another one they asked about the Diplomatic Service – my father was in it – and this time I did know the right people.

Male interviewee

INTRODUCTION

In chapter 3, I demonstrated that women continue to be concentrated at the bottom end of the occupational hierarchy and in particular types of jobs in merchant banks, although significant numbers of well-qualified young women are now graduating from the universities, and some of them are applying for and obtaining positions in banks. In chapter 4, a detailed comparison of men's and women's career patterns revealed differences in their trajectories and also in their attitudes. I now want to examine recruitment strategies. It might be argued that the patterns and behaviours revealed in the two preceding chapters reflect earlier recruitment strategies. What is important for women's future position in merchant banks is the extent to which they are now being recruited and the culture in the banks which they enter. Recruitment is an interesting area to consider in examinations of gender stereotyping as it is at this stage that the particular characteristics and attributes sought in potential employees are made most clear and that gender biases in selection procedures may become evident. The history and character of merchant banks, their national origins and familial loyalties, their specialisms and their market position affect and reflect the ways of working that have become acceptable and reinforce particular patterns of behaviour in different departments. These differentiated cultures also influence who is recruited and the ways in which particular class and gender attributes interconnect in the construction of an employee who 'fits' into the culture of the City as a whole and the different banks within it.

This chapter acts as a pivot between the overall patterns of gender segregation already explored and the focus on the social construction of self and identity in the chapters that follow. Particular sets of traits, attitudes and behaviours are differentially valued by organisations and the workers within them, who are recruited and promoted in large part on the extent to which they are seen to conform to these differential cultures. As Casey (1995) has illustrated, organisational structures result in 'the corporate colonisation of the self' (p. 138). While some employees adapt to this colonisation, others resist it in a defensive attempt to produce and maintain a non-corporate self. This creates a complex duality in the identity of some corporate employees, and I shall show in chapter 8 that it was most common in the women whom I interviewed. In this chapter, however, the recruitment and acculturation strategies of the organisation are the focus. While the culture of merchant banking in general has received a great deal of attention, the specific nature of the changes from the mid 1980s onwards as they affect individuals in different banks has been less well established. While the self-evidently masculinist attitudes of the 'old' and 'new' City have been parodied in film and fiction, it is apparent that at present we know relatively little about the detailed lives and social networks of individual employees and the ways in which they are reproduced in recruitment practices.

MONEY CULTURE: THE AMERICANISATION OF THE CITY?

The three banks in which I interviewed vary in the date of their foundation, their status, size and culture, ranging from the investment arm of a high street 'name' to an old family, blue-blooded bank with a smaller, more recent second-tier bank somewhere between the two extremes. At the time of my field work they were all in British hands. I asked all my interviewees about the culture of their organisation, phrased in terms such as 'What is it like working here?' and 'How has the City changed recently?' I wanted, first, to establish the extent of the introduction of those 'new' practices described in chapter 2, or the continuation of 'older' or British ways of doing things. Despite stated differences between the banks, I found that they were remarkably similar in their selection procedures, reproducing, to a much greater extent than earlier commentators imagined, a social elite with strong links to the earlier period before Big Bang.

To assess whether or not 'American practices' have affected business practices and social interactions in the City, I also expanded my investigation from the three case study banks. I interviewed a small number of bankers employed by US banks in London, as well as questioning in detail my respondents who had worked in other banks, especially US-owned ones, before joining their current employers. The results were unambiguous. The environment in British banks is still distinct – more leisurely, better mannered and slower paced than in US-owned institutions. According to a salesman at Bluebros, who had worked in a US financial institution earlier in his career:

It's very different in British banks than in American firms. There there's much more pressure, it's not so friendly, people were more brash and the working environment's not so pleasant.

And a woman who had thought of working for Goldman Sachs before joining Merbank was emphatic about her choice:

I talked to all the American banks but I decided not to apply for them basically on the grounds that I didn't like the culture. The very macho culture of, you know, 'we're all big swinging dicks here, if you come and be a bigger swinging dick, then that's fine, otherwise forget it'. Anyone who works less than 24 hours a day is, you know, a failure etc. and I thought I just don't want to do that with my life.

Although British-owned banks have changed with the times, progress seems to be relatively slow. The following quotes are representative of the opinions expressed by employees of both US- and British-owned banks.

Here is the view of a 31-year-old English man working as a manager in financial control at Northbank:

The City has changed slowly although it is still very cliquey. I mean you just have to go out for lunch around here, especially the traditional areas and look around. But I think that that's decreased since Big Bang and so on. I think that the blue tie,[1] my father-was-a-stockbroker image, and the progression of the family through a particular area of financial services, I think that has changed a little bit now. I think Big Bang opened things up, and indeed just the fact that you have a lot of American and Japanese banks, who maybe don't have, dare I say it, the same class structure . . . they just recruit the best people for the job, no matter what, and I think some of that has rubbed off onto the UK banks, so they've opened up a little bit more and therefore those stuffy lunches, and over the port and so on, I think they've also decreased a little bit. Having said that, I do think it definitely goes on.

Compare this cautious expression of cultural change with a description of life in a US bank:

It's terribly Darwinian around here, chuck people in and see who comes out on top. (English woman, 27, US bank)

In British banks on the other hand, respondents were as likely to argue that their place of employment was:

definitely on the caring end – that's not to say it's totally caring, because there's obviously uncertainties at the moment but the atmosphere is a lot better than in some US banks. . . . I don't think people feel the same need to assert themselves here. (female analyst, 30, Northbank)

Another interviewee suggested that the 'old-style', elitist world of British banks might actually have advantages for women compared to the 'mine-field' of a US bank:

Two friends of mine have gone to a very English institution, Barings. It's as English as it comes and we were talking about this and they said 'It's OK. It's hierarchical but at least you know where you are.' They say men say 'Oh my dear may I open the door for you' which may look incredibly heavy-handed but they say that there's this sort of English respect for women. At least you actually know there's an old-school, old-style network so you know where the barriers are. But in a firm like this it's all about who you know, stab you in the back when you are not looking, do it in a locker room. In the old-fashioned hierarchical organisation you know from day one what you are getting into and you could probably say to someone 'Look, you know, this old-school network thing isn't on', whereas here you have got to sidestep hidden minefields all the time. People say one thing but the messages are very confused. We are an equal opportunities employer, we are an affirmative action employer, but in fact we hardly recruit any women, we fire them when they go on maternity leave, we don't like practical care arrangements, we have patterns of behaviour they can and can't conform to, if you want to know the rules you have to find out for yourself. So it's actually quite difficult to negotiate, I think, for women. (English woman, 31, human resources, US bank)

The comments of respondents who had worked for a number of organisations, especially those who were not themselves English, are particularly revealing about the contrasts in workplaces cultures. Louise (whose career path was examined in chapter 4) was a 32-year-old American working in London for Northbank at director level. Here she reflects on how she decided not to behave as usual when she moved to a British institution:

I think that probably wouldn't have been the right thing to do because in America at that time the way to get by as a woman was to be really butch, really pushy and aggressive, and that sort of thing. And I think over here that wasn't admired and wasn't as necessary in the same way as over there.

She also found that workplace behaviour varied:

After a while I discovered it [Northbank] was a different kind of organisation. The US bank was a lot of fun. People worked together and they laughed together. They didn't socialise a lot after work. But people worked very hard and they worked as teams. People got on really well together. They'd go for lunch every day, for a quick drink after work or whatever. But people don't really do that here. People come in, they work their hours and then they go home. Some people are more enthusiastic than others. But it's just a totally different attitude from what I was used to. I think the difference is based on the compensation structure because at the US bank the structure was such that you got a very small proportion of their pay as salary then you had the opportunity to make an absolutely massive bonus – I mean you could earn huge sums of money as bonuses if you performed well. You could get 200 per cent of your salary. ... There were more opportunities. It was American-run and American organisations I think do tend to be more open and less bureaucratic. ... It's very different here – more hierarchical and I think people are not encouraged to really knock themselves out dead. The attitude here is different. Here if somebody is going on holiday and an important deal is going on, they do tend to go on holiday, they don't cancel their holidays, they pass it across.

It is important to remember, however, that Louise moved to the British bank in 1990 as recession bit into City profits, although this does not negate her comments about the differences in organisational and compensation structures.

Another respondent, Isobel, then 37 and working at Bluebros, and who was also not English, commented on the hierarchical nature of her place of employment and went on to explain that:

They [her immediate colleagues] are traditional English bourgeois with the habits of a particular, very self-selected, reinforcing group of people. They are quite theatrical to watch.

This image of theatre, a spectacle or masquerade, is a significant one which reappears in the consideration of gendered performances in later chapters. Bluebros is the most traditional of the three banks in my sample and has the narrowest class representation among its employees, or at least among the sample whom I interviewed. As a manager in the human resources division remarked, 'there are quite a lot of old Etonians here, I have to say'. A young woman recently recruited to the capital markets division explained part of the reason for this:

It's a job which appeals to and gets done by a certain sort of person. Probably the criteria that go with it almost inevitably mean public school, or if not actually public school then that sort of person, if you see what I mean. I suppose it's all to do with the hard work, the team playing, the families, the ethics of what we're doing. There is an implicit code of honour there which all fits the sort of public school training. Hence the sort of people who are recruited fit a certain sort of mould. (woman, 25, capital markets, Bluebros)

But Isobel argued that in this small, then family-owned bank, there was neither an automatic reproduction of a social elite nor direct nepotism.

I have certainly never come across circumstances where a family member, and there are still a number who work here, has a job or a position that depends entirely on their blood line and not on their ability. There's one remote family member who is to my mind a fool but that may be because I can't understand what he says because it comes through such a mouth of plums. But he, I can't judge his work. What I see is the arrogance and foolishness of making sure everybody knows what his blood line is. But that's an exceptional situation.

However, she continued:

There's a fair spread of educational backgrounds among the people I work with. There's a hard core of Etonian, Oxbridge types ... I think it's a narrow and self-selected band that turns up here and it's self-perpetuating, a system of patronage develops when they turn up here.

A younger woman also hinted at nepotism. Talking about how people were promoted, she commented:

In some cases it's very political, some of them went to school, have personal friends, son of our, I don't know, deputy chairman, so suddenly he's like wonder boy. (woman, 28, capital markets, Bluebros)

But patronage and family connections may also bring advantages:

You know I sit there for two hours on a Tuesday afternoon [as secretary to a committee] and there is about two centuries of banking experience and that's very impressive. Whatever you think about them, you realise that they have been through two or three cycles and they do know a lot, you are wet behind the ears. It would be nice sometimes if they could say it without such pomp, but you can't have it all.

Even in this bank, restructuring and new practices were introducing 'American' features. Two managers in their late 20s in capital markets emphasised that the bank had become lean and mean: 'people have to be very adaptable', one argued. The other phrased the same point somewhat more negatively: 'the place is very meanly staffed'. But the bank is also, in most respondents' views, friendly and non-hierarchical: 'if you have an idea, you can walk into any director's office', and 'we are all on Christian-name terms, directors too'. While the male respondents were more likely to believe that Bluebros is a meritocratic organisation, the women I interviewed were less sure. This is a representative comment: 'I think probably it is, I wouldn't use that word but I think it's close to that.' As a female manager noted:

This bank is very old-fashioned in its ideas and its philosophies and even people at my level seem to be built in the same mould as the people who are there [in senior positions], so conceivably nothing's going to change; even by the time they get up there it's going to be no different. The way the bank operates is that the directors are effectively a partnership and they are resistant to change.

In fact this bank was taken over not long after my interviews and the culture began to change. A shakeout of senior management was an immediate consequence.

The perceived image of Merbank, at least from outside, is of a more egalitarian institution than the first tier of blue-blooded banks among which Bluebros was proud to be numbered. As a woman assistant director in corporate finance explained:

It is a lot more egalitarian than a lot of other English merchant banks. Most are still very stuffy and public school dominated. . . . We mould ourselves into a type of work but by no means all Oxbridge, by no means all public school, or all landed gentry. There is a difference between Merbank and a blue-blooded bank. They give an air, a greater air, of pomposity and arrogance.

Another woman in corporate finance at Merbank, a director with almost a decade's more experience, outlined the same distinction:

The cultures in Merbank and the blue-blooded banks are perceived to be different. In the blue-blooded merchant banks there are a lot more independently wealthy people. Here at Merbank most of the men are from minor public schools compared with Eton and so on in blue-blooded banks. Generally the culture would be more old-fashioned, more traditional and more male-dominated. Somewhere like Barings probably has a very male-dominated culture and that's very blue-blooded. Or Lazards, that's very old-fashioned, more hierarchical. Here we mix freely on a social level, even a junior person would go out for drinks after work with the directors. Colleagues at Schroders and Morgan Grenfell are very surprised by this. This place was and is much less hierarchical, much more friendly and much more a meritocracy I think also.

It is important to note, however, that Merbank was the only merchant bank this woman had worked for, although she had worked for a firm of large accountants before that. She joined Merbank in the boom period of Big Bang and experienced a meteoric rise, becoming a director in four years.

An employee of Northbank who had previously worked at Merbank commented that Merbank 'is closer to the Civil Service model than most banks; you have to spend a certain amount of time in each grade irrespective of how brilliant you are' (male analyst, executive level, Northbank).

Northbank, by contrast with Merbank, is another small originally family-owned bank, relatively blue-blooded but less 'traditional' or 'prestigious' than Bluebros.

It's, umm, relatively blue-blooded ... it's not one of the extreme examples, which I quite like, as I have this belief that some of the blue-blooded characters that fill some of the merchant banks are twits. (man, 26, Northbank)

The bank expanded quite rapidly in the 1980s, after a merger and another change of ownership, finally moving into European hands in the early 1990s. By repute Northbank also has an elitist atmosphere, dominated by employees from prestigious universities: 'It is Oxbridge-dominated' (woman, 26). This view was supported by many other interviewees, but a younger employee commented that:

The recruitment policy seemed to be, when I joined, very Oxbridge-dominated. I think that's true about most merchant banks but I was surprised actually here how many people had degrees from universities that didn't seem to be of the supposed top rank and by that I mean the Oxbridge, Bristol, Durham type. I like to think that London is among the stronger universities [his degree was from London] in terms of a name, but I mean there are people here who've come from Cardiff University ... but the thing is every time you make a presentation the client wants to see the credentials of the team so it will say where you went to university. (male executive, mergers and acquisitions, Northbank)

A senior and relatively long-standing figure argued, however:

I've noticed a very radical change in hiring since I've been here – I've been here since 1982. I can actually remember somebody saying in 1984 'well, he wasn't, I mean he wasn't at Oxbridge; we are not going to take them are we?' . . . But two or three years later you'd never hear anybody saying that, never, not in this bank. (woman, 51, director, Northbank)

She also suggested that the bank was less than prestigious in its atmosphere and culture compared with the Civil Service where she had held a senior position at the end of the 1960s.

The Civil Service, which did have some women in it, was very civilised in those days – well up-market of a merchant bank, believe me. Both socially and culturally, the Civil Service is several grades up-market from a merchant bank[2] where chaps come from distinctly middle-class backgrounds, middle-class and lower-middle-class, and work all the hours that God sends ... there's not much cultural input around here. Everyone thinks how smart merchant banks are – this is not true. They are all grey, professional, middle-class places. I mean Warburgs has some slightly flashier people, but on the whole merchant banks don't have flashy people.

Warburgs seemed to be on the minds of my Northbank respondents as a younger man, suggesting that the atmosphere there is meritocratic and friendly, said:

We have an open door policy and anyone can talk to anyone, have a chat to the director. But at Warburgs, I think I am right, it is very stuffy and hierarchical. They have different dining rooms for different sorts of grades and the director's on another floor to other people and it's all very procedural. (male assistant director)

A senior male director also commented:

I think each merchant bank has an ethos, particularly in the corporate area. ... Kleinwort has a fairly arrogant self-confidence about itself, partly though success. Warburgs is very professional, if you've got a cup of coffee at Warburgs you're doing very well; it's that sort of very spartan and rather a grim place to work. Probably not in fact – this is the sort of reputation. The more blue-blooded sort of backgrounds are clearly the most professional, disciplined organisations, I suppose it's the more successful, it's sort of ... we, I think, have probably got a relatively friendly ethos – not aggressive – but straight down the middle. But innovative. (male director, Northbank)

Ruth, whose case was discussed in chapter 4, believed that part of the reason for Northbank's less aggressive culture was the entry of women:

Women have changed the culture in the Civil Service and in banking. Thirty years ago, all the senior women just assimilated to the male culture. I mean they did. I remember as a young woman sitting aghast watching someone 20 years my senior discussing something in one of the big interdepartmental meetings, discussing some issue in terms of cricket. Well, she doesn't play cricket and nor do I. 'What was this?' I thought.

Surprisingly this woman went on to discuss the impact of women's growing numbers in sporting and military language, without any recognition
of the incongruity. She suggested that the 'first row' women, as she
termed them, had had to behave differently from the second row – this
I took to be a rugby analogy. Later she referred to women 'getting in
under the wire'. The effects of sporting and sexualised language on
women's place in the workplace are discussed further in chapter 6.

For the younger employees, both men and women, at Northbank,
class divisions and gender differences remained an important aspect of
the 'atmosphere' in the bank. Most of the respondents commented on
the continuing importance of social status in the bank. A passing comment that 'it's amazing how many people ask you what your background
is, what does your father do, what does your mother do' (woman, 30,
senior communication officer) was echoed many times. 'You have to fit
in, you know, to be employed here' was another common remark. A
male interviewee remarked that:

It's a friendly culture here, I think, casual and informal in some senses but the
hierarchy is also very clearly defined. And it's fairly ruthless in career progression.
People are quite arrogant and very much career-driven. . . . The ability to get on
with people is important, but so is having the right background. (man, 26,
corporate finance)

Whereas class differences were an important aspect of recruitment as well
as of the cultural milieu of this bank, gender differences generally were
discussed in different and less material terms. Many women referred to a
sort of 'matiness' among their male peers which excluded women, although several respondents mentioned the intersections between class and
gender discrimination. Thus, for example, 'It's a sort of preference for the
old sort of environment; I think too clients are very keen on seeing traditional and male corporate finance teams working with them' (female analyst, Northbank). A detailed discussion of the mechanisms through which
women are excluded or made to feel out of place in the banks will be
postponed until the next chapter. Here I examine the ways in which
recruitment procedures are part of the explanation for the continuance of
old forms of privilege and the reproduction of a banking elite.

RECRUITING WORKERS: REPRODUCING AN ELITE

People like to recruit people like themselves, that's what happens, and to be fair
people come to merchant banks looking for a certain type of service and expecting
to see a certain type of person providing it. (male interviewee)

One of the most illuminating ways of assessing the extent to which the culture of organisations is changing is to examine their recruitment procedures. In all three case study banks, I interviewed a senior member of the personnel department who was involved in selection and in training. At the time of the interviews, the impact of recession was beginning to decline but all three banks were operating a limited recruitment drive. This had the effect of making their key assumptions more visible than they might have been in an expanding labour market. Two of the three banks had undertaken a restricted 'milk-round' in 1991 and 1992, visiting only a small number of targeted universities. Both banks included Oxford and Cambridge in their visits. Durham, Bristol, Edinburgh, Exeter and London Universities were also common choices. At Bluebros, for example, after an initial screening of applicants on the basis of examination results and 'a sort of "feel" if you like, from reading application forms', initial interviews were undertaken: 'we do two streams at Oxbridge and one stream at Edinburgh, Bristol and Durham' (manager, human resources). She continued:

There's certainly a bias towards Oxbridge. I would say probably 50 per cent of recruits are from Oxbridge. And a bias towards public schools ... not necessarily Eton, but the lower public schools as well.

At the third bank, Northbank, a set of informal mechanisms operated to filter out applicants:

We don't do a milk-round, we don't do a graduate trainee scheme any more – we are too small. When we want people they either walk in through the door or we have a head hunter. We ring him up and say 'we want another three in corporate finance. You know what we need.' 'Just what everybody needs in the City' they say amicably. (woman, 51, director)

The potential for bias towards a certain type of entrant hardly needs emphasising but when I pushed my informant to specify more accurately what 'everybody needs', she explained:

Well, we look where they were trained. They better have trained somewhere we have heard of [only trained solicitors and accountants were recruited]. And where they were at university, in the sense that it's got to be a university, and we don't take less than a 2.1.

At Merbank too, graduates who were chartered accountants and, increasingly (supporting arguments about the inflation of credentials), applicants with an MBA, were favoured. The (male) personnel director explained the history of the bank's recruitment procedure:

We were not like the old-established merchant banks, you know, who go back a long way and who are very blue-blooded. We had no real client list to talk of, we didn't have the historical, the religious or family traditions, and so we started, I think, with a much broader perspective ... [although] people in corporate finance tend to be the, certainly historically, public school, Oxbridge accountants ... though, I did say historically there. I think that has changed and it's had to change for a number of reasons. One, I don't think the City is an elitist profession as it used to be. I also think there is a lot of change going on in people's perceptions of people, like for instance, I guess for instance ten years ago you wouldn't have seen a black face in an investment bank, you certainly wouldn't have seen a black person in corporate finance; you do now. And you wouldn't have seen a woman in corporate finance but you do now.

Certainly women were conspicuous: in the last few recruitment rounds, Merbank had recruited between 12 and 15 graduates – of whom about a third were women – but very few employees from ethnic minority backgrounds worked in this or the other two banks.

On closer questioning, however, it became clear that the requirement of an all-graduate intake may have shifted the bank from a more to a less meritocratic base:

The organisation had a tradition of grammar school tea boy working his way up. People hung onto the old traditions until deregulation, I think that's when it started to change, and became an issue. Oxbridge recruits became more important then. . . . frankly, it's not cost-effective to visit every university in the country, so we made, so decisions were made on prejudices to visit Cambridge and Oxford, not the rest.

So within a credential-based system, there is a judgement between de-gree-awarding institutions. Indeed, at Northbank my interviewee made it brutally clear that a 'good' university background outweighed other fac-tors:

We started to take more girls in the mid 1980s expansion, or we would have had to look at men from the polytechnics. (woman 51, director, Northbank)

Bluebros was less restrictive in its entry requirements in the sense of the subject of a degree, and as they had their own trainee schemes they recruited from subjects other than law and accountancy. Although many of my respondents had law, economics or business-related degrees, they also had humanities degrees ranging from history to Chinese, and a small number of social scientists had found their way in: 'We look for variety really. Degree subject is not important as far as we are concerned . . . we train them once they are here.'

Of the 50 professional employees whom I interviewed, 11 had degrees from Oxbridge and a further 13 from that elite group of 'top' universities including Durham, Bristol, London, Exeter and Trinity College Dublin (48 per cent of the sample). That almost half of this sample had degrees from only seven universities (from a total of more than 80 in the UK alone) reveals the remarkable persistence of selection from among an elite group of institutions. As this group of people were relatively young – most of them between 24 and 37 – the continued dominance of the City by this group will stretch well into the early decades of the next century. Eight (three men and five women) of the professional sample had no degrees at all (although one of the women had attended a Swiss finishing school), and only two had attended one of the former polytechnics. The remainder had been to a variety of redbrick universities or to universities outside the UK.

THE IMPORTANCE OF 'FIT'

All the banks emphasised that they were looking for more than educational credentials in prospective recruits.

We also look for something called 'achievement', and that can be in anything. It can be someone who's got sporting prowess, it can be someone who is particularly committed to a cause, someone who's taken time out during a vacation to do something specific. (personnel, Merbank)

My informant continued, perhaps revealing a secret yearning of his own:

An example could be someone who wanted to collect 200 wild flowers in the Katmandu valley. Now, it wouldn't appeal to everyone, but someone who said 'I want to collect 200 wild flowers in the Katmandu valley because I'm particularly interested, and I worked and I saved my money and I stayed in teahouses etc. and I lived, and I got dysentery halfway through' – that is an achievement. We might not value the cause but it shows that someone's determined to do something. We also look for someone who is interesting. If they are boring we turn them down.

I asked how he defined 'interesting'.

That's a tough question, because if I'm going to turn someone down I ought to, hmm, I think 'interesting' is someone who shows interest during the meeting. Someone who doesn't actually sparkle when they are talking and show that they're interested and alive. . . . It's amazing the number of people who come and just sit here, very clever people and they are just not presenting themselves, so they are not exciting, they're not vibrant, people who are reluctant to put their view forward and argue with you. . . . Then there are some jobs you want boring people for [*laughter*].

It has been argued that the emphasis on these intangible qualities may disadvantage women, especially young women who are interviewed by older men (Rubin, 1995), but in this case my informant disagreed:

The type of women who we interview here are actually the pushy type. Pushy's a terrible word, I know. But they are the type of people who are extrovert, who've done their research, who push you, who do disagree and who are strong, confident and assertive. . . . But there aren't many successful women who are *not* overtly confident and assertive. But then men need to be that as well.

But his qualifying comment revealed the differential valuation of these attributes for men and for women:

I wonder, though, whether those qualities are regarded as positive in men and negative in women. (personnel director, Merbank)

At the other banks, too, a certain degree of aggression or 'push' was an essential attribute. Describing milk-round interviews, the manager from Bluebros explained that 'they [applicants] basically have to sell themselves to us'. In response to a general question (and not, interestingly, about gender differences, given her comment) about what attributes Bluebros looked for in a recruitment interview, my respondent suggested that:

You have to be self-confident, you can't have people who are wallflowers, who are going to get trodden on or as soon as somebody shouts at them they're going to go and hide under the table and cry. So it's a quite tough world to actually get into. (human resources manager, Bluebros)

Like her Merbank opposite number, she suggested that the women who were recruited, compared to the men, were 'perhaps even more self-confident, at least initially'.

Thus, it seems clear that a charismatic personality is a pre-requisite for entry to City banks.

We are also looking for flexibility, team spirit, an ability to fit in. (personnel director, Merbank)

Other interviewees also emphasised these attributes:

It's quite important that they're team players if you like. It's very much a team culture so you've got to be willing to be part of that team. (human resources manager, Bluebros)

Part of the second interview for applicants at Bluebros involved a buffet lunch with current employees – 'so that they get a feel of what it's like working here. It's very important to fit in' – and at the end of their 18-month training programme the graduate recruits are allocated to a particular area of the bank.

We have an idea right from the beginning though where we think they are going to fit; slightly different sorts of people fit into different departments. (human resources, Bluebros)

I asked for some expansion of who fits where:

Well, the type of person who has the basic qualities that you need is probably very similar, as I was saying you need a very high intellectual level and certainly academic capability. The corporate finance department, the individuals in there tend to be slightly more aggressive, I suppose, in their nature. Their nature tends to be far more that type of personality than in the traditional banking and capital markets types. . . . Someone who's slightly quieter, though there's not a great deal in it, is likely to go towards the banking side.

CONCLUSIONS

In all three banks, it was clear that recruitment procedures tended towards what might be termed 'informal' practices. Indeed, some of the people whom I interviewed in detail had been recruited by 'chance', through personal contacts, through an exchange with a more senior person and so on. It has been argued that more flexible methods of recruitment with an emphasis on personal characteristics – the 'fit' that is so important in banking – are becoming more common in a wider range of organisations in the 1990s. Thus, Brown (1995) and Brown and Scase (1994) have argued that there has been a shift in the recruitment strategies and organisational style of organisations with the move to 'flexible' methods of management. Economic restructuring and new managerial paradigms have led to a challenge to bureaucratic methods of management. Downsizing and delayering have stripped out the middle levels of management from many organisations and a new language of creativity and entrepreneurial individualism has become prominent in efforts to increase productivity. In a study of graduate employers, Brown and Scase found that recruitment specialists were adopting the discourse of a flexibility paradigm, distinguished from the bureaucratic paradigm by its emphasis on the personal characteristics of employees, forms of team-working, and informal promotion criteria based on personal achievement and compatibility with colleagues and cultural attributes valued in the organisation.

Brown (1995) argued that these features of the flexible paradigm are becoming part of a changing ideology of organisations in an attempt to solve command and control problems. He suggests that:

> the 'rules of entry' and the 'rules of the game' [have] become increasingly personalised. The distinction between the 'official' and the 'person' is weakened in the work situation, leading to an exposure of the 'whole' person in the assessment of adequate performance, which is reflected in the increasing use of student profiles, assessment centres and staff appraisal schemes. Moreover, the greater the emphasis on normative control, the greater the demand for recruits to exhibit strong cultural affiliation to colleagues and the organisation. (p. 41)

Arguments about a shift from a bureaucratic to flexible and charismatic form of selection and promotion structure clearly have more relevance in some institutions than others. It might be argued that merchant banks, with their history of connections to elite families and educational institutions, have always been on the 'flexible' end of recruitment procedures. Indeed, Brown argued that he was not suggesting 'that social qualifications were eliminated in recruitment to bureaucratic organisations. The selection of elites has traditionally been associated with a "cultural code" consistent with images of masculine managerial authority, expert knowledge and the right school tie' (Brown, 1995, p. 41).

What is interesting in the case study banks is not only their emphasis on personality and the possession of cultural capital but also the ways in which recruits from elitist backgrounds, schools and universities have retained their dominance in the period following deregulation. This finding counters the argument of Thrift and Leyshon (1990) who suggested that the social base of recruitment in the banking world was expanding. The gender of applicants, and perhaps their ethnic background (although I found little evidence to support the contention of Merbank's personnel director – my entire sample, bar one, was white), may be changing, but their class composition remains solidly bourgeois. All the banks suggested that they operated a form of equal opportunities policy, but it appeared to be in theory rather than in practice. As one of the human resources staff said in response to my question about widening the recruitment procedures, even perhaps in as minor a way as visiting a wider range of universities:

No, we wouldn't want to. We get the calibre of people that we want. I do have people who phone me up at great regularity trying to get me to advertise in all sorts of magazines and brochures but our feeling is that doing what we do, we recruit the people we want and, anyway, we are more open now and there's more women. (human resources manager, Bluebros)

But even in the case of gender, it is hard to support the claims of the interviewees with quantitative data as none of the banks recorded the ratio of men to women among their applicants. Certainly women are being recruited by investment banks. The changing gender composition of the undergraduate body at Oxbridge alone has made this more likely. As I noted earlier, women are now 42 per cent of undergraduate students. Within the subjects from which recruitment was most concentrated, women were almost 50 per cent of those leaving Cambridge in 1993 with a law degree, although still only 25 per cent of economists. The 1992 figures from Cambridge University Careers Service, for example, revealed that approximately twice as many men as women among the year's leavers were working in professional positions in banking six months after their graduation. As my Bluebros respondent remarked, 'there's still a heavy dominance of males applying in comparison to women', and, as all three representatives from the human resources divisions of the three banks were at pains to emphasise, the environment of an investment bank is a tough one which may intimidate women.

I don't want you to think the women who work here are like some modern-day Boudiccas, but I do think women need to be quite tough. It's a tough environment ... women might be frightened off by the perceived environment in which they've got to work in order to be successful, in order to get those opportunities. (male, head of personnel, Merbank)

In the next chapters, therefore, the women who were not frightened by these perceptions of the nature of merchant banking enter centre stage as I examine the ways in which women, and men, interact with each other and with clients in this apparently cut-throat world. The culture of merchant banks may be one in which the attributes of a 'whole person' are crucial, but is this 'person' in fact masculine? In chapter 6, I turn to an assessment of the ways in which women as a group are constructed as the 'Other' in the everyday social practices in banking. In chapters 7 and 8, the social construction of particular forms of masculinity and femininity at work is examined. Men and women do not come to work with their gender attributes fixed in place but rather 'do' gender in the workplace, inscribing gendered characteristics on the body in ways which conform to or transgress expected patterns of behaviour in a particular cultural milieu and physical settings. In chapters 7 and 8 the different physical spaces and places that constitute merchant banks are also examined.

NOTES

1   Did he mean blue tie or was this a confused but neat amalgam of old school tie and blue blood, I wonder?
2   It is interesting that the comment earlier by a Northbank employee that Merbank was like the Civil Service was intended as a disparaging comparison.

Part II
Bodies at Work

6

Engendered Cultures:
The Impossibility of Being a Man

To be successful women have to become honorary men.

Acker, 1990; p. 140

You have to be one of the boys to get on here.

Analyst, Bluebros

I can never be a man as well as a man is.

Director, Northbank

INTRODUCTION

We have seen that the type of person who is recruited to a British merchant or investment bank is likely to be confident and outgoing with a good brain validated by a good degree from a good university. The women as well as the men, indeed perhaps even more so than the men, are apparently self-confident and 'pushy', and in general from an upper-middle-class background. So what happens to these young people when they enter their respective banks? Do the young women find themselves equally valued in the so-called 'new' City, where more open or 'American' attitudes might lead to challenges to the elitist 'English' social practices of the City? Or do they find themselves up against the barriers that face many women in professional occupations in a range of large organisations (Davidson and Cooper, 1992)?

There is now an enormous literature, some but not all of it feminist, which documents the ways in which institutional mechanisms, procedures and everyday attitudes position women within organisations so that their 'Otherness' is emphasised. Not only do women not fit the idealised image of a rational male worker, at least as far as senior positions of responsibility and status are concerned, but the very structures of organisations are based on masculinised assumptions – about the timing of work, the structure of tasks and ways of doing things, schemes of appraisal and promotion. In the rest of the book, I look in detail at the social construction of self in everyday interactions inside organisations – in this case merchant banks.

THE DRAMA OF WORK AND THE
CONSTRUCTION OF SELF

Analyses of gendered organisations have a lengthening history from Kanter's (1977) classic study onwards (Cockburn, 1991; Knights and Willmott, 1986; Marshall, 1984; Savage and Witz, 1993; Witz, 1992; Wright, 1994). Kanter's work is notable for its comparison of men and women – a crucially important approach that apparently was forgotten by many successors who, although interested in gender divisions, interviewed only women. Despite their recognition of gender as a social construction reinforced in everyday interactions, later analysts ignored the gendering of men and the variety of masculinised behaviour, instead seeing masculinity as a singular oppositional category against which to compare the 'difference' of women. A common feature of these 'gender and organisational culture' studies is their characterisation of the position of women as performers in a drama. The ways in which women are made to feel out of place or like bit players have been outlined and the limited number of acceptable roles or scripts available to women attempting to fit into the masculinised performance of work have been detailed. Marshall's (1984) study of women managers as travellers in a male world is an exemplar of this approach.

The tradition draws in particular on the work of Goffman (1961, 1963) and Berger and Luckmann (1966) who, despite claims by contemporary postmodern theorists, never held to a modernist view of the self as a fixed or solid entity. Instead they, and the gender and organisation analysts, demonstrated the social construction of the self through display and contextual performances. Where contemporary theory perhaps differs is in a greater emphasis on the fluidity and fictional character of these performances. The notion of selfhood itself is seen as a narrative construct, created to give some coherence and stability to the unsettling fluidity. Accepting this argument about the fictional or narrative construction of self does not, however, necessitate an outright rejection of the notion of self, rather a recognition of the contingency of selfhood. As Casey (1995) suggested in her study of the relations between the changing nature of work in contempory corporations and the production of self within them, 'recognising the self as a pattern or a constellation of contingent events and processes can still enable an understanding of the person who experiences, as we moderns do, a sense of agency, inwardness and individuality. . . . the self encompasses both identity-making processes and outcomes' (pp. 3–4). Many of my respondents had a clear, modernist sense of their 'real self' and often experienced discrepancies in the relationship between this self and the fictional self they were aware of constructing and performing in the workplace.

In the next three chapters, I explore the ways in which the changes in the nature of service sector work and in organisational structures affect and are reflected in changes in gendered self formation. Micro-scale practices in the workplace – the focus of what follows – connect to the enormous technological and organisational changes in the production and marketing of services, as well as to societal changes in ideas about gender relations. I want to construct a two-stage argument that links the three chapters. First, I show how women as a group are out of place in the workplace, marked by their gender and their bodies as 'natural' and so as unsuitable participants in the rational, cerebral world of work. As earlier studies of gender and organisations have suggested, the options for women in the workplace seem to be limited to a small number of variations on their sexual and/or familial roles, or an attempt to produce a gender-neutral performance in a parody of accepted masculine norms of workplace behaviour. But, as I argued earlier, the shift towards inter-active work has altered the relationship between embodiment, the self and the ideal worker. In the new service sector occupations which are increasingly dependent on selling information and advice, the personal performance of workers, their ways of being and doing, are part of the service that is sold. This is leading to the 'feminisation' of all workers in the sense that bodies and personal appearance have become an integral element of workplace success. The old bureaucratic notion of the successful worker as disembodied brain-power, of a rational decision-maker who thinks and then acts, is being challenged. This necessitates a reappraisal of workplace attitudes and behaviour by many men and may reposition women in a more powerful place.

A second significant aspect of these new forms of work, as I also outlined in chapter 2, is a blurring of the distinctions between work and leisure (Du Gay, 1996; Leidner, 1993). My respondents often referred to work as 'enormous fun', suggesting that 'you have to have a certain love for it. There are people here who really do have a passionate love for being here' (man, 29, assistant director, Merbank). The blurring of these boundaries, between work and fun, waged labour and leisure activities, is also reflected in the new built environment of the City where, as the developers of the Broadgate Centre emphasised in their publicity material, the new buildings and the spaces around them are a 'total landscape of work and leisure'. Inside the workplace too, the lack of distinction is important. Many organisations now include sporting facilities in their redeveloped spaces, as well as atria and entrance lobbies to give new offices the feel of an hotel. This redefinition of the boundaries is leading to a greater emphasis on the cultural capital of workers, on attributes such as style and bodily form, on how they look as well as how they perform in the workplace. However, as I also suggested, the social construction of the female body as nature, not culture, for pleasure, not work, may continue to mark women as different from, and inferior to, an embodied but still ideally masculinised worker.

It may be, therefore, that the changing social characteristics of new service sector occupations are having a contradictory impact on women's position in the workforce. Certain aspects challenge their socially constructed inferiority whereas others reinforce it. In an investigation of these contradictions, in this chapter I keep a singular focus on 'woman', looking at the strategies that construct and place woman as the 'Other', different from an idealised masculine norm and so excluded from the still predominantly masculinised culture of merchant banks. Here I demonstrate the continuing strength of the binary distinction between masculine and feminine subjects or selves. In chapters 7 and 8, however, the second stage of the argument becomes dominant. The concept of the self as a narrative fiction becomes the focus as I turn to an exploration of the multiple ways in which masculinity and femininity are constructed in, affected by and reflected in the particular workplace practices in different arenas in merchant banks. In these two final, empirical chapters, the importance of place or location is also reasserted.

MARKED AS 'WOMAN' IN THE WORKPLACE

Drawing on the taped narratives, I first examined the range of ways in which the women I talked to suggested that they were marked as different from an idealised version of disembodied masculinity. All the remarks were made in the context of a general discussion about everyday working practices and were not elicited by direct questions about either embodiment or discrimination. My female interviewees openly discussed the ways in which they were reminded every day that they possessed a female body which classified them as inferior to men. They provided evidence of how the 'dynamics of desire and the pulses of attraction and aversion' identified by Young restricted the range of possible interactions with their peers, superiors and clients. From comments about size, 'attractiveness' and clothes, through sexualised jokes and gossip, to a range of behaviours verging on sexual harassment, the women I interviewed found that they were marked out and restricted to a small number of acceptable ways of presenting themselves at work.

NOTHING BUT BODY

Through gestures, behaviour and comments, the women in the three banks revealed that their embodiment as female and particularly their sexuality made everyday relationships with colleagues and clients a matter of negotiation rather than a taken-for-granted matter. The men I interviewed were equally clear about the significance of female embodiment, although they had a different interpretation of the reasons for and consequences of the mechanisms involved.

Although the differences between the social position and age of researchers and their subjects may raise particular problems when investigating embodied and sexualised images and language commonly used by young men in the workplace, I was surprised at how frank many of the men were prepared to be. I recorded many comments in which sexualised language was used to objectify and humiliate women – 'I'd like to screw/nail her if I got a chance' – as well as references to women in general or to female colleagues as 'skirts', 'slags', 'brasses' and 'tarts', synonyms for 'prostitutes'. In face-to-face interactions, women colleagues were habitually referred to as 'girls', infantilising them (although. as noted earlier, many women also refer to each other as girls). A range of practical jokes revolving around, variously, sexy computer passwords, smutty messages and faxes, underwear and blow-up dolls were reported. It was clear that the men whom I interviewed were not unaware of the impact of their behaviour and there was general agreement that:

Most guys of course will react to talking to a girl or doing business with a girl . . . I'd say there are probably disadvantages in terms of being female in this sort of environment. (man in his 30s)

I turned to women employees to explore these disadvantages and their consequences.

Many women argued that their femininity and their sexuality was a constant issue at work, influencing everyday interactions with male colleagues.

It's so hard to strike a balance – if you are seen as feminine or desirable they think you're available, and if you are not they call you a dyke. (woman, 28, trader, Northbank)

Many women suggested that the most important consequences of female embodiment occurred when promotion became an issue. In merchant banks, mentoring is an important part of getting seen, and hence promoted, for young men. Women, however, felt that they were more likely to be successful if they were not subject to sponsorship and mentoring.

I think that the slur of a woman being patronised or being a protégée of somebody is probably more detrimental than having to fight their corner and having several people who judge them and who make a sort of cocktail judgement. Everybody would make the assumption that you are sleeping with them. (female manager, Bluebros)

Interactions with clients, who are almost always men, also present problems:

So you are dealing with men and up to a point you and they are always aware that you are a woman and they are a man, but I don't think it's tremendously, sometimes they will – and I think this is cultural, I think it's cultural – they will kind of make jokes in a way that you will kind of deflect. They are not really meant to be smutty or flirtatious. As long as you sort of deflect them back gently then you clear the air. Everybody has their position established. Yes, you can say saucy things to me, but no, I'm not going to do anything about it. I think that probably happens quite a lot. It's relatively tame I think ... nothing particularly sinister. (woman, 38, manager, Bluebros)

Younger women also suggested that their age combined with their gender to doubly disadvantage them, creating difficulties in being taken seriously:

Being young and female means you have to really earn somebody's respect. One of my clients, I had quite an uphill battle with him; he used to think I was very sweet but for any important issue he'd go straight to my boss ... I know it's my age too ... On the positive side, there's certainly the novelty aspect; that can work quite well for women but I really think it is outweighed by the fact that you are not taken seriously initially. (woman, 27, manager, Bluebros)

This woman also mentioned problems, verging on sexual harassment, with colleagues who verbally abused her and also made inappropriate gestures and bodily contact with her.

I had problems with, serious problems with a couple of people in my department, one of whom was supposed to be working with me on an account and basically doesn't like working with women. And another, who airs his views very openly about where a woman's place is: the kitchen or the bedroom. And he's my age. I can understand that coming down from older generations but it's very concerning that current generations have that attitude as well.

In a whole constellation of ways, women in the workplace are constantly reminded that they are female and therefore seen as sexually available and sexually vulnerable. Tannen (1994, p. 260), drawing on Goffman (1963), suggested that being female is in itself 'faultable': women's vulnerability – in this case to sexual harassment – is constructed as if women, and not men, were responsible for it. Goffman used the concept to refer to the way in which someone can be made to feel embarrassed or in the wrong simply because of a particular characteristic they possess. Tseelon's (1995) modesty paradox, in which the woman is constructed as seduction to be ever punished for it, is a close parallel.

Tseelon also distinguished a duplicity paradox in which the woman is constructed as sexualised artifice and so marginalised for lacking authenticity. This is also demonstrated in both Tannen's study and my own work, interestingly in exactly the same example. Tannen reported how a woman who is interviewing a man is irritated by the way the man keeps letting his eyes drift to her chest, a reminder that 'You're a woman, and I'm thinking about your sex rather than your brains, your authority, the words you are saying to me' (p. 261). This example was replicated in my work, albeit in reverse. Thus, a respondent commented on the desperate efforts made by her male colleagues to avoid looking at her cleavage as they spoke to her.

Some of my colleagues talk to me looking like this [*squinting sideways*], you know I think that's either because they've got something in their eye or they have just never seen a chest before you know. They are just not comfortable with me and end up looking over my shoulder. (woman, 37, manager, Bluebros)

She spoke disparagingly of the men – colleagues and clients – who:

let themselves get distracted because it is a woman speaking to them. They are just not listening to what you are saying ... whereas if it had been a man they may be listening.

DEALING WITH SEXUALISED TALK AND BEHAVIOUR

Many women I interviewed, from the youngest to the oldest, adopted a strategy of passive resistance, trying in most circumstances to ignore rather than challenge sexist language and behaviour.

You have got to let this behaviour not affect you [talking about stripagrams on the trading floor, a condom over the mouthpiece of her phone etc.]. It all depends on your reaction. If you react badly, you know chinks in armour, if you react very badly, they're going to go for your jugular. If you take it in good humour or give it back, ... that's quite a good one. Or just take it in good humour and tell them they're being silly, being boyish again. (woman, 34, sales, Bluebros)

A slightly older woman, also at Bluebros, this time in corporate finance, said the same thing:

I'm pretty good at deflecting most things; I can just turn it into a joke; they really won't go for you once you have done that. The point is I don't think they ever mean it seriously and I think if you just bat it back in a kind of half-hearted way, it's not a problem. ... But ask women who work on the trading floor, then you might get a different answer because the environment is very different. (woman, 37, manager, Bluebros)

The difference between work sites and types of occupation is explored in more detail later.

Younger women, too, adopt the same strategy of passive resistance:

I let most things float over me rather than react because a lot of the time it's much funnier if you react. I got a whole series of chauvinistic faxes, very derogatory towards women ... it's just not really worth the time or effort or lowering yourself to that level to play the same game. If the talk does get too crude, then I'll tell them to shut up and they'll shut up. And then they'll wait until I've gone and then they'll carry on and that's fine. (woman, 28, capital markets, Bluebros)

It seemed to me, however, that carrying on behind women's backs was another mechanism of exclusion. But many women seemed to regard the jokes, language and behaviour as a professional hazard that really was not too important. In an interesting comment, a woman from a US bank suggested that 'yes, there's harassment against women as a group, but not against me as an individual'. But this distinction was not always clear, as the next comment suggests:

It's a fairly friendly environment – heaps of jokes, and rude comments and things like that. The women are as rude as the men but the place is riven with sexual metaphors. I've never had a really personal comment directed at me. I think there's a difference between, well, you hear all these cases that get taken, and you think for God's sake, can't you take a joke . . . but I am sure there does come a time when it actually becomes too personal. I'm sure we've all been in situations not necessarily at work but out where a comment has been made that really offends you. And there's just a difference, I don't know what it is, but there's a very fine line between actually making a joke that's funny, that somebody can accept, and making a joke that's totally unacceptable, because it's personal. Maybe it's a look or something. If you see someone looking at you, two feet below your face and making comments . . . (woman, 32, divisional administrator, financial control, Northbank)

This seems a clear illustration of how hard it is to draw the line between, and take preventative steps against, a style of interaction that qualifies as cultural imperialism and friendly, albeit sexualised banter. Most of the men I talked to were horrified to have their behaviour represented to them as a form of harassment or imperialism: 'No there's nothing meant by it, just a way of blowing off a bit of steam, sort of relieving the tension' (man, 31, financial control, Northbank).

One man's relief, however, is another woman's exclusion.

'BRAINS AREN'T ENOUGH': DRESSING THE BODY FOR WORK

Marked as female by their body and so seen as immodest and faultable means that for many women, clothing the body for professional work raises complex questions of style and image. Here we might add the notion of being marked. The term 'marked' is a staple of linguistic theory, referring to the way language alters the base meaning of a word by adding something, often a feminised ending, to distinguish its specific usage. The unmarked form of a word carries a meaning that goes without saying and, in English, usually conveys 'male' or masculinity. Thus, in the English language, there are endings such as '-ess' and '-ette' which are used to mark words as female. Marking words for female also, by association, marks them for frivolity and sexuality.

This description of language also applies to clothes. Every style available to women is marked, whereas men's styles are unmarked. 'A man can choose a style that will not attract attention or subject him to any particular interpretation, but a woman can't. Whatever she wears, she draws attention to herself, however she talks will be fodder for interpretation about her character and competence. In a setting where most of the players are men, there is no unmarked woman' (Tannen, 1994, p. 112). It is impossible for women to dress in a 'neutral' fashion. If a woman's clothes are too tight, too bright or too revealing, they send a message, albeit one that may be unintended, of availability, but wearing clothes that are deliberately frumpy or less sexy sends a message too, given meaning by the fact that her clothes could have been different. Even the conventional choice of a dark suit and plain blouse is an eloquent message about the place of women in the workplace; and it is a message that I found my respondents took to heart.

Without a single exception, the women I interviewed raised the question of appearance. It became clear that their male colleagues frequently commented on women's clothes, hair and make-up in an intrusive way.

The minute you walk in they comment on your clothes . . . I was teased on Friday because I was Sloaney, you see, because I wore the pearls and I had the hair and everything. (female manager, human resources, Northbank)

People always comment on your clothes. If you are wearing something slightly odd, they'll be rude about it. If you are wearing something slightly bright, they'll make a comment about it. (female divisional administrator, Northbank)

What a woman wears is also an important consideration in interactions with clients:

I make a conscious choice on days like today when I have a call and I am very determined to get the client's attention, to get them to understand what I tell them. I could have done it in my leather skirt but it would have been a silly distraction. To me it would have been irresponsible, because it has been very hard to get this man to accept an appointment so I am grittily determined that he will listen, at least for two minutes, and so I don't want anything to distract him for two minutes. (manager, Bluebros)

Several women suggested that one way of minimising distraction is to try to present a neutral appearance. As the manager at Bluebros explained, 'if I am doing a "cold call" [seeing an unknown client] I'll wear something like this [*gestured to her plain blue tailored dress*] to blend in'. And a younger women explained, 'I wear something sort of grotty or boring, so I'm not obvious, better to blend in' (executive, Merbank). It was taken for granted by both these women – and many others – that I would understand that what they were aiming to blend in with was the masculinised environment in which dark suits were the norm.

Some women went further in adjusting their appearance to 'blend in' and adopted a variant of the male business dress. Several respondents told me a version of the following story, which reveals that not only do women in professional positions have to blend in with their male peers but they also have to avoid the too-automatic association of a feminised appearance with secretarial work, where embodiment, appearance and the gender coding of workplace tasks are congruent rather than disjunctive:

I wear these men's shirts; I mean they are ladies', they are made for ladies at a men's tailors; and you should wear a jacket, women should wear jackets unless you want to be associated with a secretary, that's one of the rules; you have to wear something quite subtle, black or navy or grey; don't wear loud or garish things or they'll spot you. (administrative services, Northbank).

A compromise for many women was a feminised version of the male uniform:

I read *Women's Dress for Success* and I obeyed everything in the book. I wore my hair in a bun and I wore these little silk shirts with lazy bows at the top. Suits all the time and never dresses. And I was just extremely, extremely conservative in my dress and the way I presented myself. ... And, well I think it just became obvious there that brains weren't enough. (woman, 32, director, Northbank)

I was saddened by the continuing relevance of Virginia Woolf's comment in *Three Guineas*, written more than half a century earlier: 'And, moreover, whatever the brain might do when the professions were open to it, the body remained' (Woolf, 1977 (1938), p. 10).

CITY TALK / MEN'S TALK: BATS, BALLS AND BULLETS

I want to turn now to ways of talking *about* work. This is not to deny, of course, the significance of everyday verbal exchanges between colleagues and clients. Talking *at* work is clearly important. Indeed the language used to describe work itself is part of the everyday verbal exchanges that take place at work. As we have already seen, women are marked as 'Other' and made to feel out of place by the inappropriate ways men refer to them as sexualised bodies and by all sorts of puns, jokes and other forms of verbal harassment. It is also clear that women are often made to feel out of place in the workplace not only because of the disjunction between their bodies and the commonly accepted ideal of a professional employee but also because of the ways they talk.

Conversation, like clothes, is an important social clue: gender, class, geographic region, ethnicity, sexual orientation, age, religion and occupation all have an effect on how we speak and interact with others at work, be they colleagues, subordinates or superiors. Many of these interactions become part of the ritualised nature of daily life. The vast majority of decisions about how to speak become automatic. These behaviours are not only class-based but also gender-linked. There are gendered patterns of behavioural practices to which many men and women, although not all, conform. Psychological research shows (Carli, 1989; Hall and Braunwald, 1981; Maccoby, 1990) that when men and women are in groups, women are likely to adapt their conversational style to become more masculinised – they raise their voices, interrupt and become more assertive. But as Maccoby suggested, there is also evidence to suggest that some women become even more stereotypically female and are silenced, smile more than the men and give non-verbal cues of assent or attentiveness to what others say, especially the men. More recent work on conversational analyses in the workplace (Drew and Heritage, 1992) has revealed several ways in which women in general are disadvantaged, ranging from the pitch and tone of their voices which are associated with a lack of authority to the tendency to play 'facilitative' rather than aggressive or confrontationary roles in conversation in mixed groups. Women spend a lot of energy sustaining conversation, doing its chores and keeping it pleasant (Fishman, 1977; Tannen, 1984, 1990, 1994).

It was impossible for me to pursue these questions and analyse conversations at work between co-workers as I interviewed individuals on their own, although many respondents did comment on the ways in which conversational patterns and habitual ways of referring to each other were part of the establishment of patterns of power and hierarchy between subordinates and superiors and between supposed equals.

There is, however, another way in which women are 'othered' in the workplace and this is through the ways in which work is referred to. A number of linguistic constructions are commonly used to refer to work which tend to emphasise men's inclusion and women's exclusion. The most common tactics here are the use of sexualised, military or sporting metaphors in the workplace. Tannen (1994) argued that:

> the very language spoken is often based on metaphors from sport or from the military, terms that are just idioms to many women, not references to worlds that they have either inhabited or observed with much alacrity. Such expressions as 'stick to your guns', 'under the gun', 'calling the shots', 'an uphill battle', 'a level playing field', 'a judgement call', 'start the ball rolling', 'a curve ball', 'the ball's in their court' and many others are part of our everyday vocabulary. (p. 121)

I found from the analysis of my tapes that not only were military metaphors and sporting analogies common, but sexualised images and metaphors made a significant appearance. Common ways of referring to work in the City, particularly in the trading and dealing areas, were in sexual terms. Thus, to 'lift your skirts' means to reveal your position, a rising market is referred to as a 'hard-on' and a successful trade is greeted with cries of 'bollocks out'. Another example is 'to rape the cards' which means to exaggerate expense claims. The language of deals is also sexualised: some people referred to being 'on the scent of a deal' and told me that 'when you are building up to a deal it's a certain sort of heat', and it was common to refer to the 'consummation' of a deal. A number of interviewees suggested that work/deals are as good as/better than orgasm.

Military and sporting images were also a common part of everyday interaction between financial workers and made many appearances in the transcripts. The most common images were in terms of playing and team play. Thus, the phrase 'we are real players/key players in (such and such a market or arena)' was mentioned 14 times and 'you have to be a team player' 26 times. Talk of jungles, races and battles were also common. At least ten respondents in each case suggested that 'it's a jungle out there' or that 'it's a race to the top'. And in talking about selection and interviewing, a (woman) respondent explained that 'we see about 100 at first and then kill it down to 30'. A good illustration of how women are 'othered' by military language was the comment by a manager in financial control at Northbank that 'when things are pushed right up to the wire, when things are really tough, women are less able to say "this is the number one priority"'. Language about clothes also seemed to reflect the army/public school image or, as in the following example, both: 'you have got to wear the uniform/you have to wear the school uniform'.

Other similar terms relating to school, the army or sports were used less frequently. Marshall (1984), drawing on Kanter's earlier work (1977), suggested that the presence of one or more 'token' women in a department – and the women in my sample, apart from those in human resources and to a lesser extent in research and analysis, were all working in environments numerically dominated by men – exaggerates these forms of masculinised language and behaviour:

> They [the men in Kanter's study] brought sexual innuendo into potentially neutral activities such as training exercises. Women were sometimes cast in the role of interrupters of 'normal' activities, being asked whether it was acceptable to continue to swear in their presence, talk about football, use technical jargon, go drinking, tell jokes etc. In doing so, majority members were drawing, and probably heightening, the cultural boundary between themselves and the token. Often the tokens were thus placed in the position of giving permission for behaviour they could not engage in themselves. (p. 101)

Although I documented many reported instances of this phenomenon, where women found that their male colleagues either stopped talking or asked with exaggerated courtesy whether they might continue, I also found that many women themselves used sexualised and sporting/military metaphors, and, although here they were usually commenting on other women rather than on their own behaviour, it was suggested to me that women are just as able and likely to 'talk dirty' as their male colleagues.

We [City workers] seem to specialise in rude comments but the women are just as bad as the men ... it's all quite good humoured. (woman, 32, financial control, Northbank)

Oh yes, as far as sexual banter, the girls [*sic*] often give as good as they get. (man, 28, manager)

It seems likely, however, that dirty talk from a woman is interpreted quite differently from that from a man. I was not able to explore this supposition in detail, although many women suggested, as I show later, that women who try to become 'honorary men' usually fail and only succeed in making their male colleagues uneasy. I did find, however, that many of the women whom I interviewed used masculinised metaphors, seemingly in an unselfconscious way and with little reaction from their male peers. Women were almost as likely as men to employ military and sporting images when talking about their workplace (remember Ruth talking about women getting 'in under the wire' in an earlier chapter), although less likely to use sexualised metaphors. For example, one of the most dignified of respondents said to me, apropos a question about harassment, 'the men have no balls' and 'just bat it back to them'. While I interpreted this as sporting rather than sexual metaphor, women did occasionally refer either to themselves or to other women using sexual analogies, although I suspect the language was unintentional. Thus, a junior woman referring to successful networking activities by a senior woman in her bank suggested 'she puts it about' and, coincidentally, this same woman referred to herself as 'still hot' in talking about her work success. It seems probable that the school sports-field and army language is a much a reflection of commonalities in the social class origins of many of the respondents, many of whom had a public school education (which in the deceitful discourse of privilege in Britain is, in fact, a private education), as a device to minimise or exaggerate gender differences.

Tannen (1994) suggested from her empirical investigations in a range of firms in the USA that 'this [use of language and metaphor] is an arena in which, it seems, women are already beginning to do things in their own way, using metaphors from cooking, birthing, and sewing along with those from war and sports' (p. 121). I searched in vain for any 'feminised' metaphors among the conversations of my respondents. There were none. The 'feminising' of workplace language, however, may have a cost. Whereas the images of military and sports worlds offer models of male authority, the primary image of female authority comes from the private world of motherhood which may make men feel childlike or in the position of a supplicant.

I shall turn to the question of images of female authority in a moment. In the next chapter, however, I shall return to conversational analysis and the use of metaphor to look at differences in social interactions at different locations in banks. It is here that physical location again becomes important as patterns of discourse are always regulated through circumstances and through the places and the forms of corporate assembly in which they are produced. Stallybrass and White (1986) have commented that:

Alehouse, coffeehouse, church, law courts, library, drawing room or country mansions: each place of assembly is a different site of intercourse requiring different manners and morals. Discursive space is never completely independent of social place and the formation of new kinds of speech can be traced through the emergence of new public sites of discourse and the transformation of old ones. Each 'site of assembly' constitutes a nucleus of material and social conditions which regulates what may and may not be said, who may speak, how people may communicate and what importance must be given to what is said. (p. 80)

It may be that one of the causes of conflict between men and women in different 'sites of assembly' is women's entry into a previously masculine space characterised by particular forms of discursive interchange that were regarded as offensive for women to hear. The most extreme versions of sexualised language that were reported to me occurred on the trading floors and in the dealing rooms where a rougher, tougher type of everyday exchange was more common than in the elite atmosphere of the capital markets and corporate finance divisions. Here the school and playing field metaphors were more dominant. These locational differences have always been important in the 'old' and the 'new' City, before and after Big Bang. It may be that it is through their lack of close attention to the types of behaviour that are acceptable in different sites that commentators such as Budd and Whimster and Thrift have oversimplified the distinctions between an 'old' and 'new' city – the former apparently stuffy, hidebound and conservative, the latter more free and easy. As I show in chapter 8, the 'old' mores have a more tenacious hold in some parts of investment banking than in others.

RESTRICTED ROLES: WIFE, MOTHER, MISTRESS, MAN?

I want to turn finally in this discussion of the gendered culture of organisations to the roles which are available for women in the workplace. As I argued earlier, the metaphor of a drama is dominant in the organisational studies and women-in-organisations literature. As many earlier studies have pointed out, in professional workplaces there are ready-made roles prescribed by gender, and women's usual/expected role is a supporting one. When a woman or a man enters a setting in an atypical role, the challenged expectation is always a backdrop to the scene. Many women interviewees mentioned that they had often been mistaken for either a secretary or their male subordinate's inferior when they visited clients.

Images of authority are gender-saturated. Indeed, the very notion of authority is associated with masculinity – with, as I have shown here, male size, shape, voice and expressions. For women the images and roles that are available at work tend to be familial or sexualised. Pringle (1989), in her analysis of the roles secretaries are able to play, distinguished 'wives, mothers, spinster aunts, mistresses and femmes fatales' (p. 3). Marshall, focusing on women managers rather than secretaries, drew up a similar list – 'the positions of mother, seductress, pet and iron maiden' (and other variations on the same theme) (Marshall, 1984, p. 103) – whereas Davidson and Cooper (1992), in their study of women also in management positions, added the pet, the seductress and the honorary man to the scripts available to women. As the argument has been so well documented in numerous studies, it is hardly necessary to point out that many of these roles restrict women to servicing, nurturing and caring – apparently natural characteristics of an essentialised femaleness. It means that most professional women have to fight against incursions on their time, as supplicants assume too readily that women will be available to do a range of 'emotional' work at work.

One of the difficulties for women in male-dominated professional occupations is trying to find an image of a powerful woman which is not negative. Tannen (1994) suggested 'a whole menagerie of stereotypical images of women: schoolmarm, head nurse, headmistress, cruel stepmother, dragon lady, catwoman, witch, bitch' (p. 165) are the only powerful options. To the schoolmarm, nurse and headmistress we might add the nanny, matron and governess, all of whom are characters from the youth of the landed gentry and the prep school dormitory. These are images of women of discipline, forms of female authority that many bourgeois men are used to obeying, and it is interesting that some of the men whom I interviewed referred to senior women in these terms. Their 'public school' attributes are emphasised to construct them as a 'jolly good sort'. Mrs Thatcher, too, has been seen in terms of a school mistress or matron. Julian Barnes, for example, commenting on Thatcher's second electoral victory, predicted four more years of 'the cold showers, the compulsory cod liver oil, the finger nail inspection, and the doling out of those vicious little pills that make you go when you don't want to' (*Observer*, 12 June 1983). (His comments perhaps reveal rather more about public school men than about Mrs Thatcher.) Anthony Barnett (1982), in *Iron Britannia*, explicitly compared Mrs Thatcher with a governess (p. 71).

An alternative, also pejorative image of a successful working woman is that of 'careerist', embodying an unspoken neglect of familial responsibilities or, worse, a selfish rejection of motherhood. The hysteria of the British press in their coverage of official figures for the birthrate, released in May 1995, which showed an increase (from 16 to 20 per cent) in women who will not become mothers, is indicative. Headlines about selfish, embittered careerists predominated. Some of my younger women respondents held rather similar views about successful women, echoing the comments of Marshall's respondents a decade earlier who feared that they would become 'hard' as they became older.

A young (28-year-old) woman in my sample reflects this view of older women in the City:

Women in the City who are a generation older, and by that I mean women who are in their late 30s, perhaps tend to be much fiercer and harder and I put that down to the fact that when they joined the City the life was just so intolerable that they had to build themselves into some kind of Russian shotputter to make their point and, I mean, we've got someone in our department who's like that and she frightens clients . . . the clients appreciate how good she is but none the less she can't put things across in a particularly feminine fashion, or she feels she has to become a sort of pseudo-male to make a point. (capital markets, Bluebros)

And another woman (aged 30) remarked:

Something that sticks in my throat a bit is people tend to sort of say so and so – she's a director at – I know quite a few people now that know of women who are directors in merchant banks but it's usually 'she's the director of so and so – tough cookie' [*with emphasis*] – the sort of inference that she's more, not even feminine, but that she's harder than hard to have got where she's got to. (analyst, Northbank)

For these women – irrevocably seen by both their male and female colleagues as 'dragons', fearsome models of female authority – other options seem to have been foreclosed but, as many feminist scholars have suggested, perhaps the only option for success in institutional structures dominated by masculinised assumptions and behaviour is to become an honorary man.

THE HONORARY MAN – OR NOT?

The relationship between a female body and lack of power is, of course, part of the reason why it has been argued that women are forced to act as if they were men to achieve success. For women in senior positions in merchant banks, their gender and appearance are at odds with the masculine nature of the occupation that they fill and the tasks that they perform. Similarly, the masculinist nature of everyday interaction in merchant banking, perhaps especially on the trading floor and in the dealing rooms, constructs women as the 'Other'. Acker (1990), Fine (1987) and Rhode (1988), among others, have argued from empirical analyses that many women, to achieve success in masculinist organisations, adopt a workplace performance that constructs them as honorary men. As Rosenberg et al. (1993) suggested, women in masculinist organisations behave 'as if the fiction of gender neutrality is a reality, as if gender is inconsequential to their careers' (p. 430) but don masculine attire and adopt masculine attributes to conform to the fiction.

Several women whom I interviewed argued that it was possible to become part of masculine culture, reporting that they felt that they had been accepted as 'one of the boys'.

For most of the time I am an honorary man. They [her male colleagues] do treat me like an honorary male and that's what I prefer. It means that I can see the way they look on women. If I go out for a drink with them, then they will comment on anything that walks past in a short skirt, things that friends wouldn't say if I was there. I guess I'd rather be an honorary man than be on the other side. (salesperson, Merbank)

Many respondents, however, were sceptical of the success of this strategy.

You can't go out and get ratted with the boys in the pub; it just won't work.

Other women recognised that:

It's difficult, even demeaning, to try to be one of the boys. Don't play a man at his own game because I think quite frankly you'll fail if you try to do that.

Other research findings back up the sense of many of my respondents that there are problems involved in attempting to become an honorary man. Women who attempt to behave like men are often distressed to find not acceptance but distrust from their male peers. Barkalow (1990), for example, documenting her experiences as one of the first women to attend an elite US military academy, detailed the mistakes she made in an attempt to enhance her image in a male domain. She argued that women cannot become officers in the same way that men can but have to find another way to fulfil the masculinised requirements of a job without violating too many of the expectations of what and how a woman should be. One of my respondents explained:

Men have a real problem with women who are unfeminine. If you hide your femininity entirely you get called a lesbian – they don't handle it very well. You can be tough but you have to maintain that edge of femininity somewhere. (female trader, Northbank)

This comment supports the contention of Spurling who, in a study of masculinity and femininity in an elite British university, came to the same conclusion: 'Women who imitate the masculine professional stereotype in male-dominated environments make their colleagues uneasy' (Spurling, 1990, p. 14).

As a male respondent rather condescendingly explained to me:

There's a certain female type in the City; trying to be men, wanting to show themselves as that much more aggressive. I find it quite sad really. It more often backfires with colleagues than helps. (manager, Northbank)

But many of the men whom I interviewed seemed to want it both ways. If a masculinised demeanour is regarded as inappropriate, some of the younger men felt themselves to be placed in a disadvantaged position because of those stereotypical feminine attributes of caring and empathy. They suggested that femininity confers unfair advantages on women. In their comments, the discursive construction of feminine attributes as natural was noticeable. Women were regarded as unfair competition because:

Women are good at getting on with people. People tell them things. (male executive, Bluebros)

Women may have a natural advantage, as the majority of clients are men, and clearly their PR skills and general warmth of approach is much better than a man's. (male manager, Merbank)

There's a definite advantage to being a woman. Being feminine, even slightly sugar-coated, can be a great advantage both within the bank and with clients, because girls can manage to strike up an almost instant rapport, you know with their director and their clients.

And, what clearly worried him,

I think it will influence the choice of promotion to a degree, as long as it's somebody who has the other skills. (male executive, Northbank)

So women seem to be in an impossible position. As female bodies they are out of place at work, but should they manage to overcome the disadvantages of the masculinised environment and achieve success, this is put down to the advantages conferred by a set of naturalised female attributes.

The women, too, while understandably less positive about the advantages of femininity, accepted that becoming an honorary man was not a viable strategy. Thus, one of the women who had 'made it' to director level was adamant about the failure of the masculinised behaviour that she originally had adopted:

Over the years I've come to the conclusion 'Why should I try to be a little man? I'm not a little man. It's not going to work. *I'll never be a man as well as a man is.*' (director, Northbank, my emphasis)

Herein lies the nub of the argument. Embodiment matters. As feminist theorists, Threadgold and Cranny-Francis (1990) have pointed out that 'masculine and feminine behaviours have different personal and social significances when acted out by male and female subjects. What is valorised in patriarchy is not masculinity but *male masculinity*' (p. 31, my emphasis).

CONCLUSIONS

This may seem a negative note and the end of the story. It is not. In the final chapters, I want to show that, despite the effects of all the mechanisms that I have outlined above, there are two important factors that need to be taken into account in understanding the construction of gender in the workplace and its consequences for women. The first of these is a criticism that I have alluded to already and which lies in an omission. Too many of the studies of gendered organisations rely on a single binary distinction between men and women. By establishing masculinity or masculinism as the norm, and so focusing on women as 'Other', the consequence is that the social construction of gender, what is often called 'doing gender' (West and Zimmerman, 1987), at work is ignored. The women who are foregrounded, and the men who remain in the main as shadows in the background, seem to enter the workplace already gendered. The significance of gender as an important distinguishing factor in the workplace – albeit based on years of accumulated evidence – is assumed rather than investigated and unpacked, and so women's inferiority is taken for granted and, more significantly, seems inescapable. The ways in which multiple gendered differences become important in the culture of organisations and the ways in which these change are thus not investigated and the stories told are too undifferentiated. Instead of looking at how workplace interactions themselves gender women and men in multiple ways – some less, some more acceptable than others, some appropriate to one type of work or site of work and some, perhaps quite other ways of being female and male, to another type or site of work – the dominant model of disembodied rational masculinity that used to be so important in professional occupations is taken for granted. Those depressing sexual and familial or at best 'crazy outsider' or 'wicked witch' roles for women are compared against a singular hegemonic male model. It is increasingly clear, however, that it is important to examine how men as well as women 'do gender' in the workplace.

Second, insufficient attention is accorded in these binary models to the changing nature of work in advanced industrial societies. In the type of professional occupations that increasingly dominate service economies, new forms of working and new versions of workplace culture are challenging the old bureaucratic model of a professional organisation and automatic male dominance. As Brown and Scase (1994) illustrated in their work on recruitment, other 'ways of being' may now be more highly valued in organisations. Empathy, embodiment, feelings and team work rather than competitive individualism are the new buzz words of management science, and feminists have not been slow to point out that these characteristics are those traditionally associated with women. As I analysed the images and everyday behaviour of female and male bankers and talked to people about their bodily images, their clothes and diet, and the ways in which they presented themselves at work, it became increasingly clear to me that by focusing solely on women's bodies and comparing them to an idealised disembodied masculinity, I was missing part of the story. For merchant banking does not typify the type of masculinised bureaucratic work that organisational theorists and many feminists seem implicitly to be comparing to the feminised roles that they are analysing. Instead it is a world in which role-playing and drama, an embodied performance, is a key requirement for both men and women. Being an 'honorary man' was not the best strategy for women, nor even, at least in the classic disembodied bureaucratic sense, for many men in investment banking. The next chapters, therefore, show how male bodies matter too and demonstrate that distinctive variants of masculinity are valorised at particular sites in the banks and excluded at others.

7

Body Work 1: Men Behaving Badly

Gender is not a fixed category; rather, it is an accomplished activity – accomplished through the routine activities of daily life and embedded in the institutional structures of society.

Andersen, 1995, p. 5

In the 1980s, as many people have noted, it was money rather than the body which was suffused by eroticism.

Grant, 1993, p. 7

INTRODUCTION

In this and the next chapter, men enter the stage. Some might argue indeed that they never left it, hogging the limelight through the dominance of an image of idealised masculinity and its reality in the majority of senior positions. Even when the focus was on women, as in the last chapter, men were in the wings as an implicit role model or comparator. So far, however, the terms 'men' and 'masculinity' have been taken for granted as a single, oppositional category. I want now to focus explicitly on men and reveal the alternative ways of doing masculinity in different parts of the bank. I argue that by moving to an understanding of masculinity, as well as femininity, as a performance or masquerade, we are able to crack open that binary distinction between men and women, masculinity and femininity, that always places women in an inferior location. I want to demonstrate how the increasing significance of new forms of professional service sector employment, in their emphasis on an embodied performance, both challenge older ways of being male at work and open a space for women to achieve a certain form of visibility and success.

In this chapter, I also return to the symbolic representations of the world of merchant banking, not only in the built environment, as in chapter 2, but also in the internal spaces of City workplaces and in the media. Material social practices in the workplace clearly are deeply imbued with and are undertaken within the context of a set of cultural and symbolic meanings. The world of merchant banking and the composition of the key social actors in the City are saturated with symbolic significance. The 'old' world of the City of London with its distinctive built environment reflecting the nineteenth century expansion is paralleled by class- and gender-specific images of bankers – the white, male and bourgeois world of the public school, elite universities and masculine clubs. As I argued earlier, these 'old' images are juxtaposed to contemporary images of a 'new' City. In the mid to late 1980s, a noticeable shift occurred in the representation of the world of money and in particular the City of London. A world that was pre-eminently both serious and inaccessible became not only the subject of novels, plays and films, in which 'fast' money and slick operators were key protagonists, but also a theme in advertising (Berlei bras and Alexon clothing, for example, both used the City of London as a backdrop in advertising campaigns in the late 1980s) and the object of press attention, ranging from praise to excoriation as financial scandals become more common, or at least more visible.

This emphasis on fictional representations was paralleled by shifts in the nature of 'economic reality' as the commodities dealt with in the new financial world themselves became increasingly fictional entities: futures trading (in commodities that do not yet exist) and junk bonds, for example, are insubstantial. Invisible earnings, something called credit, which, as Grace pointed out, is really debt (1991, p. 118) and the new future – the derivative – are hard to define, let alone make visible. The men and women to whom I talked made their living by moving invisible sums around the globe or by advising companies to invest, divest and take over other firms whose products and workers would never be seen. Although the City has long dealt with variants of these commodities, the element of fiction seems heightened in recent years as extreme losses and gains predominate. For example, in 1992 the British government 'wasted' millions from the reserves trying to prop up the pound, at the same time as the financier/speculator/philanthropist Georg Soros made millions of dollars by astute currency deals. In 1995 a young man brought down a bank single-handed by 'hiding' losses of $8 million in a fictional 'errors' account known only by the numbers 88888. As Grace suggested, 'Clearly, then, a world of high fiction is observable, a daily soap opera, full of the most extreme occurrences. Everyday economic life has become a fiction of terrifying realism, a horror scenario with such convincing special effects that, at times, you really feel you too are there, in the middle of it' (p. 119).

Several of the key themes in fictional representations of high finance – the 'greed is good' ethos as well as guilt about the high-living lifestyle

– are also apparent in the media coverage of the financial world, in the pages of the broadsheet and the specialist press. As I talked to my respondents, I noticed that they too touched on these themes in the ways in which they spoke about their own lives in the City, especially in the ways they discussed the characteristics of the 'key actors'. In this chapter, fictional and 'factional' images of bankers are juxtaposed to show how the fictional images of money and banking constructed in 1980s films, novels and plays find echoes in the 'serious' pages of the '90s quality press whose editors, I am sure, would deny that they produce fictions.

READING CITY IMAGES

There's always this image, I think, which is clearly very wrong, about merchant bankers being slick guys in fast cars with loads of money . . . I haven't experienced this yet. (male interviewee, 26)

One of the most noticeable aspects of the transformation of the world of banking from serious money to fun was the number of 1980s and early 1990s films, plays and novels set in the City or on Wall Street. The 'financial films' probably reached the widest audience. In a review of this genre, Williamson (1991) argued that in the 1980s business and enterprise culture was characterised by a profound cultural unease. She suggested that the great achievement of Hollywood cinema was to dramatise both business achievement and the social indignation it engendered as a single narrative within a coherent moral framework. Probably the classic example of these films, in which the financial world is both glamorised and celebrated but also criticised, is *Wall Street* (1987), from which the motto of the decade, 'greed is good', was taken. Denzin (1990) identified *Wall Street* as a conventional morality play, in which seduction and fall precede redemption, as old-fashioned virtues triumph over fast talk and fast money. In this film, alternative models of masculinity – presented as two contrasting versions of patriarchal rule – struggle for the soul of the young protagonist. Conventional patriarchal authority vanquishes the moral ambivalence but desirable lure of easy money. The solid blue-collar origins and the simple family-centred values of the young protagonist, Bud, played by Charlie Sheen, win out, as his true father (played by Martin Sheen, his real-life father) in the end overcomes the seductive lure of the City and the wiles of his false father, his Wall Street boss Gordon Gekko (played by Michael Douglas).

A similar struggle between alternative versions of masculinity may be identified in factual, as opposed to fictional, portraits of the key male actors within merchant banking, although dramatic denouements tend to be absent. I found a distinction between a version of patriarchal authority and two versions of masculine challenge from younger men a useful way of distinguishing masculine performances by my respondents, as I demonstrate in this and the next chapter.

In Britain a different fictional genre was predominant in the 1980s where the moral edge, or perhaps the wide-eyed US belief in happy endings, was lacking. Classic British examples of fast money dramas tended to be either gangster films such as *Long Good Friday, Empire State* and *Stormy Monday* or TV series like *Capital City* which glamorised City yuppies. The typical British tale was one of trickery and facile success rather than a titanic moral struggle. Similarly, although British novels set in the City emphasise the greed, corruption and the unscrupulous nature of those tied up in the drama of high finance, moral indignation is underplayed and the stance is more one of fascinated awe and envy. The denouement, when it comes in these films, plays and novels, is seldom a reassertion of higher moral values but rather the material success of the hero, or occasionally the heroine. In real life, titanic struggles tended to have unhappy endings in Britain, often involving ruin and/or prison for the patriarchs and young challengers seduced by the lure of money.

In the Hollywood business movies, however, Williamson identified a key dualism. The 'false' values of the world of money are contrasted with the 'real' values of either family life or the 'real' products of manufacturing industry. A key feature of these films is the notion of masquerade where 'real' working-class protagonists masquerade as their boss by adopting the disguise of power-dressing in business suits. Analysts of workplace culture have also identified the ways in which 'designer employees' (the term is Casey's (1995, ch. 6)) are constructed to fit into particular cultures (see also Kondo, 1990; Kunda, 1992), often experiencing their workplace personas as false. The public/private, home/work division which has a long heritage in western thought, as I argued in chapter 2, is reflected in a duality between what is regarded as a necessary masquerade at work and an essential 'real' self that may emerge occasionally on the workplace stage but is allowed complete dominance only in off-stage activities – perhaps in leisure, but particularly in home life which has always been portrayed as more real or more authentic than the artificial and instrumental social relations of the workplace. As I shall show, the metaphors of performance, of reality versus masquerade, were also significant elements in the interviews I undertook.

'FACTION' AND REALITY?

By juxtaposing the narratives of my respondents to media photographs of real actors in the City in the 1990s I am able to give corporeal shape, a fleshy solidity to at least some of the dramatis personae. Throughout my empirical work in the three banks I longed to be able to take photographs, but the bounds of confidentiality could not be stretched so far. But public images of public actors, drawn in the main from the *Guardian*, the *Observer* and the *Financial Times*, seem reasonable and provocative substitutes. The broadcasting media, broadsheets, popular newspapers and glossy magazines alike, have played an important part in 'turning dreary dealing into spectacular battles in which the fashionable demigods emerge triumphant' (*Financial Times*, 4 March 1995, p. XVI).

The financial media, despite the appearance of objective and factual reporting in columns of figures, graphs and reports on currency movements, industrial takeovers and mergers and the like, do not merely convey 'the facts of a matter'. Through their selection of material and the construction of a story line, financial journalists, and others who comment on financial matters and comings and goings in the City, present a partial and discursive construction of an event. Even in the presentation of 'the news', the various media usually present a view of the world that reflects the ideological assumptions of the politically powerful (Glasgow Media Group, 1976, 1980, 1982). While it has been argued that the quality press has an inbuilt bias in favour of the City (Box, 1983), in recent years the presentation of material about financial dealings has changed and there is both a greater degree of questioning of the class-based assumptions about the ways in which business is done and a far greater degree of personalisation of the actors involved in financial dealings. The 'fictional' world which is increasingly common in the serious newspapers, like that of novels and films, is one which, in the words of geographers Thrift and Leyshon (1990), has become a 'sexy/greedy world' in which heroic but flawed individuals struggle against extreme forces of love, envy and greed. As Harvey has argued, 'Love and money may make the world go round . . . but love of money provides the raw energy at the centre of the whirlwind' (1989a, p. 185).

The combination of elemental sex and greed is now common in press coverage of the affairs of the City. In the financial and business pages of the serious press, photographs of key individuals in the world of money are an habitual feature. Photographs are an important part of presenting images of power and influence that are so strongly associated with money and in the representation of an image of a tragic hero engaged in a struggle against elemental forces. Grace (1991), in an analysis of the

Australian quality press, found that the visual content of business pages had significantly increased in recent years. In the British press, dramatic charts and graphs with huge peaks and troughs are now commonly used to illustrate the movement of exchange rates, share prices and, in the midst of the débâcle over the European Exchange Rate Mechanism in the summer of 1993, the relative values of different European currencies. Portraits of key financial actors, almost without exception male, are also a common feature of the more visual focus of recent business pages. In recent years the City and financial affairs seem to have gripped the imagination of the nation and coverage has increased, not only in the quality broadsheets but in the popular press. Financial scandals and sexual peccadillos are front-page news: for example, the story that the deputy governor of the Bank of England made love to an American financial journalist on the carpeted floor of his office in the bank hit all the front pages early in 1995 and precipitated his resignation. Contrary to Levi's assertion in 1987 that 'pin-striped blood does not show up very easily on the walls' (p. 13), it is clear that City blood, especially if it is blue, is just as visible and fascinating as other types.

In her analysis of the business pages, Grace defined a set of dramatis personae familiar to us from films: the hero and the villain were omnipresent. Grace also sketchily identified an ambivalent female figure – the princess – who made an extremely infrequent appearance in Australian broadsheets. On the business pages that Grace examined, representations of female figures 'speak desire rather than authority', although Grace did note the presence of smart, confident and knowledgeable women as support figures on financial programmes on Australian television. Thus, perhaps there is a possible authoritative role for women that goes beyond the matron, school mistress and honorary man that I discussed in the last chapter. In a search for this elusive feminine authority, but also to establish the complex and multiple masculine performances possible in the City of London, I juxtaposed a survey of British press images, mainly from the 'serious' press, in the first half of the 1990s with readings of the taped interviews to construct a materialist semiotics of the different characters, bodily norms and gendered performances in different arenas in investment banks.

GENDER PERFORMANCES AT WORK

In chapter 6, I began to interpret the position of women in merchant banks as a form of drama; I want now to deepen this analysis, covering the multiplicity of ways in which both men and women 'do gender' in the workplace. I have interpreted the taped narratives through the lens of

Butler's (1990a, b, 1993) theorisation of the social construction of gender as an embodied performance. Butler challenged the permanence of the sexed body and the fixity of self in her theorisation of the body as a fluid set of boundaries constructed in discourse and practice. Unlike Young, whose notion of cultural imperialism lay behind chapter 6, Butler did not take the body for granted. Indeed, Young has been accused of bodily essentialism (Molloy, 1995). By *taking for granted* women's singularity as the embodied 'Other', rather paradoxically she reinforced it in her attempt to establish a version of justice based on group membership. In Young's work, therefore, as in the gender and organisational school, women are unable to escape their embodiment as inferior femininity.

Butler's theorisation of bodily performance, with its emphasis on the possibility of transgressive acts that might disrupt 'the regulatory fiction' of heterosexuality, provides a way to construct multiple positions for women and for men. I want to stress, however, that the emphasis here on performativity and the sexed self at work is not to deny the wider social structures of power which themselves affect and reflect the organisation of firms, deep-seated patterns of occupational segregation and the large-scale restructuring of the economy. Gendered differences and the inequalities between them are constructed by more than, and extend beyond, daily cultural performances. Like Thorne, I believe that 'gender – and race, class and compulsory heterosexuality – extend deep into the subconscious and the shaping of emotions and outward into social structure and material interests' (Thorne, 1995, p. 499). Indeed, the structure of this book, moving across the spatial scales at which gendered attitudes are inculcated and reinforced, reflects this belief.

Despite the liberatory prospects of transgressive behaviours, as Butler showed, drawing on Foucault, in contemporary industrial societies an epistemic regime of compulsory heterosexuality produces and reifies an ontological binary gender division that enforces women's inferiority. But this division is a fiction. Gender is not a binary division located in biological difference, but is instead a persistent impersonation that passes as real. Being female is not a 'natural fact' but 'a cultural performance, [in which] "naturalness" [is] constituted through discursively constrained performative acts that produce the body through and within the categories of sex' (Butler, 1990a, p. viii). The aim of this fabrication is the production of a coherent identity. Through acts, gestures and clothes, through corporeal signs and other discursive means, a gendered identity is manufactured, manifested and sustained. Thus, Butler argued:

> gender ought not to be constructed as a stable identity or locus of agency from which various acts follow; rather, gender is an identity tenuously constituted in time, instituted in an exterior space through a *stylized repeti-*

tion of acts. The effect of gender is produced through the stylization of the body and, hence, must be understood as the mundane way in which bodily gestures, movements, and styles of various kinds constitute *the illusion* of an abiding gendered self. . . . Significantly, if gender is instituted through acts which are internally discontinuous, then the *appearance of substance* is precisely that, a constructed identity, a performative accomplishment through which the social audience, including the actors themselves, come to believe and to perform in the mode of belief. (Butler, 1990a, pp. 140–1, original emphasis)

Thus, the body is bounded and constituted by political forces and everyday acts within institutions which constitute systems of compulsory heterosexuality.

The workplace is, of course, one institution and arena in which discursive practices construct acceptable versions of 'men' and 'women', particular gendered appearances and sets of social relations that are seen as appropriate to the practices and structures of that institution. If gender is defined not as a fixed or stable category but as a construct congruent with the discourses and practices of particular locations, then it becomes possible to examine not only the ways in which particular hetereosexual performances become hegemonic but also the prospects of resistance. There is a whole range of acts, as Butler suggested, that may produce subversive discontinuities and dissonance among the categories of sex, gender and desire and question their alleged relations. By making it clear that what seems an inalienable part of a sexed self is actually a temporally and spatially specific performance, the disruption of the associations between particular gender performances and power in the workplace may be possible, and may, in the longer run, lead to the transformation and multiplication of acceptable fleshy styles and corporeal practices.

Butler herself investigated these dissonances through an examination of homosexuality and the incest taboo. She drew on a range of literatures – from psychoanalysis, including a paper by Riviere (1986) about femininity as masquerade, as well as the work of Lacan and Irigaray, and from anthropology, particularly Mary Douglas's work – to argue that there is 'a set of parodic practices based in a performative theory of gender acts that disrupt the categories of the body, sex, gender, and sexuality and occasion their subversive resignification and proliferation beyond the binary frame' (1990a, p. x). In reading and re-reading my transcripts I was particularly struck by the ways in which a number of the most senior women interviewees referred to parody, masquerade and subversive confusion in talking about themselves and their workplace identities. I also began to consider the extent to which transgressive gender performances are open to men. The changes I have identified in the 'new' City, whether full-scale 'Americanisation' or a smaller breach in the solid bourgeois façade of the City, may have opened new ways of doing masculinity for City men.

Drawing on the images and words used by the women and men whom I interviewed, I therefore examined the ways in which discursive strategies construct alternative versions of a heterosexual gender performance at different sites in investment banks. The physical setting of City interactions affect and reflect particular versions of masculinity and constrain the ways in which men and women are able to 'do gender'. In this chapter, trading floors and dealing rooms are the sites examined, and in the next, the offices and suites of corporate finance divisions.

WORKING SITES

One of the most significant divisions in merchant banks is between those who are actively seen to be making money and the rest – the support and service workers, the aptly named back office workers who are denied the glamour and associated rewards of both corporate finance and trading and dealing. Although money clearly cannot be made and moved without the support functions, the status of these employees is distinctly second-rate.

In merchant banking there's a tremendous divide; despite how people try and say there isn't, there is. Between revenue earners and service support staff. There is ... because if you're bringing money in you're regarded as wonderful; if you're seen as an overhead being paid, having your mortgage subsidy paid for you ... you know, you're a second-class citizen. (woman, 30, communication services, Northbank)

Although united by their wealth-generating role, there is nevertheless a parallel and significant divide between the traders and dealers and the corporate bankers. As numerous respondents explained:

There's a cultural divide between them, between traders and what I might call small 'e' executives.

A male respondent in his mid 20s, himself a product of Eton and Cambridge, was able to more clearly define the divide:

In corporate finance, the social background of people is quite narrow – Oxbridge, Bristol, Exeter – so that gives a certain social division immediately. By contrast, the trading floor is very different. Much more sort of, as they say these days, yahoo. ... With regard to social group, the trading floor's one end and the rest of the bank the other.

So divided by class and educational background, in the minds of my respondents as well as popular imagination, the staid and still elitist, old-fashioned world of quiet, dignified corporate boardrooms and offices is also physically a world away from the exchanges and dealing rooms.

These two sites of work seem to mirror the extremes of exalted and base spaces and activities. At each site, alternative ways of performing masculinity are sedimented by everyday social interactions. Bodily styles and workplace practices are utterly different. Despite the demise of certain aspects of market-based trading and its replacement by screen-based dealing in open-plan offices, the atmosphere and range of tolerated behaviour in dealing rooms continues to reflect floor trading. Stock exchanges are sites of spectacle where exotic goods are traded and the body is allowed out of control – shouting and gesticulating are required forms of interaction. Like a medieval fair, the exchange is a dual site – a market place, a site of commercial exchanges, in which goods from national and international markets are traded, but also a site of pleasure, unconnected to the 'real' world and standards of normal behaviour. On the trading floors, the senses are flooded by strange signs, and performances are stimulated by excitement and desire. The usual control of emotions expected in middle-class workplaces is not demanded. Disorder, excitement, fear and shock mingle with dreams, greed and a desire for wealth. In the carnivalesque atmosphere, with its smells, sweating and loud noises, participants cannot fail to be aware of their own bodily space. As Stallybrass and White (1986) have suggested, in capitalist societies the desire and longing for the carnivalesque is a way of transgressing bourgeois norms of work.

On the floor (and to an extent in the new electronic dealing rooms), however, the carnivalesque actually enters the workplace, and transgressive behaviours are a sanctified aspect of paid work. 'Place, body, group identity and subjectivity interconnect' here (Stallybrass and White, 1986, p. 25). The extent of transgression is not unlimited, however. As Wouters (1987) has suggested, in stock exchanges the type of behaviour commonly accepted may be a 'controlled de-control of the emotions'.

DOING GENDER IN THE DEALING ROOMS / ON THE TRADING FLOOR

A new employee, once he reached the trading floor, was handed a pair of telephones. He went on line almost immediately. If he could make millions of dollars come out of those phones, he became that most revered of all species: a Big Swinging Dick. . . . Nothing in the jungle got in the way of a Big Swinging Dick. . . . That was the prize we coveted . . . everyone wanted to be a Big Swinging Dick, even the women. Big Swinging Dickettes. (Lewis, 1989, pp. 42–3)

A trading room has never been a career, it's always been a means to an end, to get quick money. (forex dealer)

My brief is to make money, that's what success is. (forex dealer)

The ultimate trader is a heterosexual male. His characteristic site is the floor of the stock exchange, in the midst of a chaotic spectacle. The spectacle of hysterical traders is a familiar media image every time there is a stock market 'adjustment' – Black Monday in 1987, Black Wednesday in September 1992 and the demise of the ERM in 1993 were all illustrated by the same image (see plate 7.1). This image, emphasising the embodiment, the sheer physical exuberance of the characters, challenges the notion of the masculine worker as a rational disembodied being. From the taped interviews, an interesting narrative representation of the qualities needed for successful workplace performance in this arena of banking emerged. It is a representation that is both classed and gendered, but in different ways from the patriarchal representatives of the banking world to whom I turn later. On the trading floors and in the dealing rooms, a particular combination of youth, class background and masculinity is characteristic.

Some jobs in the City are the domain of younger people – trading, looking at green screens all day long and yelling, screaming . . . the selling jobs that are the domain of the younger people here are on the trading floor. . . . They have a tough time. It's very frantic if the market moves suddenly and they have to have very good nerves, and they have to suppress the emotion of an excitement like joining the ERM, or the Gulf War. They have to stand back and assess a position. The sort of personalities who are good at these jobs are the guys that are laid back, the guys who go out and drink a lot of beer at lunchtime, play football in the office. They're a mix. Some with self-important accents but I think the sort of Oxbridge type is more typically recruited into the area I am in and corporate finance. (female manager, capital markets, Bluebros)

Another interviewee argued that:

Dealing is young; it's definitely a fairly short-lived career. Ten years, then I think you're burned out. They stash away heaps of money and then they can do anything they like after that. A few good bonuses and you can buy a house outright and then maybe a business. (male financial administrator, Northbank)

Plate 7.1 Youthful exuberance on the trading floor
Source: Guardian; photo by Graham Turner

Financial journalists have the same view:

> ... out there on the floor it is the energy and speed of reaction, and hunger. Most traders on the floor are young – in their early twenties. In the good years they earn several hundred thousand pounds in bonuses. But they don't expect to last. The three-year burn out is a maxim proved by experience. (Hamilton et al., 1995, p. 23)

In the performance of youthful virility associated with success in trading and dealing, there is an emphasis on the 'natural' characteristics of a certain type of masculinity, and on the unity, rather than the dualism, of mind and body. The attributes of the tasks involved are associated with a form of rampant male libido. In the social construction of masculine and feminine sexuality, women are portrayed as passive and quiet, their role being to subdue, quieten and pacify the male. These images of male agency and female containment have a powerful hold and a continuing influence. They act against a notion of female agency, making it difficult for women to become players. As a respondent who had tried, but failed, explained:

It is difficult to be a woman on the dealing floor. It [sexism] is so overt ... I was much more conscious of being a woman to be looked at and having to put up with, you know, a lot of that kind of gutter humour and all that kind of thing and frankly I wasn't taken that seriously, really. That was difficult. ... There was a stripper once on the floor. I was so angry I stormed out. What do you do? It's very difficult to know how to deal with it. Of course, there were one or two women who were trying to show they were one of the boys – difficult. Whatever you do is difficult, because, you know, if you leave, you are conspicuous by your absence. ... There's other things ... sometimes if there is a big issue going off, we make a big fanfare for it. There'd be a French flag for a French client, or Australian flags and beer everywhere. You know Fosters because of XXXX. Women don't drink ... it is a very macho thing where it is difficult to be a woman. (former dealer, now human resources, Merbank)

Men recognise this too:

There are fewer women traders than men certainly ... it's a very high risk business, the risks are very immediate. It's a very competitive culture. You can't alter it in terms of the business, and historically I guess it's been male-dominated. And, well, some of the personal skills of the traders are perhaps a little bit lacking. (personnel, Merbank)

In the view of many of my respondents, especially those from the 'other side' of the banking world, the young men who succeed in this world are 'naturals'. 'They are natural mathematicians, good with fig-ures', 'their chief characteristic is basic raw intelligence' and they 'come to the bank at 18, no training, all natural ability, straight from school, highly numerate, amazingly quick minds'. Another respondent corrected any misunderstandings that I might harbour about the importance of qualifications:

There is much misunderstanding about the role and brightness of traders in the dealing rooms of the financial institutions. You don't need a degree or a Ph.D. in maths to deal on the floor. Degrees are the insignia of the senior management, the Ph.D. the requirement for the designers of the trading programmes, the so-called rocket scientists. (personnel director, Merbank)

Others commented:

[They are] barrow boys, natural sellers. If they weren't selling bonds, they'd be selling fruit and vegetables in the East End. (man, capital markets, Northbank)

Traders and salesmen are born not made. They used to equate it with selling apples off the barrow, if you could do that you could trade. (man, corporate finance, Bluebros)

In image, therefore, traders and dealers are constructed above all as boys, with boys' natural interests and masculine attributes like mathematical talent.

These recorded views are themselves partially fictional. They are based on prejudice, on media representations and perhaps on envy from men who work in less 'exciting' areas of investment banking, as much as on a detailed analysis of the range and variation of class backgrounds and educational credentials of employees in a sample set of dealing rooms. As one of my interviewees, who was actually working as a trader, pointed out somewhat ungrammatically, 'the trading floor's much wider in fact in regard of social group nowadays'. In fact, all but one of the respondents in my sample who were employed in this area of the banking world were graduates, differing from the corporate finance divisions only in the fact that somewhat less prestigious universities had been attended, and yet the 'barrow boy' image held sway. An excellent illustration of the strength of these representations was afforded by one of the (few) women respondents from this area of banking. Working in equity sales herself, with a degree in mathematics from Cambridge, she argued that:

Market makers traditionally are quite spivvy characters and you know typically I guess their reputation is that they'll leg you over if they can. (woman, 23, Merbank)

My respondents also pointed out that there were finer-grained distinctions in class background and attitudes between dealers/traders, the salesmen (*sic*) and the market makers:

The sales people have to be and do tend to be more diplomatic – there's a fine line to tread between keeping your clients happy, keeping your dealers happy, making money and relaying all the relevant information you hear to your dealers. Traders tend to be, not all of them but they're perceived to be more arrogant, mmm ... single-minded and sort of prima donnas than the sales people. Sales people probably have a higher level of social background than the dealers do. I would say that's the case here and everywhere else. (gilts salesman, 33, Bluebros (degree from London University))

Here, gendered associations have opened a space for women. As the young woman in equity sales, quoted above, said, 'it's not unusual now for women to be salesmen, but less common as market makers'. She expanded as follows:

The thing is as a market maker you have to be quite aggressive and women are generally less aggressive I would say. All the market makers here are men and it's also because it's not a very secure job at all and perhaps women, I tend to think, they want a little bit more security. Umm in the old market days they were all down on the floors – a very laddy atmosphere – and women, I mean typically anyone who goes into it is given a very hard time. It's just still steeped in old-style tradition. They're called blue button and they have to do a lot of fetching and carrying and going and getting breakfast in the morning and they suffer usually a lot of abuse and that's just something that goes with the job. And I don't think there are many women who want to work in that sort of atmosphere. I think a lot of women find it uncomfortable as well. The language can often be quite blue and they find the presence of women quite uncomfortable, they don't really know how to cope with it and so it probably makes it very difficult for women.

THE LEESON AFFAIR

In 1995 a remarkable coincidence of fiction and fact seemed to confirm the popular stereotypes. Nick Leeson, a derivatives trader on the Singapore Stock Exchange, brought down Barings Bank. All the elements of a fictional financial drama were in place. Leeson himself was a stereotypical trader – if not quite the barrow boy cum financial wizard of folk history, at least a council house boy from Leytonstone in the eastern outer suburbs of London. According to the press he was variously described as 'a plasterer's son whose education finished at his local comprehensive' (*London Review of Books*, 23 March 1993) and 'a scion of a working class family from a council estate' (*Daily Telegraph*, 28 February 1995, p. 3). In fact, Leeson had attended a neighbourhood grammar school (state-funded but selective), but while there he was an aggressive hustler (at least viewed in retrospect), reported to be 'proud and arrogant' and 'cocksure'. As an adult, according to an *Observer* report, 'around town, he was the typical London trader, drinking too much and behaving badly. Once on a pub crawl, he dropped his pants in front of a group of women and, when asked, refused to apologise. . . . In the world of the dealing rooms, such antics were common' (*Observer*, 5 March 1995, p. 24).

The *Guardian* described him in more flattering terms, attributing to him 'a pocket calculator mind, a ruthless gambling instinct, together with an ice-cold ability to handle risk' (*Guardian Outlook*, 4 March 1995, p. 23). But in perhaps the most satisfactory twist to the tale, it appeared that Leeson, far from being a mathematical genius, had failed his mathematics A level (a British school-leaving certificate). This was the man who, reputedly, single-handedly brought down the longest-established and one of the most blue-blooded banks in the City of London. Barings had been founded in 1762 by German merchants who throughout the succeeding centuries became important figures in the British establishment. Five members of the family received hereditary peerages and have variously been imperial governors, ambassadors and governor of the Bank of England, as well as marrying into the aristocracy. In the late 1960s, members of the Barings family further enhanced their reputation by transferring their individual shareholdings to a charitable foundation, although they remained voting directors of the bank. Despite the apparent appearance of respectability and rock solid security, it has become clear from press coverage and the Bank of England inquiry into Barings' dealings that the head office in London had little knowledge and less control of the Singapore operation. As long as Leeson was turning in huge profits, and Barings Futures Singapore made £8.8 million in 1993, he was given a long rein.

The press coverage of this affair conforms to the stereotypical images described here. The image of Barings as an entity is that of the 'old' City, characterised by a close network between elite actors. Leeson, on the other hand, was constructed as the classic outsider who had failed to understand the unwritten rules of a club to which he never should have been admitted. As the *Observer* astutely pointed out at the time, 'the search for a scapegoat is on and nobody better than a single rogue trader from the wrong side of the class divide' (5 March 1995, p. 24). In a less individualist vein, the *Observer* writers recognised that the case represented 'a classic battle between the two sides of Barings – the old merchant bank tradition and the new trading spirit' (p. 24).

While Leeson was successful, he was portrayed in the same terms of naturalistic masculinist talent that my respondents used. Thus, 'He loved trading and he did it with guts' (Singapore broker, *The Sunday Times*, 9 July 1995). But once he failed, he became an outsider, excluded from the elite world of investment banking as 'the toffs' closed ranks. In an extraordinary illustration of my argument about the significance of representations, it was reported towards the end of 1995 that a film was to be made of the Barings collapse, with Hugh Grant as Nick Leeson (*Observer*, 22 October 1995). That Grant – the quintessential English upper-class toff of *Four Weddings and a Funeral* – should be named shows the continuing strength of the elitist image of bankers in the popular imagination. Grant's carefully cultivated screen persona more nearly parallels that of the young princes in corporate finance that I discuss below, although, like Leeson, Grant has also had problems keeping his pants on.

GENDERED ATTRIBUTES

Masculinity is taken for granted in the press coverage of 'rogue traders'. As Blundy (1995) remarked at the time, 'there could never be a female Nick Leeson' (p. 47), not merely because there are so few women dealers and traders, but also because of their 'characters'. The characteristics required for success in dealing, trading and selling (be it honestly or dishonestly) are exactly those attributes conventionally associated with masculinity. In the course of many of my interviews, the nature of trading and the attributes assumed to be essential to success were pointed out. As respondents explained, 'you have to be tough and ruthless to succeed' and 'there seems to be an incredible need to bite everybody's head off and knock them out of the way and trample on their heads'. Other reasons were added. At Bluebros, for example, it was explained that in gilts sales and the dealing room women were disadvantaged because:

. . . you're very close to people. It can be very noisy and you have to be aware of everything that's going on in the room as well as listening to the phones. You tend to be, have to be quite alert the whole time and because of that, especially on busy days, people can get quite het up. Sometimes problems can boil up very quickly and then there are arguments but then if there is a problem or an argument it's over very quickly and then something else happens. It's a working environment where things happen very quickly. You don't write memos to people, you just go and shout at them. Women can't do that. (salesman, Bluebros)

And in Northbank too:

It's a very aggressive environment. If things get really heated between two guys, then all right, we may ... you know, we may shout and swear and whatever it may be, and you know really have a go at each other, but sometimes I don't think I really could, you know, really sort of go 100 per cent if I was really shouting at a girl. Maybe that's just a sort of personal thing. But personally I find it harder to argue with a woman than with a guy. (male dealer, Northbank)

This difficulty is, of course, seen as a mark of weakness rather than strength or restraint. Another salesman explained:

You have got to be able to think quickly. Take a view on something. Men are better at quick decisions. Whether you are right or wrong doesn't necessarily matter. You have to be able to decipher what you are hearing and relay what is relevant and do that on the spot. (salesman, Bluebros)

I found his admission rather unnerving as well as disarmingly honest and wondered about its connections with the huge losses in the City. Later a young man on the corporate finance side made an similar revealing comment: 'I think men are more able to inspire clients with confidence, whether it's warranted or not.' The argument that the world of money is a fictitious one began to seem disconcertingly real.

A range of other explanations of why masculinity is important were also proffered:

It's easier to work with men. You have more in common: football, cricket, sport in general but also you can deal up front ... you can be more explicit with a man, if you think something is wrong or the guy's maybe a bit selfish or whatever, if you think a man's making the wrong price or whatever you can tell him outright. Women too often get the benefit of the doubt. (male dealer, Northbank)

On the sales side, it's a phone job really, so I suppose a woman could do it [*and see the comment below*] but you have to be out there seeing clients as often as you judge is necessary really. Do anything from official visits to going go-karting with them. Lunches and some evening entertainment – theatre, squash, horse-racing – it could be anything really. (salesman, Bluebros)

This may, perhaps, make it more difficult for women to deal with male clients but it was also suggested that recent changes may have improved women's prospects. At Merbank, for example:

The sales and trading of equities is now purely screen- and telecom-based, so the dealers are sat [*sic*] in front of fairly complex screens, there's touch-screen dealing. The old stock jobbers, working on the stock exchange floor, where you actually dealt with people face to face, are all gone. So I think the skills required now are quite different, working on a screen. One, technology and two, there's the skills of conversing over the telephone. . . . There's some people who prefer talking on the telephone; I think women do actually. (male, personnel officer, Merbank)

A woman trader, however, told me that this telephone trading was not actually an advantage as:

It's hard to scream down the phone at someone, at least at first.

The view that women lack the necessary attributes of a successful trader, dealer or salesman was widespread in the essentialist reading of human nature that was common among my respondents. This common remark sums it up: 'an aggressive male dealer – well that's how dealers are, an aggressive woman – it's not natural'.

However, there was also a less evident discourse about female advantage. One of the dealers quoted above suggested that, in his view at least, 'women too often get the benefit of the doubt'. A more nuanced view of the relative strengths of men and women, as well as of the changing culture of this part of investment banking, was expressed by one of my female interviewees, Beth.

You sell by using a number of different characteristics – by being very aggressive and pushy and being really sharp or you can sell by personality, and that is much more the old-style salesman which is probably why it was possible for a few women to get in where it's a lot of chatting, a few fat lunches, wine etc. There's less of that now. It's much more competitive and you've got to have the edge in terms of having the best ideas as well as being sharp and bright etc. There's no reason why a woman can't do that any more than a bloke.

But there's still a difference. A lot of the guys will take their clients off to a strip show and I could never do that. Basically the whole point of being a salesman is you want your client to feel special, you want him, you want to make him feel he's right on the top of your sales list, erhm, you do that by, you want to get under his skin, you want to try and find out what makes this guy tick so that he trusts you and you develop this relationship. It's all about developing relationships and, as I say, there's different ways to do that. So the one thing I could never do is erhm, is uhm, you know, take people to a strip show and I don't usually get tickets for rugby and football matches which a lot of people are after. But on the other hand, uhhm, you can use your personality, and use your charm, the fact that they might like to be taken out, erhm, you know, by a ... a pleasant girl, errhm, you know, it's different and as a girl if you've actually got that you might as well use it.

Despite the hesitation, it was quite clear what she meant by 'that' – a combination of looks, brains and personality. The quotation is interesting as it substantiates Leidner's (1993) argument that men and women are able to interpret the attributes of the same job in ways which are congruent with particular gender 'regimes' and their own gendered identity. The term 'regime' is used here both in Connell's (1987) structural, sociological sense of an established way of doing gender, which although not invariant becomes sedimented by a range of social structures from the legal system to the family, and in Butler's psychoanalytical sense of a regulatory heterosexual fiction. The salesmen, and here I mean men, in investment banking, exactly like the insurance salesmen in the company Leidner studied, interpreted their task in terms of 'overcoming resistance' and aggressive selling, as well as in the construction of a 'boys together' social ambience, despite the fact that the job itself might seem to demand feminised attributes of listening well and being socially available. As my interviewee makes plain, the ways men construct and carry out their tasks are impossible for women and so the job is reinterpreted in conventional female terms – requiring sympathy and indispensability with a dash of 'personality and charm' thrown in. From Beth's hesitation, she was clearly slightly uneasy at presenting herself as a version of an escort with brains but as she concluded, 'you might as well use it'. Men certainly take advantage of their common masculinity in interactions with clients. But Beth was also aware of limitations.

You do have to be careful; as a single girl [*sic*] you can get yourself into hot water – that can be a disadvantage. The job is to be open and friendly and it can get difficult. With men that will never happen because they'll just become big buddies and go off to rugby matches together.

She concluded:

As a woman it's quite easy to get your foot in the door because you are different but if you are good, as a woman, you will get on well, but if you are bad and a woman you'll have a far worse time. Men don't suffer female fools gladly in this business.

While gender clearly makes a significant difference to acceptance and to success in this side of banking, cultural differences between the banks and the markets were also emphasised in the narratives I recorded and analysed. While these might be a matter of degree, the social construction of different markets makes it more or less easy for women to enter such masculinised domains. An interviewee suggested that:

The media image of trading is probably very accurate in some markets. It depends which market you choose. If you choose foreign exchange then it tends to be 'work hard, play hard' and it tends to attract those younger wilder types. Gilts doesn't have the same foreign exchange tag put on it. The type of dealer that appears on the television is a minority here. (gilts salesman, Bluebros)

Similarly, the respondents at Northbank were quick to suggest that the culture of their bank was more dignified, more cooperative and less competitive than elsewhere. Popular images were used as the contrast:

There's nobody here like in *Liar's Poker*. They would be in a brokers; they couldn't possibly be in a bank. They would be dealing stocks. They can't possibly be in a bank where you are advising real, serious companies as proper businesses. They can't possibly be in a merchant bank. They are in the frivolous end where you are dealing stock. (female director, Northbank)

And another Northbank director suggested that size made a difference too:

The forex dealing room at Northbank is small; eight traders share a desk on one side of the room. It's not cut-throat as it's small and we share the work, no cut-throat atmosphere or superstar traders. The bank looks for team players. If a man's got a problem in a position you'll try and help him out of it; it won't just be feet on the desk sort of thing, because the bottom line is it's the desk not the individual, so it's in everyone's best interests to help people out.

But I could not fail to remark the gendered pronoun.

At Merbank, on the other hand, the personnel officer suggested that competition rather than cooperation was more usual:

At Merbank in trading and sales they work on what they call 'desks'. So there'll be a European desk, a US desk, there'll be a Japan desk and they'll work as a group but then they'll all be doing the same thing. They may all have their own clients but they would then all be doing the same job. People have to get on with each other but they are in competition really. This is quite a tough environment in terms of performing to the standard. (male, personnel officer, Merbank)

If Merbank approached popular images of dealing and trading more closely than Northbank, what about Bluebros?

Well, it's friendly. I am in sales and I know everyone on the trading floor. But it's very masculine in the sense of day-to-day contacts. Most of the clients are men and all the dealers are men, though there are women in sales. It's also very tough and aggressive. . . . Bluebros certainly has its reputation but it is an approachable place to work. (salesman, equities)

Similarly, the woman in equity sales who was this man's 'partner' in my sample suggested that 'it's quite genteel here. It's uhm certainly not the worst.' Like her colleague, she suggested 'you have got to go to the money brokers, the forex brokers to get truly, ... if you want dirt. I mean the trading room at Bluebros is actually quite genteel.' (This woman later told me that her husband was a money broker, suggesting in fond tones that 'he's a gorilla actually – he's been let out of the zoo. I hear the stories' but, she added, 'actually he's terribly good at home, around the house'.)

CONCLUSIONS

I have demonstrated here, and in the previous chapter, how women are made to feel out of place on the trading floors and in the dealing rooms by the development of a particular type of heterosexual machismo culture in which crude bodily humour, pin-ups, practical jokes and various forms of verbal and non-verbal behaviour verging on sexual harassment are the norm. The bodily imagery that is commonplace in the everyday language and social practices of the trading and dealing rooms relies on a particularly exaggerated version of masculinity and masculine perform-ance. The most extreme example is the dubbing of successful traders as 'big swinging dicks'. Power, sexuality, desire and masculinity combine to construct femininity as deficient.

It is not only women, however, who are constructed as 'Other' and made to feel 'out of place' in these arenas of the banks. Alternative versions of masculinity are also out of place there. Sexualised language and humour centres on an idealised rampant heterosexuality that ab-hors both faithfulness and bi- or homosexuality. Young men habitually ask each other about their sexual performance in the relatively jocular language of 'getting your leg over' and 'pulling'. Disapproval of homo-erotic relationships, however, was expressed more strongly. As a woman respondent remarked of her co-workers, 'most of them are completely homophobic'. In a more coded comment, another woman suggested that 'men who are, well, perhaps artistic or sensitive are out of place here. You have got to conform, as well as have a thick skin in this world.'

In their path-breaking work on lesbian identities, Rubin (1975) and Rich (1980) documented the mechanisms that enforce 'obligatory' or 'compulsory heterosexuality', and, as Connell (1995) has more recently reminded scholars, 'compulsory heterosexuality is also enforced on men' (p. 104). The individual competitiveness, the sexual objectification of women and the emphasis on particular forms of homosocial relationships between male colleagues and clients also position gay men as the 'Other'. Consequently, a number of male respondents indicated that they had decided to conceal their sexual preferences while at work and participate in the normal practices of an overwhelmingly heterosexist workplace. The only 'out' gay man who was interviewed revealed that the homo-phobic atmosphere made him the subject of unacceptable sexist jokes and behaviour, which, like his women colleagues, he endeavoured to treat as unimportant. The following statement from one of his colleagues reveals commonly held, and disturbing, attitudes:

There's this guy who's completely queer, makes no bones about it, thinks it's hilarious. I mean he's always making jokes, and I mean once upon a time we sent him up in the lift. We stuck him to his chair, taped him up with sellotape, and sent him to the 12th floor in the lift, and this kind of stuff. I mean it goes on all the time; it's really very funny. So it's a very nice place to work; it's very friendly. (woman, Merbank)

Other male respondents, both straight and gay, talked about the camou-flage or masquerades they adopted in the workplace in order to conform to accepted versions of masculinity. So for men too, the performance of gender as traders or dealers involves the construction of a fictional narrative that is specific to the workplace. In the next chapter, I move to an alternative site in merchant banks and show that there are other ways of doing masculinity and femininity in which parody and pretence are also significant.

8

Body Work 2: The Masqueraders

Corporate finance is the last bastion of male stranglehold.
                                   Head of human resources, Merbank

It could be argued that men don't have any bodies at all . . . only the heads, the unsmiling heads, the talking heads, the decision-making heads, and maybe a little glimpse, a coy flash of suit. How do we know there's a body, under all that discreet pinstriped tailoring? We don't, and maybe there isn't.
                                                   Atwood, 1992, p. 80

The British have no bodies. They have only heads.
       Pascal Fleury, Parisian semiotician, quoted in Armstrong, 1995, p. 15

INTRODUCTION

In the previous two chapters, relationships between the genders have been the focus. I showed how women are constructed as inferior workers through the opposition of a set of naturalised feminine characters to an unspecified masculine norm (in chapter 6) and to a particular version of active masculinist and embodied performances (in chapter 7). I also suggested that the hegemonic and heterosexual version of masculinity positions gay men as 'Other' in certain types of work. There are, however, other ways of doing heterosexuality and these are the focus of this chapter.

Recognition of masculinity as a multiple social construction has been slower than the equivalent recognition about femininity. Detailed empirical investigations of the multiple variants of masculinity are still relatively rare (Connell, 1987; Kimmel, 1988) and the main comparison is between hetero- and homosexual masculinities (Bell et al., 1994; Connell, 1992, 1995). While there are several studies of masculine performance at work – in the police for example (Cornwall and Lindisfarne, 1994) – as well as studies of homosocial relations between men in leisure environments, such as social and sports clubs (Messner, 1992), there are almost no comparisons of different versions of masculinity within the same organisation or workplace. Uncovering the social construction of different masculinities and the relations between them is, however, a crucial element in revealing how the structural order of gender is maintained, reproduced or challenged. In the first part of this chapter, a challenge to the version of hegemonic, class-based, disembodied masculinity that is dominant in corporate finance divisions is examined, as younger men begin to do gender in ways that parallel the social construction of femininity. As I shall argue, this 'feminisation' is leading to a struggle between 'real' women and masculinised feminine performances or masquerades. It may be that femininity in a self-evidently masculine body will become the most highly valorised workplace performance.

DOING GENDER IN CORPORATE FINANCE

The extreme versions of heterosexual masculinity, the bodily gestures and fluids and the *déshabillé* of the thrusting wheelers and dealers of the trading floors and dealing rooms, are out of place in the offices, boardrooms, clubs and restaurants frequented by the men, and smaller numbers of women, who are employed in the corporate finance and capital markets divisions of investment banks. Here an alternative world is staged, peopled by sober-suited bourgeois men whom I term patriarchs and princes – the former distinguished from the latter most obviously by their age and seniority. These are the employees who give (though 'sell' is the more accurate word) advice on investment strategies, who arrange mergers and acquisitions and negotiate large loans for, in the main, corporate clients.

Corporate finance is seen as, has been described as, the shop window of any merchant bank, or investment bank. It's the corporate finance people that actually advise on the deals that hit the headlines. (personnel director, Merbank)

Corporate finance is an essentially serious world in contrast to the frivolity and carnival atmosphere of the markets. Here, the traditional image of the merchant banker as sober, rational and powerful, with the levers of the world financial system secure in his careful hands, is dominant. This form of masculinity is quite clearly class-specific and is perhaps the least conscious performance. None of the older men on the corporate side whom I interviewed referred to notions of image, performance or masquerade, or to selling themselves, unlike all other categories of respondents. These men are cautious and industrious, with a

Plate 8.1 Patriarchal attitudes
Source: merchant bank's annual report, 1991

solid background of a good family and a public school behind them. In some cases they are members of a dynasty of bankers whose names are still commemorated in merchant banks. In the status hierarchy of the City, these bankers are, to mix metaphors, the *'crème de la crème'* among the employees of 'blue-blooded' banks. Plate 8.1 shows these patriarchs at their most serious. Carefully posed in a statesman-like group in the pages of the company accounts, these men radiate confidence in a world in which, in the words of Sir Kenneth Kleinwort, 'a gentleman's word was his bond' (City Lives Project, 1991). This illustration is of the Barings board, a few years before their bank's collapse in 1995.

In the press, corporate financiers and bankers are presented in similar ways. Unlike the impulsive youth of the trading floor, represented on the business pages in a state of relative undress, the wise hero/patriarch seldom removes his jacket. Considered contemplation and careful assessment overheats neither the brain nor the body. It is here that the image of disembodied rational masculinity reaches its apotheosis. The hero appears alone rather than in a mob or crowd – often in a head and shoulders shot, to remind us that his world is cerebral, rather than corporeal (see plate 8.2). The patriarch is always portrayed fully clothed, a figure standing upright in a dark business suit, the photo often cropped just below the belt. As Stallybrass and White (1986) have argued, the bourgeois body ignores its lower parts and is most correctly presented upright.

> The verticalness of the bourgeois body is primarily emphasised in the education of the child as s/he grows up. The lower bodily stratum is regulated or denied, as far as possible by the correct posture ('stand up straight', 'don't squat', 'don't kneel on all fours' – the position of servants and savages) and by the censoring of lower 'bodily' references along with bodily wastes. (pp. 144–5)

This is particularly the case in representations of masculine images of authority. Women as 'Others' are more likely to be shown in non-vertical poses, as I shall illustrate below.

Plate 8.2 Head and shoulders
Source: photo by Kippa Matthews

But these sober, clothed patriarchs – perhaps the nearest image of a disembodied rational mind available – are under threat. In the corporate finance divisions in all three of the banks in my study, what we might characterise as 'the new men of the City' have made an appearance. These men, who have been recruited since Big Bang, present a different version of masculinity – that of a slick young pretender or prince, a patriarch in waiting perhaps. Despite the impeccable educational credentials of many of the younger corporate financiers – from the 'right' schools and universities, still members of a social elite – they 'do' their masculinity in different ways from their predecessors. These patriarchs in waiting are distinguished by their youthful appearance, energy, activity and virility. Interested in clothes, the body and performance, they are, as Lewis (1989) suggested, 'American' or international figures, rather than representatives of that particular bourgeois version of Englishness that dominated investment banks for a hundred years between the 1880s and the 1980s.

The world of these younger corporate heroes is no longer entirely cerebral and upright. In media representations, these young, white, clean-cut men present a particular heterosexual style (see plate 8.3). They are seriously sexy in a self-confident, moneyed way. The corporate finance division has, in the words of one interviewee, 'a special gloss to it because it's the exciting star-takers' (man, 28, Bluebros). And as an older male

Plate 8.3 Young, and sexy, princes
Source: Guardian; photo by David Ferguson

respondent remarked, 'the corporate area has always recruited high fliers. It is the glamorous side of investment banking' (director, Northbank).

But glamour has to be worked at to be achieved. Although these young high fliers are the men who eventually expect to become directors of corporate finance, their presentation of self in the workplace is different from that of their senior colleagues. They are much more conscious of the significance of an embodied performance than their 'fathers' who still dominate the most prestigious positions. Rather than regarding work as a series of bureaucratic or technical tasks to be performed by a highly trained analytical mind, these young men are perhaps even more aware of the nature of interactive service work – the inseparability of their bodily performance from the product being sold – than their peers on the floors and in the dealing rooms. A wide range of comments from younger men in corporate positions illustrates their attitudes: 'We only have one thing to sell and that's ourselves', 'Merchant bankers have to be presentable and come in and convince' and 'You have to persuade people that you know better than they do.'

Several respondents talked at length about the type of performance that is required to be successful:

Your success depends on how you persuade people to value your abilities and brain power. It's about self-confidence. 100 per cent so. (man, 28, mergers and acquisitions, Bluebros)

A fair per cent of the time is just being polite to people – getting out making new clients, keeping our relationships with existing ones. ... Some banks have calling officers who are people who literally go and take clients out to lunch and talk to them in very general terms. (man, 28, manager, capital markets, Bluebros)

It's not just the quality of your work that matters although that's important. It's only one of the things that's considered along with your personal position. I mean, I think that one of the strongest characteristics of someone in this business must be the ability to talk convincingly to their clients, and in a way it's almost a politician's job because if you really analyse it, what are you doing? You're selling somebody the idea that you know better than them. Somebody who can wheel the ... oil the wheels rather, know the right people and be convincing. So really the ability to get on with people and go out there and sell is essential to my mind. (man, 26, analyst, mergers and acquisitions, Northbank)

These men revealed how important the body, its maintenance and discipline, is in the production of a convincing performance. A wide range of unsolicited remarks were made about image and self-presentation. Almost everyone referred to their clothing, style and weight in the interviews. Weight seemed particularly significant. The second half of the twentieth century has seen the triumph of the cult of the body and thinness for men as well as women, with 'the last bastions of corpulence amongst the working class now under siege' (Featherstone, 1991b, p. 184). In an image-conscious, class-conscious and youthful occupation like merchant banking, weight (or rather lack of it) is a crucial element of success for men as much as for women. The young men in corporate finance presented an astonishingly physically uniform appearance – the majority of them of average height and suitable weight for that height, and virtually all of them white. That the respondents were aware of this uniformity is clear from the protestation: 'We are not all clones, you know' (male, 28, assistant director, Northbank). Another respondent, in a more senior position in the same bank, had remarked earlier that:

It's curious because they all look exactly the same when they pop in at 25 or 26.

But, as she went on to explain, looks are not everything; flair is important too:

Some of them turn out to be wonderful and have a natural flair for it and some of them don't. You have to like it, I think. (female director, Northbank)

So on this side of the bank, too, work performance is referred to in naturalistic and embodied ways – flair and liking: attributes that many feminists have argued are more commonly presented as feminised. But while flair is intangible and may be difficult to cultivate, it was clear that bodily appearance can be manipulated and improved. As Shilling (1993) has argued, 'the body is increasingly a phenomenon of options and choices' (p. 3). The body is a flexible object that can be disciplined by diet and exercise to achieve normalisation, and those with the necessary resources are expected to maintain and improve it. For many men in the sedentary occupations that predominate in corporate finance, the maintenance of a sleek body required considerable effort and expenditure. More than a third of the male respondents worked out on a regular basis, for example, and almost a half were actively involved in sporting activities. It was also usual for men in managerial positions to openly 'discipline' their subordinates: 'I tell people in my team to look after themselves, sort out their BO or weight. You have got to look good' argued a male interviewee who was an assistant director responsible for a team of ten people, all of them men. Another man in a similar position reported that 'I often tell people, in a nice way, if I can, to get their hair cut, or to buy a deodorant'. And, as he explained, using a revealing class metaphor, self-improvement is possible, if not limitless:

It's no good putting someone in a frock coat if they should be in a donkey jacket, but you can make yourself look better with hard work. (assistant director, Northbank)

Clearly, corporeality has a materiality that matters, and not all applicants to enter the world of high finance are given the option to manipulate their appearance. Indeed, bodily size may be a barrier to entry. There were no obviously overweight people among those who were interviewed and, as one respondent candidly admitted, 'If someone was very fat or ugly it would make a difference.' Reflecting on a recent job applicant who was, according to this respondent, three or four stones overweight, he continued:

The fact that he was very large is going to weigh on the client's mind. ... We don't recruit physical stereotypes but we are selling a service and if people don't want to buy the service from that person ... well . . . (man, 28, assistant director, Northbank)

Bourdieu (1984) also drew attention to the significance of bodily image and weight in his work on new middle-class professions in France. He too distinguished younger from older men, arguing that the new bourgeoisie is much more body-conscious than the old guard, and contrasting 'the pompous, pot-bellied patron and the slim, sun-tanned cadre' (p. 311).

Closely related to the body *per se* is personal appearance, the body's extension into dress. The appearance of a worker makes it possible to assess the extent of bodily discipline or docility, or alternatively to assess visible strategies of resistance. In professional interactive service occupations, by comparison with routine service jobs, where bodily performance is carefully controlled and standardised through an explicit script and uniform, disciplining the body through overt codes and corporate uniforms is not common. However, informal norms are clearly important and a limited set of possible dress styles is available for professional workers. Here is Fiske (1993), reporting the advice given to male candidates for professional employment in the USA:

'The lower tip of the tie should come to the top or center of the belt buckle and the back of the tie should go through the label so it cannot escape control and reveal its undisciplined self to the interviewer. The belt should not only be new, but should show no sign of weight loss or gain. The body of the candidate should be totally disciplined, and should indicate that it is always controllable. Weight gain or loss are signs of a body breaking out of control and having to be redisciplined. The tie relates to the belt symmetrically, producing the body as aesthetically balanced around both vertical and horizontal axes. the aesthetics of symmetry, of the repetition and balance of form, represents human control over nature. Nature is asymmetrical, ever changing and growing. Aesthetic form is static, completed, controlled.' (p. 59)

The male body must not be associated, like the female body, with nature or sexuality.

In the corporate world, the standard male dress is a dark suit, shirt and tie and black shoes. A male assistant director explained the position at Bluebros:

There is an unwritten rule here about dress. Of course guys are going to come in here in suits, but there's a lot about the sort of style and colour of the suits for example. I mean you, I don't think you'd find anyone in here in a brown suit for example. But I mean even something like this, which is light grey, is a little bit different and causes a little bit of a, well it's just a little bit out of the ordinary, you know. Dark blues and greys are very acceptable, and anything else is noticeable really. Little things, like Barbour jackets, which basically are unofficially not allowed to be worn, because you've got to wear long overcoats and so on and so forth. So I think dress is a code, I mean the whole sort of image.

For a man so astute about male distinctions, he had a curious blindness when it came to women. When I asked 'what about women?' he replied, 'I'm sure the dress code applies equally, um ... I couldn't sort of give you the detail of it, but I'm sure it does.'

Other respondents in the other banks confirmed the generality of these rules of masculine dress. Thus, a male senior executive at Merbank routinely advised his subordinates that 'only dark suits are permissible. To wear a brown suit in the City is unforgivable.'

The cut, style and quality of men's clothing, as well as its colour, are crucial distinguishing characteristics which are read by clients and co-workers alike to place and evaluate both the adviser and the advice he or she is giving.

I may advise them where to buy their shirts, not to wear a Marks and Spencer's suit but to buy something a bit better.

And deviations from these norms are not sanctioned:

Someone wore short sleeves instead of long ones with cuff links and he's been, I mean, berated so many times for not having a proper shirt on ... you see, there's all these codes. (female financial administrator, Northbank)

Male resistance to bodily normalisation is possible only through the manipulation of details. Signs of rebellion may be demonstrated in the choice of tie and braces:

The most men can do is wear tartan socks, and nobody can really see them, or a large tie or braces. Some of the braces are amazing and some look as if the dog barfed on them. (woman, 37, executive, Bluebros)

There's no ponytails and earrings here – they are the preserve of traders. Braces are about the only experiments seen. (woman, 30, analyst, Northbank)

A slightly more visible form of rebellion for men is through individual variations on the theme of short hair, although even this form of transgression attracts ridicule. Thus:

One younger dealer saw *Wall Street* and got a Gordon [Gekko] haircut. But he got the mickey taken so badly he changed it. (female financial administrator, Northbank)

Instead of workplace transgressions, a number of men resorted to the language of masquerade, regarding their performance at work as just one part of their identity. This comment on the appearance of a subordinate is representative:

There's somebody who works for me who's only 22 years old, and you know he has a very short haircut, but apart from that, I mean I've seen him on a weekend and I know he's a young guy basically, and he's very sharp and he's good, but on a weekend . . . I'm sure if Robert [the director of their section] saw him on a weekend with a bandanna on his head and so on, then it would be a whole different ball game ... and his two earrings and everything else, but the bottom line is this guy comes in, conforms during the week, and umm, to be honest, it doesn't really bother me. (man, 31, financial control, Northbank)

I detected, however, a distinct note of yearning to be ten years younger with pierced ears in this man's comments.

I shall return to the metaphor of masquerade at the end of the chapter, suggesting that the ways in which it has been used in theories of feminine identity might profitably be extended to investigations of multiple ways of doing masculinity. Rather than the centred and singular concept of a masculine identity that is used as a comparison to a more fluid feminine sense of self, it seems that young men in service occupations have a view of themselves and their gendered subjectivity as complex and multiple. First, however, I turn briefly to everyday interactions with colleagues and clients, to examine the evidence for the continuation of that 'old' style of City working that revolves around personal contacts, networking and 'old boys' clubs'.

HYBRID SUBJECTS: MALE BONDING
AND NETWORKING

Business does get done in the club and there are some clients who go off and have cosy dinners with the directors but it's not all done like that. (female manager, Bluebros)

In both general analyses of the changing nature of work and specific studies of the 'new' City, theorists have argued that the interpenetration of work and leisure is producing a new hybrid subject of service-class worker who is always on display. I want to argue that the hybrid male subjects of the 'new' City are not new at all, but are direct descendants of their 'fathers' who also mixed work and play, albeit in different locations. The dominance of a new, slim and fit bodily image has merely displaced the location from old-style male clubs to the sports field and club. In the displacement, however, women remain largely excluded.

Investment banking is, by definition, about networking and developing personal contacts. As the dealers, market makers and salesmen explained earlier, it all lies in making the client feel special and corporate finance is no exception to this rule. It is the ways in which relationships are made, developed and cemented that vary. The interpenetration of the worlds of work and leisure is habitual: 'hard to separate' in one director's words. Senior employees in particular are expected to participate in a range of activities, both sporting and cultural, outside 'working hours'. And as a number of women pointed out, many of their male colleagues further blurred the links between home and work by inviting their wives or female partners to elite social occasions, disadvantaging women without partners or with partners who were not prepared to participate to order. Senior women bankers were thus seen as doubly different: they were neither wives nor appropriately sexed as workers.

The image of this side of investment banking as a high-status, high-class arena was confirmed by the list of social events patronised by the bankers whom I interviewed. Key sporting features, tennis at Wimbledon and rugby at Twickenham were mentioned many times, as were cultural events such as the opera at Covent Garden and Glyndebourne. Indeed, the best illustration of the cultural capital of these elite bankers is an explanation by one respondent, a woman from the Antipodes, of why she did *not* fit into the cultural ambience of Bluebros:

I'm not interested in beagles, I don't want a wine cellar, I'm not interested in horse trials, it doesn't matter to me who wins Wimbledon, if I go to the opera it doesn't have to be Glyndebourne because I go to listen to the music.

Although networking in an informal or leisure-based way is clearly important in developing good client relationships, the men whom I interviewed no longer conformed to mores of the 'old' City in the sense of belonging to the conventional London clubs. Indeed, the younger men expressed scorn at the notion and suggested that 'those days are gone for good' or more strongly, 'I wouldn't be seen dead in one of those places'. Only three men among the entire group of interviewees belonged to what may be regarded as the traditional gentleman's club.

However, both men and women argued that informal social networks among men, whether built up at school and university or in sports clubs, were still an aspect of women's exclusion in this side of investment banking.

I think men have always been quite sort of good at networking, bonding, whether it's from going to public school or to rugby matches together. I always think it probably operates at a subconscious level but it's none the less quite powerful. I don't think anybody thinks consciously 'Right, we'll give that job to J. Bloggs because he's a good sort or we went to the rugby with him.' It's more likely to be in their subconscious 'he seems to be, he seems OK' maybe because of some sort of networking or bonding that has taken place elsewhere that they think they like him. (female assistant director, venture capital, Northbank)

I think the clubby City has changed. I think it has changed but there is still this informal kind of male networking that, perhaps, makes it even harder for women to get in and challenge. (woman, 29, assistant director, corporate finance, Merbank)

For the young princes it was this sort of informal networking – in pubs and clubs, on the football or rugby pitches at the weekend – as well as their shared school experiences that constructed bonds between them and excluded women. Although these young princes were different from their more macho colleagues elsewhere in the banks, their way of doing masculinity still left women on the outside. So although the older form of patriarchal masculinity may now be vanishing, women still have to find a way of doing gender at work that constructs them as not only different but acceptably different and equal.

REPRESENTING WOMEN: PRINCESSES AND OLDER WOMEN

What about representations of women? I have already broached the question of how women present themselves and construct a workplace performance in the worlds of banking when they are clearly not masculine, neither patriarchs nor princes. In chapter 6 the impossibility

Plate 8.4 Princesses: objects of male desire?
Source: Rapho; photo by Lily Franey

of a successful performance as an honorary male was illustrated. Other performances or roles based on familial and sexualised imagery tend to reaffirm women's exclusion or subordinate position. In a move from the language of roles to that of performance, I want to suggest here that parodic forms of femininity operate as subversive performances in highly masculinised workplaces like investment banks. Such parodies may enable powerful and successful women to challenge male dominance. The rub arises in the way I have phrased this statement. It seemed from my interviews that it was only women who had achieved a certain level of power and status who were able to transgress accepted feminine norms. Parodic femininity may thus enhance the position of women but it seems to be rather a consequence of power rather than a cause of it, although cross-sectional studies cannot fully substantiate this assertion.

Before turning to the words of powerful women, images of women on the pages of the financial press are evaluated. Photographs of women so rarely appear on the business pages that when they do, their presence is marked. The style of photography and the location of the women immediately marks out their difference from representations of powerful men. There is often an emphasis on the whole body or on a close-up shot of the face rather than a head and shoulders business-like shot. In plate 8.4, a conventional image of femininity is portrayed – the women are young, long-haired and attractive.

A second noticeable feature of images of women in the financial sector is that they are often pictured either without an identifiable location, outside or in their homes rather than in their offices in the bank, let alone on the trading floor. Countering the images of energetic, active and virile masculinity, women tend to be represented as passive and domestic, as private rather than public, and so out of place in the public arena of work. Images of more senior women also emphasise their difference, but the difference is not always straightforwardly that of sexual difference or of passivity. Although the femininity of these women is emphasised, they are also women 'of a certain age', smart, confident, knowledgeable and experienced. These women are no longer 'princesses', nor even mistresses. Plate 8.5 shows a woman who was, at the time, a director of Charterhouse. Although she is portrayed in a typically feminine pose, a close shot, a sideways glance, the object of the masculinist gaze, the impression is still one of somebody to be reckoned with. This is a woman who is clearly no longer a girl but nor is she in the conventional image of middle-aged women – neither a housewife nor a schoolmarm. This woman is clearly at ease with herself.

I was also intrigued by the echo of a reference to Madonna's track 'Material Girl' in the (inappropriate) headline to the accompanying article, 'Material girls know how to spend it'. Madonna is the arch manipulator of gender and sexual identities (Schwichtenberg, 1993), a prime example of a woman both constructed through representations and able to sell multiple versions of herself.

As women enter powerful positions in the workplace, and older women even scale the pinnacles of power, a certain anxiety among men has become evident. A displacement of women as the exclusive representations of desire and pleasure has begun to take place. Increasingly, the sex objects are men, partly in terms of their bodily attributes (the hair and sultry pout, perhaps, of the young men in plate 8.3) but partly because of what also might be termed their mind attributes. Thus, 'the bright young executive or bond dealer, who outsmarts the competition' is now a sex object (Grace, 1991, p. 118). However, the limits of the displacement of (hetero)sexual desire suggested by Grace – in media images at least – are made clear in plate 8.6. This photograph of young French women traders so challenged conventional images of the trading floor and its associations with masculine virility that it appeared on the front page of every British daily paper in August 1993, with the sole exception of the *Financial Times* which carried it on page 3. That this image was so widely circulated demonstrates how unusual – even shocking – the association of young, sexy women and the financial and masculine power of traders

Plate 8.5 Female authority?
Source: Observer, 1992; photo by David Rose

is. Their emphatic gestures and facial grimaces challenge conventional images of feminine passivity and, no doubt, induced a good dose of the anxiety that Grace detected. It seems here that the masculinised power of traders might be disruptable, albeit through the sexualised power of young women. This clearly is an image of women who can, in the inimitable words of one of my respondents, 'give as good as they get'. And yet, parodic femininity causes an unease among young women. In an unsettling move, the two young French women, rather than celebrating their evident power in the press image, were appalled at the way in which they had been represented and demanded publication of a different image in the British national press on the following day. The image

Plate 8.6 Outrageous femininity
Source: Guardian; photo by Lionel Cironneau

they chose was the conventional representation of passive femininity, outside rather than inside their workplace (already illustrated in plate 8.4). The soft waves of their hair, the gesture of the hand, allow desire rather than authority to be read from their poses. The princess is re-established in her proper place.

FEMININE PARODIES AND MASQUERADES

I want now to present material from the transcripts that demonstrates feminine parodies. In chapter 6, I argued that a masculinised perform- ance by women in the workplace is doomed to failure. A number of commentators, drawing on their case studies of women in male-domi- nated organisations, have suggested that it is not until the post-menopau- sal period in women's lives that such a parody has any chance of success at all. Thus, Rodgers (1981) argued, in the context of her work on women in the British parliament, that older women who have estab- lished their position with difficulty are often overtly hostile to younger women who display attributes of embodied femininity, such as preg- nancy, too openly. She suggests that:

> Women whose success has been geared to the male construct have dis- carded the symbols by which they would be anchored into the traditional domain of domesticity and nature. The fear that if one of their women colleagues openly combines the public symbols with the female domestic ones, they themselves will be at risk of being seen as women, which, on some levels they, of course, are. Their position in the dominant category is after all a tenuous one. (pp. 60–1)

In the case of the three banks, however, I found exactly the reverse situation. As I showed in chapter 6, it was younger rather than older women, in the main, who attempted a masculine masquerade. Older women seem to recognise that a display of overt femininity confers ad- vantages, realising that ' "feminine" decorativeness may function "subversively" in professional contexts which are dominated by highly masculinist norms' (Bordo, 1993, p. 193). Bordo's arguments are close to Butler's suggestion that parodies of the regulatory norm cause 'gender trouble'.

A good number of the women I interviewed, both young and older, in junior as well as senior positions, clearly recognised the advantages of being a woman:

> You obviously stand out because you are a woman … it could be to your advantage; they remember you more if you are a woman. But equally, they might also … think 'oh, that awful woman from Northbank with that dreadful laugh'. So it can cut both ways. (woman, 30, senior analyst, Northbank)

Earlier in the interview, this woman had been less ambivalent about the advantages of being female.

Respondents at the other banks made similar remarks. For example a

25-year-old executive in the corporate finance section of Bluebros suggested:

As long as you are very competent you can use being a woman to your advantage. It might be easier to gain a client and his confidence. I worked for clients briefly because someone was off on holiday and they demanded me back because they just love having a girl on the account.

Another woman spoke very clearly about what she termed tricks and methods of manipulation:

It's a strength being a female and you should use it, use it to your best advantage. You get a chance to speak maybe when others don't; you can dress for a certain meeting in a way that will instantly change the atmosphere slightly or I mean you start to learn that there are things you can do that manipulate things. You can influence things by being more female or less female. (woman, 30, manager, corporate finance)

This description of 'being more female or less female' is a clear recognition of the significance of a fluid gender performance in the workplace. This woman expanded on her method of 'doing gender' at work:

If you walk in the door and you're properly dressed and you've got a smile on and you just a little bit like, you know, you're reasonably put together, uhm, you know, that instantly takes them back a tiny bit because they, they usually expect a woman to look slightly like the back end of a bus. There is a sort of perception that some women in business are very aggressive and harsh, and so the next trick is not to be. ... It's all tactics. The other thing that you do that surprises them even more having been female and hopefully feminine is you talk business. And so that comes as a surprise because then that doesn't add up, you know it doesn't, it's a bit confusing and you make sure that you ask them some pretty pertinent questions.

It was in general only the most senior women who recognised the unambivalent advantages of a subversive feminised performance. Several women commented in similar words that they have to 'be careful not to give the wrong vibes'. Age was not a significant factor, as some of the most senior women were relatively young. It is rather an ability to command respect at the same time as constructing a fluid and varying performance. One woman expressed particularly clearly the ways in which she deliberately adopted different stereotypical images of femininity to suit the circumstances and the location.

It depends who I'm going to be seeing. Sometimes I'll choose the 'executive bimbo' look; at other times, like today when I've got to make a cold call, it's easiest if I look as if I'll blend into the background. I think this [a plain but very smart tailored blue dress] looks tremendously, you know, professional. No statement about me at all. 'Don't look at me, look at these papers I'm talking to you about.' But I wear high heels too, so I'm six feet tall when I stand up. And I think that commands some small sense of 'well, I'd probably better listen to her, at least for a little while'. I do dress quite consciously because you've got to have some fun in life, and sometimes wearing a leather skirt to work is just fun because you know they can't cope with it. (manager, Bluebros)

The parallels between this quotation and Judith Williamson's (1992) reflections on her own sense of self in her introduction to the work of the feminist photographer Cindy Sherman, that mistress of masquerade, are striking.

When I rummage through my wardrobe in the morning I am not merely faced with a choice of what to wear. I am faced with a choice of images: the difference between a smart suit and a pair of overalls, a leather skirt and a cotton frock, is not just one of fabric and style but one of identity. You know perfectly well that you will be seen differently for the whole day, depending on what you put on; you will appear as a particular type of woman with one particular identity which excludes others. The black leather skirt rather rules out girlish innocence, oily overalls tend to exclude sophistication, ditto smart suit and radical feminism. Often I have wished I could put them on all together, or appear simultaneously in every possible outfit, just to say, Fuck you, for thinking any one of these is me. But also, See, I can be all of them. (p. 222)

An older woman suggested that while she may be past a sexualised feminine parody, it works as a strategy of confusion for other women:

I just use what I am. I don't turn up disguised as an executive bimbo because I'm not really of an age to do that. Some women do use that image. Some women are disguised as bimbos and it turns out there's a first-class brain hammering away underneath all that. (51-year-old director, Northbank)

The image of the body as a disguise for the brain is vivid.

It was noticeable that almost half of the (tiny) number of the most senior women whom I interviewed were not English. Their 'double out-sider' status seemed to give them an additional freedom to break hegemonic norms of under-stated femininity and expected social behaviour.

I have a real advantage. Since I'm American nobody has any particular idea of what I should be like or they expect me to be a little bit loud. I can say something naff or ask a question that is indiscreet or things like that and it's not out of character for what people expect an American to do. And they don't mind if an American woman is in a business role. American women don't stay at home necessarily and their wife isn't an American woman so they don't compare me to her.

Another respondent was also, in her own words, able to 'play the outrageous wild colonial girl' and behave in meetings in ways that challenged British conventions. There are interesting parallels here with the earlier work of Epstein (1973) on the status of black women lawyers in the USA. Epstein found that black women explained their success by the multiple 'deviant' statuses undermining narrow stereotypical responses – what she terms 'the positive effects of the multiple negative' and I have called the double outsider status.

It must be emphasised, however, that the women in my study were not only a minority, but also seemed secure in their own version(s) of femininity and in their careers. As I suggested above, it is hard to conclude whether their femininity was a cause or a consequence of their success. Similar findings about the adoption of a parodic femininity by women in high-status professional occupations have been documented by Watson (1992) in her study of the professional Civil Service in England and by Pringle (1993) in her comparison of women medical consultants in Australia and Great Britain, although both scholars are as hesitant as I am about the direction of the relationship between parody and power.

UNEASY SEDUCTION: MASQUERADE OR THE 'REAL' SELF

While metaphors of performance, disguise and masquerade were commonly used by women respondents, it became clear from the transcripts that many women felt uneasy about the ways in which they used feminised parodies at work. Significant numbers of women spoke openly to me about how they used their sexuality and femininity to seduce their colleagues, but particularly their clients, albeit not in the literal sense. They described the ways in which the majority of interactions between themselves and clients were based on the manipulation of conventional heterosexual norms of attraction between the opposite sexes. The language in the following quotations, for example, is that of flirtation:

I'm no good with a client I am not interested in or he in me ... if there is no spark in a relationship, you just can't turn it on.

I have the ability to listen and make polite noises. I gain clients' confidence. It's a different way of doing things.

And, more explicitly:

Women seduce their clients, not literally. I'm quite certain it's done that way. (female director, Northbank)

While this woman was confident in her power to attract and control clients, others enunciated feelings of unease about their performance, unhappy in their adoption and exploitation of a parodic femininity which they found demeaning.

If you are an attractive woman in this environment it can help on the male side of things. Frankly you have to learn to use all your assets and swallow your pride sometimes because in some form or other, obviously not in the literal sense, but in some form or other, it can be a form of prostitution of your sex ... and you, hmm, and you ... you have to learn to cope with that. (woman, 34, sales, Bluebros)

This respondent confirms Hochschild's contention that interactive service work, where the manipulation of bodily images and emotions is an integral part of selling a product, may lead to workers becoming alienated from their feelings. Many women not only explicitly used the language of performance to describe everyday social interaction in the workplace but also suggested that their workplace persona was unreal. They talked about 'building up a shell', of 'adopting a different sense of myself', of 'not using my real personality'. It seemed that many of the women whom I interviewed held to an essentialist notion of a unitary self and were troubled by what they saw as their falsehoods at work. Here, we might return to feminist theorists in order to understand these feelings of unease.

In a provocative paper, originally published in 1929 but recently influential again, Joan Riviere (1986) documented the implications for women who took on a masculine identity in order to compete in the professions. She suggested that women who take on a masculine identity may also put on 'a mask of womanliness' or masquerade in a feminine guise in order to 'avert anxiety and the retribution feared from men' (p. 35). And here we see the echoes of the male bankers who were at ease neither with masculine women nor with feminine women. In Riviere's case notes, which focus on a woman university lecturer, it is suggested that she copes with her male colleagues by being flippant or frivolous; that 'she has to treat the situation of displaying her masculinity to men as a "game", as something not real, as a "joke"' (p. 39). Irigaray (1977) also understood femininity in similar ways. She described the mimicry that she saw as constitutive of feminine subjectivity as a 'masquerade of femininity' in which 'the woman loses herself by playing on her femininity'. The game of femininity is one which is imposed on women by male values and language. The sense of loss identified by Irigaray parallels an unease felt by many of my respondents. Work in cultural studies and film theory on analyses of representations of women in the media also emphasises that the cultural category of gender is constituted on the terrain of representation. These theorists have shown how the representation of femininity rests on structures of oppression that necessitate the dominated group seeing through the eyes and categories of the dominant culture (Mulvey, 1989; Kuhn, 1985; Wolff, 1990). In negotiating this alienation of identity, women are led into simulating appearances of femininity through masks and masquerade in an infinite regress. As Schwichtenberg argued, we might understand 'the mutable cultural underpinnings of femininity as an exaggeration in which woman "plays" at herself, playing a part' (1993, p. 133).

CONCLUSIONS

It is not clear, however, from Butler's work, and indeed from mine, quite what are the implications of the notion of masquerade for an individual's sense of themselves. Masquerade may either be theorised as the performative production of a sexual ontology, an appearing that makes itself convincing as a 'being', or it can be defined as a denial of a feminine desire. This latter case, which is closer to Irigaray's understanding of woman, seems to presuppose some prior ontological femininity, unrepresented by the phallic economy. These two views have different consequences both for the interpretation of actions and for strategic decisions about workplace reform. As Butler (1990a) argued, 'the former task would engage a critical reflection on gender ontology as parodic (de)construction and, perhaps, pursue the mobile possibilities of the slippery distinction between "appearing" and "being". . . . The latter would initiate feminist strategies of unmasking in order to uncover or release whatever feminine desire has remained suppressed within the terms of the phallic economy' (p. 47). As I have shown, my respondents spoke in terms of the second belief. To them a particular feminine performance at work masked their being, what they termed the 'real me'.

In her own arguments about the possibilities for gender politics, however, Butler (1990a) seems to reject this latter position in suggesting that there can never be any version of a transcendent gender, an idealised freedom in the classical liberal mode. Power, she argued, 'can neither be withdrawn nor refused, but only redeployed . . . the normative focus for gay and lesbian practice [and I would suggest for straight feminist politics] ought to be on the subversive and parodic redeployment of power rather than on the impossible fantasy of its full-scale transcendence' (p. 124). Thus, she argues, it is impossible to refuse to engage with the norms of heterosexuality: all transgressive actions are in an important sense an engagement with them, but 'parodic contest and display . . . rob compulsory heterosexuality of its claims to naturalness and originality' (p. 124). But the problem with this strategy, as Butler herself recognised, is that such a politics requires the category from which it is excluded.

It seems to me, however, that this is the place to start. It is impossible to deny the strength of the discourses that construct an idealised and oppositional masculinity and femininity. This seems to explain the first position – a belief in a transcendent femininity. As other feminist theorists have long argued, it is important to explore 'the problem of the investments that subjects have in complying with the practices of representation' (Threadgold and Cranny-Francis, 1990, p. 7). The idea of loss of self/femininity seems a fruitful way forward in an exploration of why so many women do not achieve the really powerful positions, and why some feel dismayed when they do. But it also seems apparent that an investigation of the different ways in which the compulsory heterosexual gender regime – the norms of heterosexuality which structure and dominate organisations from the workplace to the school to the family – might be displaced, disrupted and parodied will assist in the dismantling of that very regime. It is increasingly clear that not only are there multiple femininities but there are different ways of doing masculinity and in the shift to a service-based economy and a growing emphasis on interactive work practices, alternative embodied performances are gaining ground. While the idealised notion of an individual continues to dominate the social practices of many organisations, shaping, among other areas, career structures, working patterns and daily interactions, it is evident that the new forms of work and alternative ways of doing gender are mutually constitutive. This recognition applies with as much force to the constitution of masculinities as to femininities.

In this study, the dominance of a version of hegemonic masculinity was uncovered, revolving around a variant of an embodied, manly, heterosexualised class-based masculinity, specific to the setting (the arena or location of everyday social interactions), the age and, to a lesser extent, the class of the participants. It is clear that these variations on a theme disempower a range of 'Others', not only women but men from different class, ethnic and educational backgrounds. The disruption and transgression of this regime, in the main by women in powerful positions but also through alternative versions of masculinity, should open a space for other ways of being. In this way, progress may be made towards Butler's demand for thorough-going critique and redeployment of the categories of gendered identity themselves. Although notions of gender are tightly bound up with the workplace and with notions of work, it is in the current reconfiguration of the social division of labour and the reorganisation of work in the service sector that the possibilities for change perhaps lie.

9

Conclusions: Rethinking Work/Places

I would say that the City is still relatively male-dominated and the reason for this is that it's always been male-dominated. Historically and in the early days it was an old boy's club, the emphasis on old boy's club, and I don't think there's been any fundamental changes in City practice and/or technology, which have caused men who are running the place, in general terms, to say 'hey, lads, this is an opportunity for women'. I don't think it's worked like that. I think what's happened is there've been a number of women, bright women, determined women, who've actually broken down the barriers. I don't think one barrier has been put down. They've all stayed up. . . . Even if there is such a thing as a woman's way of doing things, I don't think that the environment and the City in general offer women the opportunity to turn things on its [sic] head and do things totally differently.

Male personnel director, Merbank

CITY CHANGES

Since the mid 1980s, the City of London has been marked by expansion and change. Its physical environment has been altered and rebuilt, new computerised systems of trading have been introduced, some successful, others a failure. Banks have expanded, declined, been taken over and even bankrupted. New workers have entered and left the City during rapid expansion, recession and slower recovery. Some have made and others have lost fortunes. However, despite unprecedented numbers of women gaining professional positions in the City, occupational sex stereotyping and the institutional and everyday structures of workplace interactions have maintained and reproduced gendered patterns of inequality at work. As I have shown here, both the embeddedness of patterns of domination and subordination in the institutional and organisational structures of the City and its constituent organisations, and local or small-scale daily inter-actions – the everyday 'doing' of gender and gender relations – are part of the construction of City women as different. Even though many occupa-tions in the 'new' City exemplify the traits of interactive or performative work, traits which are often characterised as feminine, men have, to a large extent, retained their old hegemonic dominance.

In order to uncover and explain this vexed persistence of gendered inequalities in the City, I have argued that it is necessary to link together the analysis of material structures of power and the subjective constitution of the self. I hope I have demonstrated how a materialist/semiotic analysis of the workplace as a physical artefact and as an organisational structure, combined with an investigation of gendered performances, helps to explain the persistence of gender and class divisions in a 'new' City. I have set this dual approach in the context of overall changes in the structure of work in a service-based economy such as Britain's and in an outline of the growing importance of the financial services sector therein. In so doing, I have ranged across a variety of geographical or spatial scales. The analysis of situated conduct cannot reveal the whole story about the structures and mechanisms of inequality in the workplace, but neither can a singular focus on structures reveal all that is important about individuals' accommodation and resistance to structural circumstances. Thus, in the story told here, I have tried to show how widespread social attitudes about women's work, the changing circumstances of the City of London in the 1980s and early 1990s, popular images and representations of investment banking, and cultures of British banks combine to construct and regulate a restricted range of gender performances at work. A corresponding multiplicity of methods of analysis is needed to uncover the multidimensional and interconnected construction of inequality in the workplace. Consequently, I have drawn not only on historical and statistical analyses but also on contextual, narrative, ethnographic and interactional approaches.

In speculations about the changing nature of work in industrial economies in the second half of the twentieth century, two alternative scenarios about the links between work, education, class and gender have been common. In the first, the post-industrial model associated with Daniel Bell (1973), it was argued that recruitment to and social mobility within the ranks of the state and private sector professions and scientific occupations would increasingly depend upon the possession of the right educational qualifications rather than tradition and status-based distinctions resulting from family connections. The ranks of high-status professional and scientific workers would therefore expand from a small elite to include a broader-based and more equitable group of workers. These arguments have their parallel in Crompton (1992), and Crompton and Sanderson's (1990) arguments about credentialism. If women are among those with the right qualifications and if Bell was correct, then clearly women should be among the new and expanded professional elite. There has, indeed, been an increasing demand for qualifications in the British economy, and increasingly large numbers of women now possess such qualifications. And yet, as numerous studies have demonstrated, their

penetration of the highest levels of occupational power and status remains limited.

An alternative relationship between credentialism and the occupational structure was suggested by Collins (1979), drawing on Weberian
notions of social exclusion. Rather than the increasing possession of
credentials being connected to greater social mobility, Collins suggested
that it leads instead to a deflation in their value. A struggle therefore
arises within the middle class for access to elite institutions and to the
most socially valued professions, as the middle class becomes increasingly
dependent on professional qualifications and occupations as a means of
the intergenerational reproduction of social status and a privileged lifestyle rather than on familial connections. Thus, access to particular elite
institutions retains, and even gains in, its significance for entry to the
highest-status, or highest-paid, occupations.

In the case of merchant banking, it seems that both processes are at
work. The expansion of the industry in the 1980s led to the entry of
growing numbers of workers from less elite backgrounds and a somewhat
wider range of educational institutions, and yet there remains a bias
towards the elite schools and universities. Indeed, in banking it is clear
that the old processes of selection and exclusion based on family background still maintain some strength. For women, the possession of educational credentials and the right class background is a partial counter to
the disadvantage of their sex, at least in their initial entrance to the world
of banking. This was made brutally clear to me in the comment made by
a senior woman and already quoted. Replying to my question about why
women had been recruited in growing numbers during the late 1980s
expansion, she explained, 'otherwise we would have had to have taken
men from the polytechnics' (a set of less elite British higher education
institutions now known as the 'new universities').

What both explanations of the relationships between class background,
gender and social mobility ignore, however, is the changing nature of
work at the end of the century. As I have illustrated, the British economy
is now dominated by occupations and jobs in which the ability to conform to a particular embodied workplace performance is crucial. Investment banking is among these occupations. The possession of a certain set
of personal characteristics and skills by bankers is crucial, not only in
recruitment and selection programmes but also in the production of an
acceptable workplace performance. Race, skin colour, weight and age
are important aspects of the suitability of prospective employees and of
how successful they become in selling the product they are promoting.
The disembodied ideal of the male bureaucrat in which rational advice
was constructed as a cerebral product, purportedly unconnected to the
specific embodiment of the purveyor of the advice, has been largely, if

not entirely, displaced in the contemporary world of high finance. The ability to construct a distinctive bodily image and gendered identity is an integral part of selling financial advice, making money and attaining power. In merchant banks, as in other interactive service occupations, corporeality – in the threefold sense of anatomical sex, gender identity and gender performance – is a crucial part of selling a service. However, as I have shown, there are several gender performances that are acceptable and appropriate fictions in the particular circumstances of the different arenas of merchant banking, with the important proviso that they are within an exclusively heterosexual scenario. I have suggested that in these circumstances the characteristics associated with femininity, conventionally assumed to be part of the reason for the disadvantaged position of women, may become a positive advantage. The establishment of masculine corporeality, the disruption of conventional dichotomised gender divisions and the acceptance, albeit limited, of 'complex and generative subject positions' (Butler, 1990b, p. 339) for men and for women seem to contain a liberatory promise. These changes may open a potential space for the development of a variety of coalitional strategies in the workplace, that neither fix the binary gender divide in place nor rely on a singular notion of equal opportunities or social justice.

And yet a less optimistic note needs adding. As I demonstrated in the first part of the book, women are still not well-represented in the highest-level occupations in merchant banks. Men continue to score more highly on evaluation and assessment schemes and are promoted more quickly. In addition, strong affiliation to the culture of a particular bank is an important part of success, and, as I have shown, the cultural construction of the banking world remains elitist and masculinist. Thus, the positional advantage of public school, elite university men on the one hand and well-educated but 'wild' traders and dealers on the other has not been as undermined as many commentators predicted by the changing nature of work in the City. The women I interviewed who have become successful seem to have done so by emphasising their difference from men in a parodic performance of femininity. However, among the small sample of the most senior women, they are also distinguished as different by their nationality. In such a small sample, it clearly is impossible to argue definitively that non-British origins, or at least a period of working elsewhere in the world, are crucial requirements for women's entry to the exclusive world of the City. Clearly, more comparative work is needed here, especially in banks based in the City of London but owned by US, Japanese and other capital. The specificity of British banks in the City of London, and indeed the differences between them, as I demonstrated, affect the cultural appropriateness of different social characteristics and gendered performances. These performances may not be valued in the same way, even in the same occupations, in banks imbued with the cultural values of other nations.

A further note to temper optimistic readings of women's potential for greater success also needs adding. It is clear that men in merchant banks have not been slow in seizing the advantages of an embodied and individualised performance. They have shown that they are just as able, even more able in many cases, to adopt the strategies required to 'sell themselves'. Optimistic commentators about the feminisation of management cultures and women's growing credentialism, and thus their prospects as managers and professionals, assume that gendered identities and behaviours in the workplace are fixed, that men and women enter into their working lives with a masculinised or feminised way of doing things already determined. But as recent work has shown, including this study, gendered identities and interactions in the working environment are, within bounds, fluid and negotiable. Men, as well as women, are able to construct differential performances in the workplace, while continuing to interpret them in ways congruent with hegemonic notions of masculinity. As Moore (1988) has argued, men, in a whole range of circumstances from leisure to work, are able to 'don the trappings of femininity without so much as a glance at the women whose clothes they have stolen' (p. 185). If, in the 1990s, workplace performances are changing, increasingly influenced by what we regard as feminine characteristics, then to retain their power and the monopoly of key positions, it is in men's interests to co-opt femininity, or a version of it. As Chapman (1988) has suggested, 'the future may be female, but I fear it may still belong to men' (p. 248). Feminine characteristics in a masculinised body may offer the best of all worlds. After all, if femininity is a masquerade, men can be women just as well as, if not better than, women.

THE CHANGING NATURE OF WORK AND EQUAL OPPORTUNITIES POLICIES

Where does this conclusion leave us in terms of the implications for equal opportunities policies in the workplace? In the wider economy, the growing polarisation of the workforce and the deepening of 'flexible' workplace practices, of casualisation, contract employment and general economic insecurity, have increased the risk of taking risks, of troubling the dominant gender regime and challenging hegemonic versions of masculinity and femininity. Creating gender trouble may not be the way to succeed. Nor is the overall political climate for utopian policy prescription auspicious: a sullen *fin de siècle* lack of confidence in both economic and social relations as an administration that has been in power too long struggles not to be defeated,[1] combined with a theoretical emphasis on difference and diversity that threatens to drift into a paralysing relativism, seems to have smothered critical thinking about equal opportunities and the introduction of measures based on a recognition of differences and divisions between women as well as between men and women.

Studies of gender relations in the workplace, and especially those whose dominant focus is women, often end with a discussion of 'women's way of doing things' – not only policies for altering hours, increasing maternity benefits, even introducing parental leave, but also stirring words about 'feminised' practices including praise at work, greater cooperation, fewer hierarchical structures and multi-skilling. Despite a certain unease with the essentialised notions that lie behind the concept of 'a woman's way' – evident in the quotation at the head of this chapter – it is clear that women's large-scale entry into the labour market, and their halting and uneven progress, but progress nevertheless, through the professions and into the new middle-class occupations in finance, advertising, and the media, have affected workplace practices. Drawing on more recent work on organisational culture and management styles, Raper (1994) has suggested that women benefit from the turn away from 'emotionless management' to a specifically female form of management that valorises an 'ethics of care' (Gilligan, 1982). Rosener (1994) similarly suggested that 'women are succeeding because and not in spite of certain characteristics generally considered to be feminine and inappropriate in leaders' (p. 122). To some extent, my findings substantiate Rosener's remark, although parodies of femininity are hardly what is usually intended by a 'woman's way of doing things'. And in banking, as one of my respondents noted, 'behind all that [the feminine masquerade] there's a fine brain [that is rational, cool and calculating, and so masculinist] ticking away'.

As the so-called feminine characteristics, which are somewhat uncritically advocated in the new management literature, have been developed in the face of long years of disadvantage, I feel less able to celebrate their significance than many psychologists or management specialists. Indeed, I would argue, the consequences of these 'female ways of doing things' have too often been negative. In a range of workplaces, management and employers have seized on a feminised rhetoric to downsize, delayer, restructure, and replace men by women in middle management in particular, in order to introduce new working practices and increase profits. It is also clear that the movement towards personalised styles and individualistic criteria of evaluation has undermined the meritocratic notions of worth and achievement that used to typify bureaucracies. The net result is that the relative evaluation of individuals against universalistic criteria is increasingly difficult. While not denying an iota of the pertinent critique of the implicit masculinist nature of the old attributes valued by purportedly universalistic assessment and evaluation schemes, it is ironic that, just as women are gaining access to formal examinations and professional credentials, the formal criteria of access to positions of power and status are becoming less valued. In the banks which I studied, equal opportunities policies became part of the official rhetoric of re-cruitment and promotion in the 1980s but it was clear that the shift away from older bureaucratic ways of comparing workers undermined their efficacy.

Conventional equal opportunity policies are based on the liberal no-tion of individual justice, in which similarly qualified individuals are ensured equal treatment, and cannot grapple with the deeply engrained attitudes about gender differences that construct women as a group as inferior. As has been shown here, women still do not present themselves in equal numbers for recruitment to merchant banks and seem not to progress through the hierarchy as quickly once recruited because the norms of City workplaces are inimical to women's interests, experiences and perspectives. Clearly attention to these differences by investment banks is in order, if only because they may be ignoring or losing highly qualified and skilled women employees. As Rhode (1990) has argued in her work on equal treatment, 'women ought not to have to seem just like men to gain equal respect, recognition and economic security' (p. 7), and, as I have shown here, the impossibility of being a man rules out this option for women. The alternative basis for policy – to stress women's difference from men – brings a different set of problems in its wake. If policies based on the affirmation of equal treatment of women run the risk of reinforcing the sets of values and institutional structures that they set out to challenge, strategies that emphasise women's differences from men tend to reinforce, even to celebrate, the very conditions that pro-duced the inequalities. An emphasis on difference tends to serve as 'in-equality's *post hoc* excuse for itself ... the outcome presented as its origin' (MacKinnon, 1990, p. 224) with 'the danger that measures apparently designed for women's special protection may end up by protecting them primarily from the benefits that men enjoy' (Jaggar, 1988, p. 244).

Clearly maternity is a special case, but while each bank had a scheme for maternity leave, for example, and the prospect of part-time work on return, these schemes were neither well defined nor well used. Many of the women, and the men, whom I interviewed argued that it is impossi-ble to work effectively on a part-time basis in a professional capacity in the financial world which involves close and daily interactions in the markets and with clients. However, many interviewees also stressed the difficulties of constructing a 'private' home life in an occupation where the boundaries between work and leisure are increasingly blurred. This seemed to be an issue for women in particular, leading to different career choices for some women compared with their male colleagues. Interesting work remains to be done on the women, and the small number of men, who choose not to compromise their 'other lives' and who leave merchant banking for less demanding careers.

Women's working lives still differ from men's, even among the highly educated, well-paid and mainly childless women whom I interviewed. As I showed in chapter 3, the most senior women in the sample had a different career pattern from men in equivalent positions, moving between occupations more frequently, or achieving success, in the memorable words of one, 'by accident'. As Bateson (1990) argued, for many women 'life is a work in progress, an improvisation' (p. 1). This is a pattern that perforce is becoming more common for men as well as for women in contemporary Britain (Dex and McCulloch, 1995). As women and growing numbers of men have to move between careers, ideally training and retraining to meet technological and other changes, the metaphor of work as performance takes on an increasing significance, as it begins to describe life-time changes as well as behaviour and interactions within any single occupation. The figures for stress among male professionals made insecure by the growing moves towards discontinuous or contract employment, even in such previous bastions of security as the British Civil Service, indicate that women may have an advantage here, accustomed as they are to more 'flexible' working lives. To seek to identify advantages for women in male disadvantage, however, is hardly ideal. Secure yet flexible employment, in which individual needs are considered by employers and the state alike in the context of a negotiated collective vision of more equitable workplace relations, seems a utopian impossibility at present, but should remain a long-term goal. As Young suggests in her vision of a more just society, what is required is attention 'to the institutional conditions necessary for the development and exercise of individual capacities and collective communication and cooperation' (Young, 1990a, p. 39). Perhaps above all, the aim is to dislodge gender difference, 'to challenge its centrality and its organising premises and to recast the terms in which gender relations have traditionally been debated' (Rhode, 1990, p. 7).

Theoretical dislodgement may be easier to achieve than material change. As I have shown here, in a particular sector of financial services the huge technological and regulatory changes of the last decade have not been reflected in changes in the social composition of the workforce. The City is a central element in British society, not only a leading edge sector in the economy but also a dominant part of the built environment of Greater London. These spaces of power are imbued with class and gender divisions which they, in turn, reinforce, and huge vested interests are bound up in the maintenance and reproduction of urban land use and spatial divisions. Land use divisions separate the spaces of power from the surrounding vernacular landscapes of residential and mixed shopping and industrial uses; the buildings of the financial powerscape remind the working class, people of colour and women of a history that has excluded them, while the internal spaces of these buildings reflect the continuing dominance of a predominantly white, male middle class. While the structure and nature of employment in the City may have changed, through the advent of new technologies, with increasing global interdependencies and with new, somewhat less paternalistic and patriarchal, even 'American' workplace practices, the class and gender composition of the City remains solidly biased towards middle-class men who are mirrored in the old and new City landscape. The places and practices of the City tell these men who they are – the masters of the universe with global money at their fingertips. Women may have entered investment banks in unprecedented numbers after Big Bang, but their presence remains marked as exceptional. While difference, diversity and multiple gendered performances are increasingly valued in many workplaces, it is clear that the City is resistant to radical change in its gendered construction. 'Fast' and serious money remains dominantly in the hands of men, and the love of money is a male affair.

NOTE

1   The success of 'New Labour' in the general election held on 1 May 1997 may alter this conclusion – I hope so! Just three weeks after the election, the Chancellor, Gordon Brown, had already given the Bank of England powers to determine interest rates and proposed to strengthen the regulatory powers of the Securities and Investment Board to restore confidence in Britain's financial services sector after the scandal-filled decade discussed in this book. As Hutton suggested in the *Observer* (25 May 97, p. 21), 'two of the key peices on the chessboard defending gentlemanly capitalism have, at a stroke, been removed'.

Appendix: The Field Work

The field work was carried out in a number of stages. In the first stage all investment banks with an address within or adjacent to the City of London were identified from business directories. There were 362 in total and a short postal questionnaire survey was sent to them in early 1992. Of these, 166 replied, a response rate of 46 per cent, which is more than respectable for a postal survey. More than 22,000 people were employed by the banks that responded. From an initial analysis of these data, there seemed to be few differences between the banks that replied and those that did not in terms of size or ownership.

The next stage was to select three banks within which to carry out detailed interviews with samples of employees. While I had planned to select these on the basis of the proportion of women in their professional staff, it turned out that there was no significant difference between the banks. Women were a small percentage of the professionals in all investment banks. It also became clear that the ownership structure, history and traditions of different banks might prove a more interesting basis for comparison, and with this in mind a range of banks were approached. I undertook some pilot work in a small number of banks, testing ideas out on a few men and women who were willing to help, at the same time as negotiating access elsewhere. It would be foolish to pretend that the banks who were eventually included were selected on the basis of any notion of representativeness. The City of London in the early 1990s was a difficult place in which to do research. Recession, scandals and terrorism added to conventional needs for secrecy in the financial world and made almost all the banks I approached reluctant to let a social scientist through the doors. But three banks agreed, and I owe them a huge debt

for the way in which they made me welcome and allowed me to interview a range of employees. My debt to Merbank in particular is out-
standing, as there I not only interviewed but was given unparalleled
access to personnel data, all of it, I hasten to add, without names attached. I have given both the banks and the individuals involved pseudonyms to preserve confidentiality.

I had initially planned to administer a diary form of questionnaire to
collect work history information, as well as the details of individuals'
workplace interactions, but this proved impossible as professionals in the
financial services sector cultivate a surface appearance, and perhaps a
reality, of extreme workplace pressure. The confidentiality of client and
collegiate interactions also militated against recording daily contacts.
Thus, all the information was collected in the course of detailed interviews lasting between one and three hours. These were undertaken between April 1992 and September 1993. Most people were interviewed in
their workplace, a few in the immediate environs of the bank. While
most people were extremely willing to discuss a wide range of issues, I
found there was a slight disadvantage to interviewing in the workplace:
a small minority of people, mainly among those in the highest-status
occupations, were somewhat reluctant to talk about their home lives. I
also found in the pilot interviews that asking personal questions first
seemed to jeopardise rapport and openness and so factual details of
education and career moves were collected at the beginning of each
interview. All the interviews were carried out either by Gill Court, who
held a research post for 18 months, or by me. We are both white,
middle-class women, university educated, quietly spoken and neat and
unobtrusive in appearance. We dressed in smartish suits while we were
in the banks and their environs to blend in with the overall ambience and
with the most typical female appearance.

To analyse the taped narratives I used a combination of what has been
termed 'immersion' by Marshall (1984) and the 'listening guide' approach developed by Brown et al. (1991). Marshall, who has worked with
women managers, analysed her transcripts by looking for key themes.
This is how she explained her method:

> As I read through, sorted and categorised the managers' accounts, profiles
> of significant events, influencing factors, attitudes, commonalities and dif-
> ferences gradually emerged for particular individuals, groups within indus-
> tries, each of the two industries and the sample as a whole. My approach
> to the material can best be described as 'immersion' and involves trying to
> appreciate inherent patterns rather than impose preconceived ideas on the
> data. The researcher becomes an interpreter rather than a manipulator,
> concerned with capturing other people's meanings rather than testing
> hypotheses. (Marshall, 1984, p. 116)

Marshall claimed that she used her identification of common experiences, attitudes and feelings as the basis for developing theories and models, although these inevitably also depended on her location within an existing set of literatures about women's workplace experiences. Adopting a similar approach, I found the 'listening guide' a helpful addition to the immersion method. The listening guide is an interpretative methodology that joins hermeneutics and feminist standpoint epistemology (Brown et al., 1991). It is a voice-centred, relational approach by which a researcher becomes a listener, taking in the voice of respondents, and developing an interpretation of their experiences. Through multiple readings of the same text, this method makes audible the 'polyphonic and complex' nature of voice and experience (Brown and Gilligan, 1992). Both speaker and listener are recognised as individuals who bring thoughts and feelings to the exchange and the resulting 'text'. Tolman (1994) has argued that this approach is particularly appropriate for the understanding of girls' and women's experiences and the ways in which they give voice to them, as it acknowledges that patriarchal culture tends to silence and obscure women's experiences and so it is important to listen attentively to silences, allusions and omissions as well as to the voiced comments. Thus, according to Tolman:

> the method is explicitly psychological and feminist in providing the listener with an organised way to respond to the coded or indirect language of girls and women, especially regarding topics such as sexuality that girls and women are not supposed to speak of. This method leaves a trail of evidence for the listeners' interpretation, and thus leaves room for other interpretations by other listeners consistent with the epistemological stance that there is multiple meaning in such stories. (p. 327)

This method raised a series of questions for me, however, as men as well as women were interviewed. Are men's voices more direct than women's in taped interviews? Are all men more direct or dominant than all women, regardless of seniority? And are young men able to speak to an older woman about their sexuality? It was clear that the subject matter under discussion at times disconcerted some male respondents. Several transcripts revealed various apologetic gestures and phrases: for example, a 28-year-old man in capital markets mentioned women behind the counter at Barclays and then said 'or rather people; sorry I shouldn't say women in an interview like this, should I?', despite my very low-key introduction to the topic of gender divisions at work. Overall, however, the respondents were remarkably open and willing to discuss all manner of subjects. We were not directive in the interviews and attempted to allow subjects' voices and opinions to 'emerge', although, of course, the manner in which we presented ourselves and the purpose of

Bibliography

Acker, J. (1990) Hierarchies, jobs, bodies: a theory of gendered organisations. *Gender and Society* 4, 139–58.

Allen, J. (1992) *The Nature of a Growth Region: the peculiarity of the South East.* The South East Programme Occasional Paper 1, Faculty of Social Sciences, The Open University, Milton Keynes.

Allen, J. and Henry, N. (1996) Fragments of industry and employment: contract service work and the shift towards precarious employment. In R. Crompton, D. Gallie and K. Purcell (eds), *Changing Forms of Employment: Organizations, skills and gender.* Routledge, London, 65–82.

Allen, J. and Pryke, M. (1994) The production of service space. *Environment and Planning D: Society and Space* 12, 453–75.

Amsden, A. (1980) *The Economics of Women and Work.* Penguin, Harmondsworth.

Andersen, M. (1995) From the Editor. *Gender and Society* 9, 5–7.

Arber, S. and Gilbert, N. (1992) *Women and Working Lives.* Macmillan, London.

Armstrong, S. (1995) Bodies of opinion. *Media Guardian,* 6 November, p. 15.

Atwood, M. (1992) *Good Bones.* Bloomsbury, London.

Barkalow, C. with Rabb, A. (1990) *In the Men's House: an inside account of life in the army by one of West Point's first female graduates.* Poseidon, New York.

Barnes, T. J. (1995) Political economy I: 'the culture, stupid'. *Progress in Human Geography* 19, 423–31.

Barnes, T. J. and Duncan, J. S. (1992) *Writing Worlds: discourse, text and metaphor in the representation of landscape.* Routledge, London.

Barnett, A. (1982) *Iron Britannia.* Allison and Busby, London.

Baron, R. and Norris, G. (1976) Sexual divisions and the dual labour market. In D. L. Barker and S. Allen (eds), *Dependence and Exploitation in Work and Marriage.* Longman, London.

Bateson, M. C. (1990) *Composing a Life.* Penguin, London.

Bauman, Z. (1992) *Mortality, Immortality and Other Life Strategies.* Polity Press,

Cambridge.

Beaverstock, J. (1994) Re-thinking skilled international labour migration: world cities and banking organisations. *Geoforum* 25, 323–38.

Beechey, V. (1977) Some notes on female wage labour in capitalist production. *Capital and Class* 3, 45–66.

Beechey, V. (1987) *Unequal Work.* Verso, London.

Beechey, V. and Perkins, T. (1987) *A Matter of Hours: women, part-time work and the labour market.* Polity Press, Cambridge .

Bell, D. (1973) *The Coming of the Post-industrial Society.* Basic Books, New York.

Bell, D., Binney, J., Cream, J. and Valentine, G. (1994) All hyped up and no place to go. *Gender Place and Culture* 1, 31–47.

Bell, D. and Valentine, G. (eds) (1995) *Mapping Desire.* Routledge, London.

Benhabib, S. and Cornell, D. (eds) (1987) *Feminism as Critique.* Blackwell, Oxford.

Beresford, P. (1990) Britain's rich: the top 200. *Sunday Times Magazine*, 8 April, pp. 19–21.

Berger, P. and Luckmann, T. (1966) *The Social Construction of Reality.* Doubleday, New York.

Blundy, A. (1995) The Leeson affair. *Cosmopolitan*, June, pp. 46–8.

Bordo, S., (1993) *Unbearable Weight: feminism, western culture and the body.* University of California Press, Berkeley, Calif.

Borrie, G. (1994) *Social Justice: strategies for national renewal.* Vintage Books, London.

Bourdieu, P. (1984) *Distinction: a social critique of the judgement of taste.* Routledge, London (first published in French in 1979).

Bowen, D. (1992) Business class connections. *Independent on Sunday*, 4 October, pp. 14–17.

Box, S. (1983) *Power, Crime and Mystification.* Tavistock, London.

Bradley, H. (1989) *Men's Work, Women's Work.* Polity, Cambridge.

Brannen, J. (1989) Childbirth and occupational mobility: evidence from a longitudinal study. *Work, Employment and Society* 3, 179–201.

Brannen, J. (1992) *Mixing Methods: qualitative and quantitative research.* Avebury, Aldershot.

Brannen, J. and Moss, P. (1991) *Managing Mothers: dual career households after maternity leave.* Unwin Hyman, London.

Braverman, H. (1974) *Labour and Monopoly Capital.* Monthly Review Press, New York.

Brontë, C. (1992) (1853) *Villette.* Everyman, London.

Brown, L., Debold, E., Tappen, M. and Gilligan, C. (1991) Reading narratives of conflict for self and moral voice: a relational method. In W. Kurtines and J. Gewirtz (eds), *Handbook of Moral Behaviour and Development: theory, research and application.* Lawrence Erlbaum, Hillsdale, N.J.

Brown, L. and Gilligan, C. (1992) *Meeting at the Crossroads: women's psychology and girls' development.* Harvard University Press, Cambridge, Mass.

Brown, P. (1995) Cultural capital and social exclusion: some observations on recent trends in education, employment and the labour market. *Work, Employment and Society* 9, 29–51.

Brown, P. and Scase, R. (1994) *Higher Education and Corporate Realities: class, culture and the decline of graduate careers.* UCL Press, London.

Budd, L. and Whimster, S. (eds) (1992) *Global Finance and Urban Living.* Routledge, London.

Burchell, B. (1993) A new way of analysing labour market flows using work history data. *Work, Employment and Society* 7, 237–58.

Burdett, R. (1992) *City Changes: architecture in the City of London 1985–1995.* Corporation of London and the Architecture Foundation, London.

Butler J. (1990a) *Gender Trouble: feminism and the subversion of identity.* Routledge, London.

Butler J. (1990b) Gender trouble, feminist theory and psychoanalytic discourse. In L. Nicholson (ed.), *Feminism/Postmodernism.* Routledge, London.

Butler, J. (1992) Contingent foundations: feminism and the question of 'Postmodernism'. In J. Butler and J. W. Scott (eds), *Feminists Theorise the Political.* Routledge, London.

Butler, J. (1993) *Bodies that Matter.* Routledge, London.

Campbell, B. (1993) *Goliath: Britain's dangerous places.* Methuen, London.

Carli, L. L. (1989) Gender differences in interaction style and influence. *Journal of Personality and Social Psychology* 56, 565–76.

Casey, C. (1995) *Work, Self and Society: after industrialism.* Routledge, London.

Cassis, Y., Feldman, G. and Olsson, U. (1995) *The Evolution of Financial Institutions and Markets in Twentieth Century Europe.* Scolar Press, Aldershot.

Castells, M. (1989) *The Informational City.* Blackwell, Oxford.

Champion, A. (1994) International migration and demographic change in the developed world. *Urban Studies* 31, 653–77.

Chaney, D. (1993) *Fictions of Collective Life: public drama in late modern culture.* Routledge, London.

Chapman, R. (1988) The great pretender: variations on the new man theme. In R. Chapman and J. Rutherford (eds), *Male Order: unwrapping masculinity.* Routledge, London, 225–48.

Charman, P. (1989) The hardest of sells. *The Times*, 21 March, p. 3.

Christopherson, S. (1989) Flexibility in the US service economy and the emerging spatial division of labour. *Transactions of the Institute of British Geographers* 14, 131–43.

Churchill, C. (1987) *Serious Money.* Methuen, London.

City Lives Project (1991) *Unpublished Interviews with Key Decision Makers in the City of London.* National Sound Archive, London.

City Research Project (1995) *The Competitive Position of London's Financial Services: final report.* Corporation of London.

Coakley, J. (1992) London as an international financial centre. In L. Budd and S. Whimster (eds), *Global Finance and Urban Living.* Routledge, London.

Coakley, J. and Harris, L. (1983) *The City of Capital: London's role as a financial centre.* Blackwell, Oxford.

Cockburn, C. (1983) *Brothers: male dominance and technological change.* Pluto Press, London.

Cockburn, C. (1991) *In the Way of Women: men's resistance to sex equality in organisations.* Macmillan, London.

Cohen, R. B. (1987) *The New Helots: migrants in the international division of labour.*

Gower, Aldershot.

Collins, R. (1979) *The Credential Society: an historical sociology of education and stratification.* Academic Press, New York.

Collinson, D. and Hearn, J. (1994) Naming men as men: implications for work, organization and management. *Gender, Work and Organization* 1, 2–22.

Collinson, D., Knights, D. and Collinson, M. (1990) *Managing to Discriminate.* Routledge, London.

Colomina, B. (ed.) (1992) *Sexuality and Space.* Princeton Architectural Press, New York.

Committee to Review the Functioning of Financial Institutions (1980) *Report,* HMSO, London.

Connell, R. W. (1987) *Gender and Power.* Polity Press, Cambridge.

Connell, R. W. (1992) A very straight gay: masculinity, homosexual experience and the dynamics of gender. *American Sociological Review* 57, 735–51.

Connell, R. W. (1995) *Masculinities.* Polity Press, Cambridge.

Corbridge, S., Thrift, N. and Martin, R. (eds) (1994) *Money, Power and Space.* Blackwell, Oxford.

Cornwall, A. and Lindisfarne, N. (1994) *Dislocating Masculinity.* Routledge, London.

Craig, C., Rubery, J., Tarling, R. and Wilkinson, F. (1982) *Labour Market Structure, Industrial Organisation and Low Pay.* Cambridge University Press, Cambridge.

Craig, S. (ed.) (1992) *Men, Masculinity and the Media.* Sage, Newbury Park, Calif.

Crang, P. (1994) It's showtime: on the workplace geographies of display in a restaurant in South East England. *Environment and Planning D: Society and Space* 12, 675–704.

Crilley, D. (1993) Architecture as advertising: constructing the image of redevelopment. In G. Kearns and C. Philo (eds), *Selling Places: the city as cultural capital past and present.* Pergamon, London.

Crompton, R. (1992) Where did all the bright girls go? Women's higher education and employment since 1964. In N. Abercrombie and A. Warde (eds), *Social Change in Britain.* Polity Press, Cambridge.

Crompton, R., Gallie, D. and Purcell, K. (eds) (1996) *Changing Forms of Employment: organizations, skills and gender.* Routledge, London.

Crompton, R., Hantrais, L. and Walters, P. (1990), Gender relations and employment. *British Journal of Sociology* 41, 329–50.

Crompton, R. and Jones, G. (1984) *White Collar Proletariat.* Macmillan, London.

Crompton, R. and Sanderson, K. (1990) *Gendered Jobs and Social Change.* Unwin Hyman, London.

Crompton, R. and Sanderson, K. (1994) The gendered restructuring of employment in the finance sector. In A. M. Scott (ed.), *Gender Segregation and Social Change.* Oxford University Press, Oxford.

Daniels, P. (1993a) *Service Industries in the World Economy.* Blackwell, Oxford.

Daniels, P. (ed.) (1993b), *The Geography of Services.* Frank Cass, London.

Davidson, M. J. (1985) *Reach for the Top: a women's guide for success in business and management.* Piatkus, London.

Davidson, M. J. and Cooper, C. (1992) *Shattering the Glass Ceiling: the woman manager*. Paul Chapman Publishing, London.

Davis, M. (1990) *City of Quartz*. Verso, London.

Debord, G. (1983) *Society of the Spectacle*. Verso, London.

Debord, G. (1990) *Comments on the Society of the Spectacle*. Verso, London.

Denzin, N. (1990) Reading 'Wall Street': postmodern contradictions in the American social structure. In B. S. Turner (ed.), *Theories of Modernity and Postmodernity*. Sage, London.

Department of Employment (1992a) Economic activity and qualifications: results from the Labour Force Survey. *Employment Gazette* 100, 101–33.

Department of Employment (1992b) Results of the (1991) Labour Force Survey. *Employment Gazette* 99, 153–72.

Dex, S. (1985) *The Sexual Division of Work: conceptual revolutions in the social sciences*. Wheatsheaf, Brighton.

Dex, S. (1987) *Women's Occupational Mobility: a lifetime perspective*. Macmillan, London.

Dex, S. (ed.) (1991) *Life and Work History Analysis: qualitative and quantitative developments*. Routledge, London.

Dex, S. and McCulloch, A. (1995) *Flexible Employment in Britain: a statistical analysis*. Equal Opportunities Commission, Manchester.

Dezalay, Y. (1990) The Big Bang and the law. In M. Featherstone (ed.), *Global Culture: nationalism, globalisation and modernity*. Sage, London.

Diamond, D. (1991) The city, the 'Big Bang' and office development. In K. Hoggart and A. Green (eds), *London: a new metropolitan geography*. Edward Arnold, London.

Donaldson, M. (1991) *Time of our Lives: labour and love in the working class*. Allen and Unwin, Sydney.

Donaldson, M. (1993) What is hegemonic masculinity? *Theory and Society* 22, 643–57.

Drew, P. and Heritage, J. (1992) *Talk at Work: interaction in institutional settings*. Cambridge University Press, Cambridge.

Du Gay, P. (1996) *Consumption and Identity at Work*. Sage, London.

Duncan, J. S. (1990) *The City as Text: the politics of landscape interpretation in the Kandyan kingdom*. Cambridge University Press, Cambridge.

Duncan, J. S. and Duncan, N. (1988) (Re)reading the landscape. *Environment and Planning D: Society and Space* 6, 117–26.

Duncan, J. S. and Ley, D. (1993) *Culture/Place/Representation*. Routledge, London.

Elder, G. (1978) Family history and the life course. In T. K. Hareven (ed.), *Transitions: the family and the life course in historical perspective*. Academic Press, New York.

Elias, P. (1983) *Occupational Mobility and Part-Time Work*. Institute of Employment Research, University of Warwick.

Elias, P. (1994) Occupational change in a working-life perspective: internal and external view. In R. Penn, M. Rose and J. Rubery (eds), *Skill and Occupational Change*. Oxford University Press, Oxford.

Elias, P. and Main, B. (1982) *Women's Working Lives: evidence from the National Training Survey*. Institute of Employment Research, University of Warwick.

Epstein, C. F. (1973) The positive effects of the double negative: explaining the

222   *References*

success of black professional women. In J. Huber (ed.), *Changing Women in a Changing Society*. University of Chicago Press, Chicago.

Epstein, C. F. (1980) The new women and the old establishment: Wall Street lawyers in the 1970s. *Sociology of Work and Occupations* 7, 291–316.

Fainstein, S. S. (1994) *The City Builders*. Blackwell, Oxford.

Featherstone, M. (ed.) (1990) *Global Culture: nationalism, globalisation and modernity*. Sage, London.

Featherstone, M. (1991a) *Consumer Culture and Postmodernism*. Sage, London.

Featherstone, M. (1991b) The body in consumer culture. In M. Featherstone, M. Hepworth and B. Turner (eds), *The Body: social process and cultural theory*. Sage, London.

Featherstone, M., Hepworth, M. and Turner, B. (eds) (1991) *The Body: social process and cultural theory*. Sage, London.

Felmlee, D. H. (1982) Women's job mobility, processes within and between employees. *American Sociological Review* 47, 142–51.

Fielding, A. J. (1992) Migration and social mobility: South East England as an escalator region. *Regional Studies* 26, 1–15.

Financial Times (1992) NHS is accused of sexism. 28 January, p. 9.

Fine, G. (1987) One of the boys: women in male-dominated settings. In M. Kimmel (ed.), *Changing Men: new directions in research on men and masculinity*. Sage, Newbury Park, Calif.

Fishman, P. (1977) Interactional shiftwork. *Heresies: a feminist publication on arts and politics* 2, 99–101.

Fiske, J. (1993) *Power Plays, Power Works*. Verso, London.

Forester, J. (ed.) (1985) *Critical Theory and Public Life*. MIT Press, Cambridge, Mass. and London.

Foucault, M. (1977) Nietzsche, genealogy, history. In D. Bouchard (ed.), *Language, Counter-memory, Practice: selected interviews by Michel Foucault*. Cornell University Press, Ithaca, N.Y.

Foucault, M. (1979) *History of Sexuality Volume 1*. Allen Lane, London.

Frobel, F., Heinrichs, J. and Kreye, O. (1980) *The New International Division of Labour*. Cambridge University Press, Cambridge.

Fromm, E. (1949) *Man for Himself: an inquiry into the psychology of ethics*. Routledge, London.

Fuss, D. (1990) *Essentially Speaking: feminism, nature and difference*. Routledge, London.

Gabriel, Y. (1988) *Working Lives in Catering*. Routledge, London.

Gallie, D. (ed.) (1988) *Employment in Britain*. Blackwell, Oxford.

Game, A. (1991) *Undoing the Social: towards a deconstructive sociology*. Open University Press, Milton Keynes.

Game, A. and Pringle, R. (1984) *Gender at Work*. Pluto, London.

Gammon, L. and Marshment, M. (eds) (1988) *The Female Gaze*. Verso, London.

Gatens, M. (1991) A critique of the sex/gender distinction. In S. Gunew (ed.), *A Reader in Feminist Knowledge*. Routledge, London, 139–157.

George, S. (1988) Several pounds of flesh. *New Internationalist 189*, 18–19.

Gibson, J. W. (1994) *Warrior Dreams: paramilitary culture in post-Vietnam America*. Hill and Wang, New York.

Giddens, A. (1990) *The Consequences of Modernity*. Polity Press, Cambridge.

Giddens, A. (1991) *Modernity and Self-identity: self and society in the late modern age.* Polity Press, Cambridge.

Giddens, A. (1992) *The Transformation of Intimacy: love, sexuality and eroticism in modern societies.* Polity Press, Cambridge.

Gilligan, C. (1982) *In a Different Voice: women's psychological development.* Harvard University Press, Cambridge, Mass.

Gilmore, D. (1990) *Manhood in the Making: cultural concepts of masculinity.* Yale University Press, New Haven, Conn.

Giuffre, P. A. and Williams, C. L. (1994) Labeling sexual harassment in restaurants. *Gender and Society* 8, 378–401.

Glasgow Media Group (1976) *Bad News*. Routledge and Kegan Paul, London.

Glasgow Media Group (1980) *More Bad News*. Routledge and Kegan Paul, London.

Glasgow Media Group (1982) *Really Bad News*. Routledge and Kegan Paul, London.

Goffman, E. (1961) *Asylums*. Anchor Books, New York.

Goffman, E. (1963) *Behaviour in Public Places*. Free Press, Glencoe, Ill.

Goodhart, D. (1991) Women in few of top civil posts. *Financial Times*, 23 October, p. 10.

Gottdiener, M. (1995) *Postmodern Semiotics*. Blackwell, Oxford.

Government Statistical Service (1992) *Education Statistics for the United Kingdom, 1991 Edition*. HMSO, London.

Grace, H. (1991) Business, pleasure, narrative: the folktale in our times. In R. Diprose and R. Ferrell (eds), *Cartographies: poststructuralism and the mapping of bodies and spaces*. Allen and Unwin, Sydney.

Granovetter, M. (1985) Economic action and social structure: the problem of embeddedness. *American Journal of Sociology* 91, 481–510.

Grant, L. (1993) *Sexing the Millennium*. HarperCollins, London.

Grossberg, M. (1990) Instituting masculinity: the law as a masculine profession. In M. C. Carnes and C. Griffen, C. (eds), *Meanings for Manhood: constructions of masculinity in Victorian America*. University of Chicago Press, Chicago.

Grosz, E. (1990) A note on essentialism and difference. In S. Gunew (ed.), *Feminist Knowledge: critique and construct*. Routledge, London.

Grosz, E. (1992) *Bodies–Cities*. In B. Colomina (ed.), *Sexuality and Space*. Princeton Architectural Press, New York.

Gudeman, S. (1986) *Economics as Culture: models and metaphors of livelihood*. Routledge, London.

Habermas, J. (1985) Modern and postmodern architecture. In J. Forester (ed.), *Critical Theory and Public Life*. MIT Press, Cambridge, Mass. and London.

Halford, S. (1991) *Gender and Employment in Midland Bank*. School of Urban and Regional Studies, University of Sussex, Brighton.

Halford, S. and Savage, M. (1995) Restructuring organisations, changing people: gender and restructuring in banking and local government. *Work, Employment and Society* 9, 97–122.

Hall, J. A. and Braunwald, K. G. (1981) Gender cues in conversation. *Journal of Personality and Social Psychology* 40, 99–110.

Hamilton, A. (1986) *The Financial Revolution*. Penguin, Harmondsworth.

Hamilton, A., Keegan, W., Vincent, L. and Field, C. (1995) Busting the bank. *The Observer*, 5 March, pp. 23–4.

Hamilton, K. (1992) Troubles at the top people's bank. *Evening Standard*, 16 January, p. 33.

Hamnett, C. and Seavers, J. (1994) *A Step up the Ladder: home ownership and careers in the south east of England*. South East Programme, Faculty of Social Sciences, The Open University, Milton Keynes.

Handy, C. (1994) *The Empty Raincoat: making sense of the future*. Hutchinson, London.

Hannah, L. (1976) *The Rise of the Corporate Economy*. Methuen, London.

Hannerz, U. (1989) Notes on the global ecumene. *Public Culture* 1, 12–27.

Hannerz, U. (1990) Cosmopolitans and locals in a world culture. In M. Featherstone (ed.), *Global Culture: nationalism, globalisation and modernity*. Sage, London.

Hanson, S. and Johnston, I. (1985) Gender differences in work trip length: explanations and implications. *Urban Geography* 6, 193–219.

Hanson, S. and Pratt, G. (1991) Job search and the occupational segregation of women. *Annals of the Association of American Geographers* 81, 229–53.

Hanson, S. and Pratt, G. (1992) Dynamic dependencies: a geographic investigation of local labour markets. *Economic Geography* 68, 373–405.

Hanson, S. and Pratt, G. (1995) *Gender, Work and Space*. Routledge, London.

Haraway, D. (1990) *Simians, Cyborgs and the Reinvention of Nature*. Free Association Books, London.

Hareven, T. K. (ed.) (1978) *Transitions: the family and the life course in historical perspective*. Academic Press, New York.

Hartmann, H. (1979) Capitalism, patriarchy and job segregation by sex. In Z. Eisenstein (ed.), *Capitalist Patriarchy and the Case for Socialist Feminism*. Monthly Review Press, New York.

Harvey, D. (1989a) *The Condition of Postmodernity*. Blackwell, Oxford.

Harvey, D. (1989b) *The Urban Experience*. Blackwell, Oxford.

Harvey, D. (1992) Class relations, social justice and the politics of difference. In J. Squires (ed.), *Principled Positions*. Verso, London.

Hearn, G. and Parkin, P. W. (1987) *Sex at Work*. Wheatsheaf, Brighton.

Helgasen, P. (1990) *The Female Advantage*. Sage, London.

Hennig, M. and Jardim, A. (1978) *The Managerial Woman*. Marion Boyars, London.

Herdt, G. (ed.) (1992) *Gay Culture in America*. Beacon Press, Boston, Mass.

Herzfeld, M. (1985) *The Poetics of Manhood: contest and identity in a Cretan mountain village*. Princeton University Press, Princeton, N.J.

Heward, C. (1988) *Making a Man of Him: parents and their sons' education at an English public school 1929–1950*. Routledge, London.

Hewitt, V. (1994) *Beauty and the Banknote: images of women on paper money*. British Museum Press, London.

Hochschild, A. (1983) *The Managed Heart: commercialisation of human feeling*. University of California Press, Berkeley, Calif.

Humphries, J. and Rubery, J. (eds) (1995) *The Economics of Equal Opportunity*.

Equal Opportunities Commission, Manchester.

Hutton, W. (1995a) A city without controls. *The Guardian*, 6 March, p. 14.

Hutton, W. (1995b) *The State We're In.* Jonathan Cape, London.

Irigaray, L. (1977) *Ce Sexe qui n'en est pas un*. Les Editions de Minuit, Paris.

Jack, A. (1992) 30,000 job losses forecast in financial services. *Financial Times*, 21 January, p. 8.

Jackson, K. (1995) *The Oxford Book of Money*. Oxford University Press, Oxford.

Jackson, P. (1991) The cultural politics of masculinity: towards a social geography. *Transactions, Institute of British Geographers* 16, 199–213.

Jacobs, J. (1992) Cultures of the past and urban transformation: the Spitalfields market redevelopment in East London. In K. Anderson and F. Gale (eds), *Inventing places: studies in cultural geography*. Longman Cheshire, Melbourne.

Jacobs, J. (1993) The city unbound: qualitative approaches to the city. *Urban Studies* 30, 827–48.

Jacobs, J. (1994a) Negotiating the heart: heritage, development and identity in post-imperial London. *Environment and Planning D: Society and Space* 12, 751–72.

Jacobs, J. (1994b) The battle of Bank Junction: the contested iconography of capital. In S. Corbridge, M. Martin and N. Thrift (eds), *Money, Power and Space*. Blackwell, Oxford.

Jaggar, A. (1988) *Feminist Politics and Human Nature*. Rowman and Allenhead, Totowa, N.J.

Jensen, M. C. and Meckling, W. H. (1976) The theory of the firm: managerial behaviour, agency costs and ownership structures. *Journal of Financial Economics* 3, 306–60.

Johnson, P. S. and Apps, R. (1979) Interlocking directorships among the UK's largest companies. *Antitrust Bulletin* 24, 357–69.

Johnston-Anumonwo, I. (1992) The influence of household type on gender differences in work trip distance. *The Professional Geographer* 44, 161–9.

Jones, C. (1992) Fertility of the over thirties. *Population Trends* 67, 10–16.

Kanter, R. (1977) *Men and Women of the Organization*. Basic Books, New York.

Kanter, R. (1991) The future of bureaucracy and hierarchy in organizational theory: a report from the field. In P. Bourdieu and J. Coleman (eds), *Social Theory for a Changing World*. Westview Press, Boulder, Colo.

Kanter, R. (1992) *The Challenge of Organizational Change*. Free Press, New York.

Kaufman, M. (1993) *Cracking the Armour: power, pain and the lives of men*. Viking, Toronto.

Kearns, G. and Philo, C. (1993) (eds) *Selling Places: the city as cultural capital past and present*. Pergamon, London.

Kerfoot, D. and Knights, D. (1994) The gendered terrains of paternalism. In S. Wright (ed.), *Anthropology of Organisations*. Routledge, London.

Kimmel, M. (1988) *Changing Men: new directions in research on men and masculinity*. Sage, London.

King, A. (1990a) Architecture, capital and the globalisation of culture. In M. Featherstone (ed.), *Global Culture: nationalism, globalization and modernity*. Sage, London.

King, A. (1990b) *Global Cities: post-imperialism and the internationalisation of London*. Routledge, London.

King, A. (1990c) *Urbanism, Colonialism and the World Economy*. Routledge, London.

King, A. (1993) Identity and difference: the internationalization of capital and the globalization of culture. In P. Knox (ed.), *The Restless Urban Landscape*. Prentice Hall, Englewood Cliffs, N.J.

King, A. (ed.) (1996) *Re-presenting the City*. Macmillan, London.

King, M. (1977) *Public Policy and the Corporation*. Chapman Hall, London.

Klein, A. M. (1993) *Little Big Men: bodybuilding subculture and gender construction*. State University of New York Press, Albany, N.Y.

Knights, D. and Willmott, H. (eds) (1986) *Gender and the Labour Process*. Gower, Aldershot.

Knox, P. (ed.) (1993) The *Restless Urban Landscape*. Prentice Hall, Englewood Cliffs, N.J.

Kondo, D. K. (1990) *Crafting Selves: power, gender and discourse of identity in a Japanese workplace*. University of Chicago Press, Chicago.

Kuhn, A. (1985) *The Power of the Image: essays on representation and sexuality*. Routledge and Kegan Paul, London.

Kunda, G. (1992) *Engineering Culture: control and commitment in a high-tech organisation*. Temple University Press, Philadelphia.

Labour Research (1992) *Challenging the Men in Suits*. March, pp. 7–9.

Lash, S. and Friedman, J. (eds) (1992) *Modernity and Identity*. Basil Blackwell, Oxford.

Lash, S. and Urry, J. (1994) *Economies of Signs and Space*. Sage, London.

Lawless, P., Martin, M. and Hardy, S. (1996) *Unemployment and Social Exclusion: landscapes of labour inequality*. Jessica Kingsley, London.

Lefebvre, H. (1991) *The Production of Space*. Blackwell, Oxford.

Leidner, R. (1991) Selling hamburgers and selling insurance: gender, work and identity in interactive service jobs. *Gender and Society* 5, 154–77.

Leidner R. (1993) *Fast Food, Fast Talk: service work and the routinization of everyday life*. University of California Press, Berkeley and Los Angeles, Calif.

Levi, M. (1987) *Regulating Fraud: white collar crime and the criminal process*. Tavistock, London.

Lewis, M. (1989) *Liar's Poker: two cities, true greed*. Hodder and Stoughton, London.

Lewis, M. (1991) *The Money Culture*. Hodder and Stoughton, London.

Leyshon, A., Thrift, N. and Daniels, P. (1987) *The Urban and Regional Consequences of the Restructuring of World Financial Markets: the case of the City of London*. Working Papers on Producer Services 4, University of Bristol and Service Industries Research Centre, Portsmouth Polytechnic.

Lindley, R. M. and Wilson, R. A. (eds) (1993) *Review of the Economy and Employment 1992/3: Occupational Assessment*. Institute for Employment Research, University of Warwick.

Lisle-Williams, M. (1984a) Beyond the market: the survival of family capitalism in the English merchant banks. *British Journal of Sociology* 35, 241–71.

Lisle-Williams, M. (1984b) Merchant banking dynasties in the English class structure: ownership, solidarity and kinship in the City. *British Journal of Sociology* 35, 333–62.

Lodge, D. (1988) *Nice Work*. Secker and Warburg, London.

Maccoby, E. E. (1990) Gender and relationships: a developmental account.

American Psychologist 45, 513–20.

MacKinnon, C. A. (1990) Legal perspectives on sexual difference. In D. Rhode (ed.), *Theoretical Perspectives on Sexual Difference.* Yale University Press, New Haven, Conn. and London.

Mangan, J. A. and Walvin, J. (1992) *Manliness and Morality: middle class masculinity in Britain and America 1800 to 1940.* Manchester University Press, Manchester.

Marcus, T. A. (1993) *Buildings and Power: freedom and control in the origin of modern building types.* Routledge, London.

Marquand, D. (1995) A new scandal with an old sting in the tale. *Guardian,* 3 March, p. 22.

Marshall, J. (1984) *Women Managers: travellers in a male world.* John Wiley, London.

Marshall, J., Gentle, C., Raybould, S. and Coombes, M. (1992) Regulatory change, corporate restructuring and the spatial redevelopment of the British financial sector. *Regional Studies* 26, 453–68.

Martin, J. and Roberts, C. (1984) *Women and Employment: a lifetime perspective.* DE/ OPCS Social Survey Report SS1143, HMSO, London.

Massey, D. (1984) *Spatial Divisions of Labour.* Macmillan, London (2nd edition 1994).

Massey, D. (1995) Masculinity, dualisms and high technology. *Transactions of the Institute of British Geography* 20, 487–99.

Massey, D. (1994) *Space, Place and Gender.* Polity Press, Cambridge.

Massey, D. and Allen, J. (1994) High-tech places: poverty in the midst of growth. In C. Philo (ed.), *Off the Map: the geography of poverty in the UK.* Child Poverty Action Group, London.

Massey, D. and Henry, N. (1992) *Something New, Something Old: a sketch of the Cambridge economy.* South East programme, Faculty of Social Sciences, The Open University, Milton Keynes.

McDowell, L. (1989) Gender divisions. In C. Hamnett, L. McDowell and P. Sarre (eds), *The Changing Social Structure.* Hodder and Stoughton, London.

McDowell, L. (1991) Life without Father and Ford: the new gender order of post-Fordism. *Transactions, Institute of British Geographers* 16, 400–19.

McDowell, L. (1995) Body work: heterosexual gender performances in City workplaces. In D. Bell and G. Valentine (eds), *Mapping Desire.* Routledge, London.

McDowell, L. and Court, G. (1994a) Missing subjects: gender, power and sexuality in merchant banking. *Economic Geography* 70, 229–51.

McDowell, L. and Court, G. (1994b) Performing work: bodily representations in merchant banks. *Environment and Planning D: Society and Space* 12, 253–78.

McDowell, L. and Massey, D. (1984) A. woman's place. In D. Massey and J. Allen (eds), *Geography Matters!* Cambridge University Press, Cambridge (also reprinted in Massey, D. (1994) *Space, Place and Gender,* Polity Press, Cambridge).

McElhinny, B. (1994) An economy of affect: objectivity, masculinity and the gendering of police work. In A. Cornwall and N. Lindisfarne (eds), *Dislocating Masculinity.* Routledge, London.

McRae, H. and Cairncross, F. (1991) *Capital City: London as a financial centre.* Methuen, London.

McRae, S. (1991) Occupational change over childbirth: evidence from a national survey. *Sociology* 25, 589–605.

Messner, M. A. (1992) *Power at Play: sports and the problem of masculinity*. Beacon Press, Boston, Mass.

Metcalf, A. and Humphries, M. (eds) (1985) *The Sexuality of Men*. Pluto, London.

Michie, R. (1992) *The City of London: continuity and change, 1850–1990*. Macmillan, London.

Miliband, R. (1969) *The State in Capitalist Society*. Basic Books, New York.

Milkman, R. (1987) *Gender at Work: the dynamics of job segregation by sex during World War II*. University of Chicago Press, Chicago.

Mincer, J. (1962) Labour force participation of married women: a study of labour supply. In National Bureau of Economic Research, *Aspects of Labour Economics*. Princeton University Press, Princeton, N.J.

Molloy, M. (1995) Imagining (the) difference: gender, ethnicity and metaphors of nationalism. *Feminist Review* 51, 94–112.

Moore, S. (1988) Getting a bit of the other: the pimps of postmodernism. In R. Chapman and J. Rutherford (eds), *Male Order: unwrapping masculinity*. Routledge, London, 165–92.

Morgan, G. and Knights, D. (1991) Gendering jobs: corporate strategy, managerial control and the dynamics of job segregation. *Work, Employment and Society* 5, 181–200.

Morgan, K. and Sayer, A. (1988) *Micro-circuits of Capital: 'Sunrise' industries and uneven development*. Polity Press, Cambridge.

Mulvey, L. (1989) *Visual and Other Pleasures*. Macmillan, London.

Noyelle, T. (ed.) (1989) *New York's Financial Markets*. Westview, London.

Nye, R. A. (1993) *Masculinity and Male Codes of Honor in Modern France*. Oxford University Press, New York.

Oakley, A. (1985) *Taking It Like a Woman*. Flamingo, London.

OPCS (1991) *General Household Survey 1989*. OPCS Series GHS No. 20, HMSO, London.

Pahl, R. (1984) *Divisions of Labour*. Blackwell, Oxford.

Pahl, R. (1988) *On Work*. Blackwell, Oxford.

Pahl, R. (1995) *After Success*. Polity Press, Cambridge.

Pateman, C. and Grosz, E. (1986) *Feminist Challenges: social and political theory*. Allen and Unwin, Sydney.

Payne, G. and Abbott, P. (eds) (1990) *The Social Mobility of Women: beyond male mobility models*. Falmer, London.

Penn, R., Rose, M. and Rubery, J. (1994) *Skill and Occupational Change*. Oxford University Press, Oxford.

Petit, C. (1995) Accidental death of a bank manager. *Guardian*, 3 November, pp. 4–5.

Phillips, A. (1989) *Divided Loyalties: dilemmas of sex and class*. Virago, London.

Phillips, A. and Taylor, B. (1980) Sex and skill: notes towards a feminist economics. *Feminist Review* 6, 79–88.

Philo, C. (1989a) 'Enough to drive one mad': the organisation of space in nineteenth century lunatic asylums. In J. Wolch and M. Dear (eds), *The Power of Geography*. Macmillan, London.

Philo, C. (1989b) Thoughts, words and creative locational acts. In F. Boal and D. Livingstone (eds), *The Behavioural Environment*. Routledge, London.

Philo, C. (ed.) (1994) *Off the Map: the geography of poverty in the UK*. Child Poverty Action Group, London.

Picciotto, S. (1988) The control of transnational capital and the democratization of the international state. *Journal of Law and Society* 15, 12–23.

Porter, R. (1994) *London: a social history*. Hamish Hamilton, London.

Pratt, G. and Hanson, S. (1988) Gender, class and space. *Environment and Planning D: Society and Space* 6, 15–35.

Pratt, G. and Hanson, S. (1990) On the links between home and work: family strategies in a buoyant labour market. *International Journal of Urban and Regional Research* 14, 55–74.

Pratt, G. and Hanson, S. (1991) Time, space and the occupational segregation of women: a critique of human capital theory. *Geoforum* 22, 149–57.

Pringle, R. (1989) *Secretaries Talk*. Verso, London.

Pringle, R. (1993) *Femininity and Performance in the Medical Profession*. Paper presented at Newnham College Geography Society, Newnham College, Cambridge.

Pryke, M. (1991) An international city going 'global': spatial change in the City of London. *Environment and Planning D: Society and Space* 9, 197–222.

Rajan, A. and Fryatt, J. (1988) *Create or Abdicate: the City's human resource choice for the '90s*. Institute of Manpower Studies, Sussex.

Rajan, A., Rajan, L. and van Eupen, P. (1990) *Capital People: skills and strategies for survival in the nineties*. The Industrial Society, London.

Raper, M. (1994) *Masculinity and the British Organisation Man since 1945*. Oxford University Press, Oxford.

Reskin, B. and Hartmann, H. (eds) (1986) *Women's Work, Men's Work: sex segregation on the job*. National Academy Press, Washington DC.

Rhode, D. (1988) Perspectives on professional women. *Stanford Law Review* 40, 1164–207.

Rhode, D. (1990) *Theoretical Perspectives on Sexual Difference*. Yale University Press, New Haven, Conn. and London.

Rice, R. (1991) Law Society reports rise in number of women solicitors. *Financial Times*, 15 October, p. 11.

Rich, A. (1980) Compulsory heterosexuality and lesbian existence. *Signs: Journal of Women in Culture and Society* 5, 631–60.

Rifkin, J. (1996) *The End of Work*. Tarcher Putnam, New York.

Riley, B. (1992) Upheaval on the high street. *Financial Times*, 2 March, p. 8.

Riviere, J. (1986) Womanliness as a masquerade. In V. Burgin, J. Donald and C. Kaplan (1986) *Formations of Fantasy*. Methuen, London.

Roberts, S. (1994) Fictitious capital, fictitious spaces: the geography of off-shore financial flows. In S. Corbridge, N. Thrift and R. Martin (eds), *Money, Power and Space*. Blackwell, Oxford.

Robins, K. (1991) Tradition and translation: national culture in its global context. In J. Corner and S. Harvey (eds), *Enterprise and Heritage*. Routledge, London.

Robson, B. (1994) No city, no civilization. *Transactions of the Institute of British*

Geographers 19, 131–41.

Rocco, F. (1991) Women who work too much. *Independent on Sunday*, 23 December, p. 20.

Rodgers, S. (1981) Women's space in a men's house: the British House of Commons. In S. Ardener (ed.), *Women and Space: ground rules and social maps*. Croom Helm, London.

Roper, M. and Tosh, J. (eds) (1991) *Manful Assertions: masculinities in Britain since 1800*. Routledge, London.

Rose, G. (1993) *Feminism and Geography: the limits of geographical knowledge*. Polity Press, Cambridge.

Rosenberg, J., Perlstadt, H. and Phillips, W, (1993) Now that we are here: discrimination, disparagement, and harassment at work and the experience of female lawyers. *Gender and Society* 7, 415–33.

Rosener, J. B. (1994) Ways women lead. In N. Nichols (ed.), *Reaching for the Top*. Harvard Business School Press, Cambridge, Mass.

Rowntree Foundation (1995) *The Distribution of Income and Wealth vols I. and II.* Rowntree Foundation, London.

Royal Commission on the Distribution of Income and Wealth (1974) *Report*. HMSO, London.

Rubery, J. (ed.) (1988) Wome*n and Recession*. Routledge and Kegan Paul, London.

Rubery, J. and Fagan, C. (1994) Occupational segregation: plus ça change? In R. Lindley (ed.), *Labour Market Structures and Prospects for Women*. Institute for Employment Research, University of Warwick and Equal Opportunities Commission, Manchester.

Rubery, J. and Wilkinson, F. (eds) (1994) *Employer Strategy and the Labour Market*. Oxford University Press, Oxford.

Rubin, G. (1975) The traffic in women: notes on the 'political economy' of sex. In R. Reitner (ed.), *Toward an Anthropology of Women*. Monthly Review Press, New York.

Rubin, J. (1995) Selecting gender: women, management and the corporate interview. Unpublished Ph.D. dissertation, Faculty of Social and Political Science, University of Cambridge.

Sahlins, M. (1976) *Culture and Practical Reason*. Chicago University Press, Chicago.

Said, E. (1978) *Orientalism*. Routledge and Kegan Paul, London.

Salt, J. (1992) Migration processes among the highly skilled in Europe. *International Migration Review* 26, 484–505.

Sampson, A. (1992) The anatomy of Britain 1992. *Independent on Sunday*, 29 March.

Sassen, S. (1990) *The Global City: New York, London and Tokyo*. Princeton University Press, Princeton N.J.

Sassen, S. (1996) Analytic borderlands: race, gender and representation in the new city. In A. King (ed.), (1996) *Re-presenting the City*. Macmillan, London.

Savage, M., Barlow, J., Dickens, P. and Fielding, T. (1992) *Property, Bureaucracy and Culture: middle class formation in contemporary Britain*. Routledge, London.

Savage, M. and Witz, A. (1993) *Gender and Bureaucracy*. Routledge, London.

Sayer, A. (1982) Explanation in economic geography. *Progress in Human Geography*

6, 68–88.

Sayer, A. (1994) Cultural studies and 'the economy, stupid'. *Environment and Planning D: Society and Space* 12, 635–7.

Sayer, A. and Morgan, K. (1985) A modern industry in a declining region: links between method, theory and policy. In D. Massey and R. Meegan (eds), *Politics and Method*. Methuen, London.

Sayer, A. and Morgan, K. (1988) *Micro-circuits of Capital*. Polity Press, Cambridge.

Sayer, A. and Walker, R. (1992) *The New Social Economy: reworking the division of labour*. Blackwell, Oxford.

Schoenberger, E. (1994) Corporate strategy and corporate strategists: power, identity and knowledge within the firm. *Environment and Planning A* 26, 435–51.

Schwichtenberg, C. (ed.) (1993) *The Madonna Connection: representational politics, subcultural identities and cultural theory*. Westview Press, Oxford.

Scott, A. and Storper, M. (1986) *Production, Work and Territory: the geographical anatomy of industrial capitalism*. Allen and Unwin, London.

Scott, A. M. (ed.) (1994) *Gender Segregation and Social Change: men and women in changing labour markets*. Oxford University Press, Oxford.

Scott, A. M. and Burchell, B. (1994) 'And never the twain shall meet'? Gender segregation and work histories. In A. M. Scott (ed.), *Gender Segregation and Social Change: men and women in changing labour markets*. Oxford University Press, Oxford.

Scott, J. (1979) *Corporations, Classes and Capitalism*. Hutchinson, London.

Scott, J. (1988) Deconstructing equality versus difference; or, the uses of post-structuralist theory for feminism. *Feminist Studies* 14, 33–50.

Scott, J. (1991) *Who Rules Britain?* Polity Press, Cambridge.

Segal, L. (1990) *Slow Motion: changing masculinities, changing men*. Virago, London.

Sennett, R. (1977) *The Fall of Public Man*. Knopf, New York.

Sennett, R. (1992) *The Conscience of the Eye: the design and social life of cities*. Norton, New York.

Sennett, R. (1994) *Flesh and Stone*. Faber and Faber, London.

Shields, R. (1991) *Places on the Margin*. Routledge, London.

Shields, R. (1996) A. guide to urban representation and what to do about it: alternative traditions of urban theory. In A. King (ed.), *Re-presenting the City*. Routledge, London.

Shilling, C. (1993) *The Body and Social Theory*. Sage, London.

Shillingford, J. (1992) Americans go home. *The Banker*, March, p. 17.

Smith, C., Knights, D. and Willmott, H. (eds) (1991) *White Collar Work: the non-manual labour process*. Macmillan, London.

Smith, D. (1992) *The Apartheid City and Beyond*. Routledge, London.

Smith, N. (1993) Homeless/global: scaling places. In J. Bird and G. Robertson (eds), *Mapping the Futures*. Routledge, London.

Spivak, G. C. (1987) *In Other Worlds: essays in cultural politics*. Methuen, London.

Spurling, A. (1990) *Report of the Women in Higher Education Research Project*. King's College Research Centre, King's College, Cambridge.

Stallybrass, P. and White, A. (1986) *The Politics and Poetics of Transgression*. Methuen, London.

Stanworth, P. and Giddens, A. (1974a) An economic elite: a demographic profile of company chairmen. In P. Stanworth and A. Giddens (eds), *Elites and Power*. Cambridge University Press, Cambridge.

Stanworth, P. and Giddens, A. (1974b) The modern corporate economy: interlocking directorships in Britain, 1906–1970. *Sociological Review* 23, 5–28.

Stewart, M. and Greenhalgh, C. A. (1982) The training and experience dividend. *Employment Gazette*, August, pp. 329–40.

Stewart, M. and Greenhalgh, C. A. (1984) Work history patterns and occupational attainment of women. *Economic Journal* 94 (375), 493–519.

Stoller, R. (1979) *Sexual Excitement: the dynamics of erotic life.* Pantheon, New York.

Storper, M. (1994) Analytics, universals, norms: the view from the 'new social science' of conventions. Paper presented at the Association of American Geographers 90th annual meeting, San Francisco, 29 March–2 April.

Storper, M. and Walker, R. (1989) *The Capitalist Imperative: territory, technology and industrial growth.* Blackwell, Oxford.

Strange, S. (1986) *Casino Capitalism.* Blackwell, Oxford.

Summers, D. (1991a) No room for new faces at the top. *Financial Times*, 7 May, 9.

Summers, D. (1991b) Opportunity knocks for women. *Financial Times*, 29 October, 10.

Summers, D. (1992) Female directors report widespread inequality. *Financial Times*, 19 March, 9.

Tannen, D. (1984) *Conversational Style: analyzing talk among friends.* Ablex, Norwood, N.J.

Tannen, D. (1990) *You Just Don't Understand: women and men in conversation.* William Morrow, Ballantine, New York.

Tannen, D. (1994) *Talking 9 to 5: how women's and men's conversational styles affect who gets heard, who gets credit, and what gets done at work.* Virago, London.

Thorne, B. (1995) Symposium on 'Doing Difference'. *Gender and Society* 9, 497–9.

Thornley, A. (ed.) (1992) *The Crisis of London.* Routledge, London.

Threadgold, T. and Cranny–Francis, A. (1990) *Feminine, Masculine and Representation.* Allen and Unwin, London.

Thrift, N. (1989) Images of social change. In C. Hamnett, L. McDowell and P. Sarre (eds), *The Changing Social Structure.* Sage, London.

Thrift, N. (1994) On the social and cultural determinants of international financial centres: the case of the City of London. In S. Corbridge, R. Martin and N. Thrift (eds), *Money, Power and Space.* Blackwell, Oxford.

Thrift, N. and Leyshon, A. (1988) The gambling propensity: banks, developing country debt exposures and the new international financial system. *Geoforum* 19, 55–69.

Thrift, N. and Leyshon, A. (1990) *In the Wake of Money: the City of London and the accumulation of value.* Working Papers in Producer Services 16, University of Bristol and Service Industries Research Centre, Portsmouth Polytechnic.

Thrift, N. and Leyshon, A. (1992) In the wake of money: the City of London and the accumulation of value. In L. Budd and S. Whimster (eds), *Global Finance and Urban Living.* Routledge, London.

Thrift, N., Leyshon, A. and Daniels, P. (1987) *'Sexy Greedy': the new international financial system, the City of London and the South East of England.* Working Papers in Producer Services 8, University of Bristol and Service Industries Research Centre, Portsmouth Polytechnic.

Tolman, D. L. (1994) Doing desire: adolescent girls' struggles for/with sexuality. *Gender and Society* 8, 324–42.

Tseelon, E. (1995) *The Masque of Femininity.* Sage, London.

Tucker, E. (1992) The Square Mile stays out in front. Financial Times survey: foreign exchange. *Financial Times,* 29 May, Section IV, p. 3.

Unseem, M. (1984) *The Inner Circle.* Oxford University Press, New York.

Unseem, M. (1990) Business and politics in the United States and Britain. In S. Zukin and P. DiMaggio (eds), *Structures of Capital: the social organization of the economy.* Cambridge University Press, Cambridge.

Urry, J. (1986) Capitalist production, scientific management and the service class. In A. Scott and M. Storper (eds), *Production, Work and Territory.* Allen and Unwin, London.

Urry, J. (1995) *Consuming Places.* Routledge, London.

Valentine, G. (1993) Desperately seeking Susan: a geography of lesbian friendships. *Area* 25, 109–16.

Villeneuve, P. and Rose, D. (1988) Gender and the separation of employment from home in metropolitan Montreal, 1971–1981. *Urban Geography* 9, 155–79.

Vogel, L. (1983) *Marxism and the Oppression of Women.* Pluto Press, London.

Walby, S. (1986) *Patriarchy at Work.* Polity Press, Cambridge.

Walby, S. (ed.) (1988) *Gender Segregation at Work.* Open University Press, Milton Keynes.

Walby, S. (1991a) Labour markets and industrial structures in women's working lives. In S. Dex (ed.), *Life and Work History Analysis: qualitative and quantitative developments.* Routledge, London.

Walby, S. (1991b) *Theorising Patriarchy.* Blackwell, Oxford.

Watson, S. (1992) *Is Sir Humphrey Dead? The changing culture of the Civil Service.* Working Paper 103, School of Advanced Urban Studies, University of Bristol.

Weeks, J. (1986) *Sexuality.* Horwood and Tavistock, London.

West, C. and Fenstermaker, S. (1995) Doing difference. *Gender and Society* 9, 8–37.

West, C. and Zimmerman, D. H. (1987) Doing gender. *Gender and Society* 1, 125–51.

Westergaard, J. and Resler, H. (1975) *Class in Capitalist Society.* Heinemann, London.

Westwood, S. (1984) *All Day, Every Day.* Pluto Press, London.

White, H. (1981) Where do markets come from? *American Journal of Sociology* 87, 517–47.

Whitley, R. (1974) The city and industry. In P. Stanworth and A. Giddens (eds), *Elites and Power.* Cambridge University Press, Cambridge.

Whittington, G. (1972) Changes in the top 100 quoted manufacturing companies in the United Kingdom, 1948 to 1968. *Journal of Industrial Economics* 21, 17–34.

Wigley, P. (1992) Untitled: the housing of gender. In B. Colomina (ed.), *Sexuality and Space.* Princeton Architectural Press, New York, 327–90.

Wilkinson, H. and Mulgan, G. (1994) *Freedom's Children*. Demos Publications, London.

Williams, S. (1992) The coming of the groundscrapers. In L. Budd and S. Whimster (eds), *Global Finance and Urban Living: a study of metropolitan change*. Routledge, London.

Williamson, J. (1991) 'Up where you belong': Hollywood images of big business in the 1980s. In J. Corner and S. Harvey (eds), *Enterprise and Heritage: crosscurrents of national culture*. Routledge, London.

Williamson, J. (1992) Images of 'Woman': the photography of Cindy Sherman. In H. Crowley and S. Himmelweit (eds), *Knowing Women: feminism and knowledge*. Polity Press, Cambridge, 222–34.

Williamson, O. E. (1975) *Markets and Hierarchies*. Free Press, New York.

Wills, J. (1996) Geographies of trade unionism: translating traditions across space and time. *Antipode* 28, 352–78.

Wittig, M. (1992) *The Straight Mind and Other Essays*. Harvester Wheatsheaf, London.

Witz, A. (1992) *Professions and Patriarchy*. Routledge, London.

Wolfe, T. (1988) *The Bonfire of the Vanities*. Jonathan Cape, London.

Wolff, J. (1990) *Feminine Sentences: essays on women and culture*. Polity Press, Cambridge.

Woodward, R. (1993) One place, two stories: two interpretations of Spitalfields in the debate over its redevelopment. In G. Kearns and C. Philo (eds), *Selling Places: the city as cultural capital past and present*. Pergamon, London.

Woolf, V. (1977) *Three Guineas*. Penguin, Harmondsworth (originally published in 1938).

Wouters, C. (1986) Formalization and informalization: changing tension balances in civilizing processes. *Theory, Culture and Society* 3, 1–18.

Wouters, C. (1987) Developments in the behavioural codes between the sexes: the formalization of informalization in the Netherlands 1930–1985. *Theory, Culture and Society* 4, 405–28.

Wouters, C. (1990) Social stratification and informalization in global perspective. *Theory, Culture and Society* 7, 66–90.

Wright, S. (ed.) (1994) *Anthropology of Organisations*. Routledge, London.

Young, I. M. (1990a) *Justice and the Politics of Difference*. Princeton University Press, Princeton, N.J.

Young, I. M. (1990b) The ideal of community and the politics of difference. In L. Nicholson (ed.), *Feminism/Postmodernism*. Routledge, London.

Young, I. M. (1993) Together in difference: transforming the logic of group political conflict. In J. Squires (ed.), *Principled Positions: postmodernism and the rediscovery of value*. Lawrence and Wishart, London, 121–50.

Zelizer, V. (1987) *Morals and Markets: the development of life insurance in the United States*. Columbia University Press, New York.

Zellner, H. (1975) The determinants of occupational segregation. In C. Lloyd (ed.), *Women and the Labour Market*. Columbia University Press, New York.

Zukin, S. (1988) *Loft Living: culture and capital in urban change*. Radius, London.

Zukin, S. (1991) *Landscapes of Power: from Detroit to Disney World*. University of California Press, Berkeley and Los Angeles, California.

Zukin, S. (1992) The city as a landscape of power: London and New York as global financial capitals. In L. Budd and S. Whimster, *Global Finance and Urban Living*. Routledge, London.

Zukin, S. (1995) *The Cultures of Cities*. Blackwell, Oxford.

Zukin, S. and DiMaggio, P. (eds) (1990) *Structures of Capital: the social organization of the economy*. Cambridge University Press, Cambridge.

Index